To Brian
from Colin
Xmas 1974

To Brian
from Colin
Xmas 1974

CIVIL WAR
THE YEARS ASUNDER

Above: *The Wounded Drummer Boy*, by Eastman Johnson, The drummer boy was a sentimental rallying point for Civil War soldiers. Though wounded, in legend he was never disheartened. *(Private collection. Photo courtesy Parke-Bernet, New York.)*
Backleaf: Conrad Wise Chapman captured the spirit of waning Confederate hopes in *Evening Gun, Fort Sumter, 1863.* The shredded rebel banner still flew after the fort had sustained two years of Federal shelling. *(The Museum of the Confederacy.)*

CIVIL WAR
THE YEARS ASUNDER

By the Editors of Country Beautiful

Publisher and Editorial Director: Michael P. Dineen

Executive Editor: Robert L. Polley

Edited by Dorothy Hennessy

Art Direction: Gerald E. Beyersdorff

Country Beautiful
Waukesha, Wisconsin

Acknowledgements

Excerpts from ABRAHAM LINCOLN: THE WAR YEARS, Volume II, by Carl Sandburg, copyright 1939 by Harcourt Brace Jovanovitch, Inc.; copyright 1967 by Carl Sandburg. Reprinted by permission of the publisher.

Excerpt from the ANTI-SLAVERY CRUSADE, by Jesse Macy, Volume 28 of *The Yale Chronicles of America*. Reprinted by permission of United States Publishers Association.

Excerpt from CONFEDERATE CHAPLAIN: A WAR JOURNAL OF REV. JAMES B. SHEERAN, edited by Rev. Joseph T. Durkin, S.J. (©The Bruce Publishing Company, 1960).

Excerpt from DOCTORS IN GRAY: THE CONFEDERATE MEDICAL SERVICE, by H. H. Cunningham. © 1960 by Louisiana State University Press. Reprinted by permission of Louisiana State University Press.

Excerpt from THE ERA OF RECONSTRUCTION, 1865-1877, by Kenneth M. Stampp. Copyright © 1965 by Kenneth M. Stampp. Reprinted by permission of Alfred A. Knopf, Inc.

Excerpts from THE FABULOUS FORTIES 1840-1850: A PRESENTATION OF PRIVATE LIFE, by Meade Minnigerode. Copyright 1924 by Meade Minnigerode. Reprinted by permission of G. P. Putnam's Sons.

Excerpt from GRANT AND LEE: A STUDY IN PERSONALITY AND GENERALSHIP, reprinted from GRANT AND LEE: A STUDY IN PERSONALITY AND GENERALSHIP, by John F. Fuller. © 1957 by Indiana University Press, Bloomington. Reprinted by permission of the publisher.

Letter from Jefferson Davis to his wife, Varina, from JEFFERSON DAVIS CONSTITUTIONALIST: HIS LETTERS, PAPERS AND SPEECHES, edited by Dunbar Rowland. Copyright 1923. Reprinted by permission of State of Mississippi Department of Archives and History.

Excerpts from JOHN BROWN'S BODY, by Stephen Vincent Benét, Holt, Rinehart and Winston, Inc. © 1927, 1928 by Stephen Vincent Benet. © renewed 1955, 1956 by Rosemary Carr Benét. Reprinted by permission of Brandt and Brandt.

Excerpts from THE LIFE OF BILLY YANK and THE LIFE OF JOHNNY REB. Copyright © 1971 by Bell Irvin Wiley, copyright 1943 by the Bobbs-Merrill Company, Inc. Reprinted by permission of Doubleday & Company, Inc.

Excerpt from NEVER CALL RETREAT, by Bruce Catton. © 1965 by Bruce Catton. Reprinted by permission of Doubleday & Company, Inc.

Excerpts from POINT LOOKOUT PRISON CAMP FOR CONFEDERATES, by Edwin W. Beitzell. Copyright 1972. Reprinted by permission of Edwin W. Beitzell, Gerard's Cove, Maryland.

Excerpts from THE RAVING FOE, THE CIVIL WAR DIARY OF MAJOR JAMES T. POE, C.S.A. AND THE 11TH ARKANSAS VOLUNTEERS. Copyright 1967 by Longhorn Press, Eastland Texas. Reprinted by permission of J.C. Poe, Eastland, Texas.

Excerpts from A REBEL'S RECOLLECTIONS, by George Cary Eggleston, edited by Donald David. Copyright 1959 by Indiana University Press, Bloomington. Reprinted by permission of the publisher.

Excerpt from THE WAR THAT NEVER ENDED: THE AMERICAN CIVIL WAR, by Robert Cruden. © 1973, p. 192. Reprinted by permission of Prentice-Hall, Inc.

Letters of Private John Brobst to Mary Englesby from WELL, MARY: CIVIL WAR LETTERS OF A WISCONSIN VOLUNTEER, edited by Margaret Brobst Roth. (Madison: University of Wisconsin Press; © 1960 by the Regents of the University of Wisconsin).

COUNTRY BEAUTIFUL: *Publisher and Editorial Director:* Michael P. Dineen; *Executive Editor:* Robert L. Polley; *Senior Editors:* Kenneth L. Schmitz; James H. Robb; *Art Director:* Buford Nixon; *Managing Editor:* John M. Nuhn; *Contributing Editor:* Dorothy Hennessy; *House Editor:* D'Arlyn Marks; *Associate Editor:* Kay Kundinger; *Editorial Assistant:* Nancy Backes; *Production Manager:* Donna Griesemer; *Editorial Secretary:* Jane Boyd; *Administration:* Brett E. Gries, Bruce Schneider; *Administrative Secretary:* Kathleen M. Stoner.

Country Beautiful Corporation is a wholly owned subsidiary of Flick-Reedy Corporation: *President:* Frank Flick; *Vice President and General Manager:* Michael P. Dineen; *Treasurer and Secretary:* August Caamano.

Union gun and gun crew. *(National Park Service.)*

Contents

Preface

More has been written about the American Civil War than about any war in the history of the world. Its fascination and its relevance have never dimmed, and the war years comprised an era of internal crisis unparalleled in the chronicle of the American experience. Like all such civil conflicts it brought out the best and the worst in both individual citizens and governments, but it is the only time Americans have found it necessary to fight each other as the price for sealing their national destiny. After 1865, Daniel Webster's earlier plea toward "Liberty and Union, now and forever, one and inseparable," became reality.

The reasons Northerners and Southerners took up arms against each other were many, and while the existence of slavery was by no means alone among the ideological tensions which tore at the nation, it was a central and crucial factor. The questions surrounding the continuation and extension of the peculiar institution could not be resolved by political means. As John Brown prophesied, blood had to be shed before the black man could be free.

It is difficult for Americans today to comprehend the scope of personal suffering and deprivation inflicted upon those who served in that war so distant in time. Generations of our citizens have lived and died never having witnessed the devastations of such a conflict at first hand. They take for granted advances in medical knowledge which were only in their infancy or non-existent during the Civil War: the use of general anesthesia, antibiotics, sterile techniques in the dressing of wounds and in surgery. They do not think of diarrhea, dysentery and malaria as killers, but during that war these diseases took their hideous tolls. Transportation of the wounded from a battlefield is now made swiftly by helicopter. In those years, horse-drawn ambulance wagons, when they were available, carried their screaming burdens over bumpy dirt roads.

The tactics of war were still based upon Napoleonic traditions. Lines of closely packed troops still made their assaults on defensive positions, even though the use of the muzzle-loaded rifle, with its greater accuracy and increased range, made this method suicidal. Ponderous generals, unwilling or unable to change, wasted countless lives as they sent waves of men against fire from entrenchments.

In total, over 350,000 Federals and 250,000 Confederates lost their lives either the victims of battlefield wounds or of disease. The distinction was unimportant for the soldier. He was as dead one way or the other.

Anxious to assume the privileges of their new freedom, black families left their homes in ever larger numbers after 1863. Usually they followed whatever yankee army happened to be passing. The government opened "refugee" camps, supposedly to deal with the problem in some organized manner. In truth, these camps, set up far enough from the army's quarters so as not to provide a disturbing influence, but close enough to be under their protection, were filthy centers of detention, lacking in the most basic sanitary facilities. The food these people ate was the food they could beg or forage. At times it was literally garbage. Small wonder that the mortality in such camps was extremely high, due mainly to malnutrition and the high prevalence of infectious disease.

When the black man was allowed to enlist in the army, he found that many white officers did not want to serve with him. He was often relegated to non-combat duty, but those who fought proved their worth.

Analysis of the whirlpool of issues encompassing the war era continues a century later as it becomes clear that we are still reaping some of the more bitter fruits.

The Civil War put an end to slavery, and Americans, Northern and Southern alike, subsequently found more insidious and vicious legal and extrajudicial methods of denying the black people their human and civil rights. As it turned out, blacks were to be free, but they were not to be equal.

The war preserved the Union and brought to the Federal government an increasing security and power it would be loath to relinquish in the twentieth century.

The war made fortunes for many who would become the robber barons of nineteenth-century capitalism and gave business a dignity and political influence it had never known. However, all too often business did not have a conscience, and those who managed the great wealth accumulated during the war had as little concern for their hirelings as the most callous slave owner before the conflict. A new system of exploitation would grow, which would be tempered with the success of trade unions, but which would still carry over into our own time.

When Johnny finally came marching home after his arduous years of service he faced problems with which many American veterans today can sympathize. Work was often scarce and it was said the returning soldiers didn't have the job skills of those who had chosen to stay at home. There was a generally widespread belief that life in the army had corrupted their morals to such an extent that they were bad risks for permanent employment. The Civil War veterans demonstrated and rioted, as did their twentieth-century counterparts. Finally they found that organization, and the political pressure it could bring to bear, was the only way of improving their lot.

The Johnnys who were rebels, and had lost the war through no fault of their own, faced an even more depressing situation as they returned home to a countryside shorn and devastated. On their home soil were the hated yankee victors, carpetbaggers ready to take over local and state governments, and the blacks with their new and dangerous freedom. Southerners could not turn to the government for help. In their anger and bitterness they turned instead violence and such organizations as the Ku Klux Klan to spread terror among the carpetbaggers and the more assailable blacks.

The legacy of the Civil War extends beyond legend and romance, beyond the delight in the myraids of anecdotes and brave deeds, to the sterner realities of life in America over one hundred years later.

Prelude to Battle

They who have been bred in the school of politics fail now and always to face the facts. Their measures are half measures and makeshifts merely. They put off the day of settlement indefinitely, and meanwhile the debt accumulates . . . .

From Henry David Thoreau's "Slavery in Massachusetts," an address to the Anti-slavery Convention, July 4, 1854

On a February evening in 1861, two figures shrouded by the early darkness entered a closed carriage outside the Jones Hotel in Harrisburg, Pennsylvania. One of the men was Abraham Lincoln, the other, his bodyguard and friend, Ward Hill Lamon. They proceeded quickly to the depot where a special car and engine took them on to West Philadelphia Station and to detective Allan Pinkerton. Again by carriage, the three took a roundabout way to the station of the Philadelphia, Wilmington and Baltimore Railroad. Beyond that point, reservations for berths had been arranged under fictitious names on the regular midnight train to Baltimore. The reason for the abrupt changes in timing and route was that Pinkerton was convinced an attempt would be made in Baltimore to murder Lincoln. The diversions worked, the alleged conspiracy was thwarted, and the passengers in the sleeping car where the President spent the night were blissfully unaware of their distinguished companion. But the secretive arrival of the President in Washington the next day was not an auspicious beginning to Lincoln's first term.

There were other more ominous events at hand, for on that February day the nation was poised on the brink of a destructive war which would forever seal its unity and destiny. The American Civil War, like all such conflicts, would be most wounding to the nation's young. North and South together would lose 600,000 soldiers, many of them mere boys who had never fired a shot in anger.

The politicians and their compromises had failed to solve the deepening sectional divisions over slavery, states' rights, tariffs and other economic issues. America was a country ready to split in half and only awaited the signal to do battle.

In the North, craftsmanship and industry had wed. Full-scale industrialization was imminent. Blessed with an abundance of manpower which could be hired cheaply and stung by qualms of conscience, Northerners had phased out slavery and slave trade. As they became more dependent upon machines, and as human resources swelled with the arrival of immigrants to the eastern shores, their understanding of Southern economic reliance upon bondage dimmed and the institution's existence became a moral question increasingly difficult to put down.

Economic development in the South lagged behind. Southerners were still tied to an agricultural lifestyle, with little inclination toward change. They produced sugar and rice, but cotton was king and slave labor the key to its production at a profit. As lands long under unskilled tillage were no longer fit for cultivation, planters looked to the west and they wanted to be certain that when the new territories opened, slavery would not be prohibited.

Congress had wrestled with the issues for thirty years prior to the war, attempting to reconcile diverse and antagonistic Northern and Southern interests. And as men like Henry Clay of Kentucky, who

A Ride for Liberty, by Eastman Johnson, forcefully re-created the escape of a young slave and his family on a "borrowed" horse. (*Courtesy of The Brooklyn Museum, gift of Miss Gwendolyn O. L. Conkling.*)

had fought slavery for sixty years of his life, and John C. Calhoun of South Carolina, firmly committed to states' rights, argued the questions in the Senate and desperately tried to hold the Union together, two streams of settlers swarmed to the new Kansas and Nebraska territories. They both wanted free land and railroads, and they wanted the rewards for hard work which America promised all her sons, but in their deep convictions regarding slavery they were unalterably divided. They were also armed. In bloody border clashes these settlers fought the first battles of the larger conflict to come.

By the 1850's some Northern abolitionists were beginning to embrace violence to gain their ends and Southerners were often openly in favor of secession. The dissolution of the Union became inevitable after John Brown's raid into West Virginia in 1859, and as historian Jesse Macy has suggested, Brown became the "personification of the irrepressible conflict." He has also perhaps answered a larger question, and that is why did Americans fight such a deadly and costly war on their own soil:

> Of all the men of his generation John Brown is best fitted to exemplify the most difficult lesson which history teaches: that slavery and despotism are themselves forms of war, that the shedding of blood is likely to continue so long as the rich, the strong, the educated, or the efficient, strive to force their will upon the poor, the weak and the ignorant. Lincoln uttered a final word on the subject when he said that no man is good enough to rule over another man; if he were good enough he would not be willing to do it.

In the Land of Promise: Castle Garden, by Charles F. Ulrich. As newly arrived immigrants waited at debarkation points, their faces were poignant with anticipation of life in the new world. (*In the collection of the Corcoran Gallery of Art.*)

From Henry Adams' *History of the United States during the Administration of James Madison:*

The traits of American character were fixed; the rate of physical and economical growth was established; and history, certain that at a given distance of time the Union would contain so many millions of people, with wealth valued at so many millions of dollars, became thence forward chiefly concerned to know what kind of people these millions would be. They were intelligent, but what paths would their intelligence select? They were quick, but what solution of insoluble problems would quickness hurry? They were scientific, and what control would their science exercise over their destiny? They were mild, but what corruptions would their relaxations bring? They were peaceful, but by what machinery were their corruptions to be purged? What interests were to vivify a society so vast and uniform? What ideals were to ennoble it? What object, besides physical content, must a democratic continent aspire to attain? For the treatment of such questions, history required another century of experience.

Henry Wadsworth Longfellow, *The Warning:*

Beware! The Israelite of old, who tore
   The lion in his path—when, poor and blind,
He saw the blessed light of heaven no more,
   Shorn of his noble strength and forced to grind
In prison, and at last led forth to be
A pander to Philistine revelry—

Upon the pillars of the temple laid
   His desperate hands, and in its overthrow
Destroyed himself, and with him those who made
   A cruel mockery of his sightless woe;
The poor blind Slave, the scoff and jest of all,
Expired, and thousands perished in the fall!

There is a poor blind Samson in this land,
   Shorn of his strength and bound in bonds of steel,
Who may, in some grim revel, raise his hand,
   And shake the pillars of this Commonweal,
Till the vast Temple of our liberties
A shapeless mass of wreck and rubbish lies.

Americans in the mid-century were fully enjoying the last vestiges of national innocence. For perhaps the final time in their history the interests of agriculture outweighed those of the burgeoning manufactories on the Atlantic Seaboard. Most people still lived on farms and in small towns, but in the North the mask of a rural lifestyle would soon fall away to reveal the face of a rapidly advancing industrial society. That society would carry its own burden of human exploitation as increasing demands for cheap labor brought immigrants and women into the work force.

12

From the *New York Weekly Tribune,* May 2, 1846:

As we understand it, a large number of Irish labor-ers have been at work in winter for certain contrac-tors for sixty-five cents per day, and the days were made pretty long at that. With this compensation, amounting to $3.90 per week, the laborers must of course live as they best could, some of them having large families to support. As the rent of any decent tenement in Brooklyn would absorb nearly the entire earnings of a laboring man at this rate, they were allowed to build miserable shanties on ground allotted them by the contractors on the plot occupied by them in performing the work.

As spring opened and days became longer, labor more effective and employment more general, the poor laborers began to grumble at their hard lot, and at last united in an effort to improve it. They asked for 87 1/2 cents per day (about equal to 50 in Vermont or 37 1/2 in the West) and to have ten hours recognized as the limit of a day's work. The contractors refused to comply with their demands; whereupon the laborers struck work.

The contractors hired a cargo of freshly landed Germans to take their places, and ordered the old laborers to quit the premises, which they refused to do, and resorted to the lawless, unjustifiable step of endeavoring to drive the Germans from the work by intimidation and violence. Of course the military were called out, the Irish overawed, the Germans protected in their work, and thus the matter stands. So far, the contractors may be said to have triumphed . . . .

Bostonians, hailed for their achievements in education and the arts, took pride in the city's designation as the "Athens of America." (*Courtesy of the Print Department, Boston Public Library*.)

To many foreign visitors it seemed that most Northeasterners were solely engaged in the pursuit of the almighty dollar, and European literati delighted in turning up continental noses at a society they considered almost devoid of cultural achievement and inclination. But in Boston travelers such as Charles Dickens found Americans worshipped "better gods."

Dubbed the "Athens of America," the city was not only an intellectual center but the summit of antislavery sentiment in the North.

One son of Massachusetts, John Greenleaf Whittier, with pervasive Quaker indignation and a strong sense of social consciousness, devoted thirty years of his life to the cause, to a "moral warfare" against the "crime and folly of an evil time."

From Meade Minnigerode's *The Fabulous Forties 1840-1850: A Presentation of Private Life:*

In Boston 93,000 people maintained twenty-nine benevolent institutions, including the Society for the Moral and Religious Instruction of the Poor and the Society for the Diffusion of Useful Knowledge; supported five circulating libraries; . . . attended lectures at the Boston Lyceum, the Social Lyceum, the Mechanics' Lyceum, and the Massachusetts Lyceum; lived, some of them, on Pearl Street and Summer Street, and on Park Street and Beacon Street and the Common, in elegant houses furnished with porticoes and iron railings, surrounded by tree shaded grass plots fronting on clean, well-paved streets, and displayed, all of them, a quality of culture which moved Mr. Dickens to remark that:

There is no doubt that much of the intellectual refinement and superiority of Boston is referable to the quiet influence of the University of Cambridge. . . . The golden calf they worship at Boston is a pygmy compared with the giant effigies set up in other parts of the vast counting house which lies beyond the Atlantic; and the almighty dollar sinks into something comparatively insignificant, amidst a whole Pantheon of better gods.

John Greenleaf Whittier, *Massachusetts to Virginia:*

The voice of Massachusetts! Of her free sons and
    daughters,
Deep calling unto deep aloud, the sound of many
    waters!
Against the burden of that voice what tyrant
    power shall stand?
No fetters in the Bay State! No slave upon her
    land!

We wage no war, we lift no arm, we fling no torch
    within
The fire-damps of the quaking mine beneath your
    soil of sin;
We leave ye with your bondmen, to wrestle, while
    ye can,
With the strong upward tendencies and godlike
    soul of man!

But for us and for our children, the vow which we
    have given
For freedom and humanity is registered in heaven;
No slave-hunt in our borders—no pirate on our
    strand!
No fetters in the Bay State—no slave upon our
    land!

Mammy and Infant, by William J. Hubard, ca. 1840.
(*Valentine Museum, Richmond, Virginia.*)

The South bore its own façade, for beyond the refinements of Richmond and Charleston or the gracious and languid pleasures of plantation life lay the true Southern experience. The Magnolia-scented myths which were perpetuated by succeeding generations of writers cast a hazy and romantic glow over the fact that many in the Deep South lived an inelegant and difficult life.

However, such an existence had few apologists, for it was the aristocratic lifestyle of the Tidewater gentleman, so despised by the more egalitarian North, which consistently drew observers and biographers.

Among these was George Cary Eggleston who typified the *haute monde* attitudes of the Southern planter when he wrote: "The Virginians were not much given to travelling beyond their own borders, and when they did go into the outer world it was only to find a manifestation of barbarism in every departure from their own prescriptive standards and models."

When men like Eggleston spoke of slavery, it was in an offhand manner, as he described it, "at least productive of more good than evil." He would undoubtedly have taken the word of his overseer that the slaves on his large holdings were treated humanely, within the reasonable limits demanded by discipline and order.

From George Cary Eggleston's *A Rebel's Recollections:*

It was a very beautiful and enjoyable life that the Virginians led in that ancient time, for it certainly seems ages ago, before the war came to turn ideas upside down and convert the picturesque commonwealth into a commonplace, modern state. It was a soft, dreamy, deliciously quiet life, a life of repose, an old life, with all its sharp corners and rough surfaces long ago worn round and smooth. Everything fitted everything else, and every point in it was so well settled as to leave no work of improvement for anybody to do. The Virginians were satisfied with things as they were, and if there were reformers born among them, they went elsewhere to work changes. Society in the Old Dominion was like a well-rolled and closely packed gravel walk, in which each pebble has found precisely the place it fits best. There was no giving way under one's feet, no uncomfortable grinding of loose materials as one walked about over the firm and long-used ways of the Virginian social life.

From Frances Anne Kemble's *Journal of a Residence on a Georgia Plantation in 1838-1839:*

. . . With regard to the indifference of our former manager upon the subject of the accommodation for the sick, he was an excellent overseer, *videlicet* the estate returned a full income under his management, and such men have nothing to do with sick slaves; they are tools, to be mended only if they can be made available again; if not, to be flung by as useless, without further expense of time, money or trouble.

. . . I told my husband, with much indignation, of poor Harriet's flogging. . . . He said he would ask the overseer about it, assuring me, at the same time, that it was impossible to believe a single word any of these people said. At dinner, accordingly, the inquiry was made as to the cause of her punishment, and Mr. O___ then said it was . . . for having answered him impertinently; that he had ordered her into the field, whereupon she had said she was ill and could not work; she replied: "Very well, I'll go, but I shall just come back again!" meaning that when in the field she would be unable to work, and obliged to return to the hospital.

"For this reply," Mr. O___ said, "I gave her a good lashing; it was her business to have gone into the field without answering me, and then we should have soon seen whether she could work or not; I gave it to Chloe too for some such impudence."

The domestic side of plantation life had its own overseer, the wife or daughter of the master of the house. George Cary Eggleston proudly related some of her daily duties, but Harriet Martineau, an Englishwoman who traveled through the South in the 1830's, drew a different picture. In her descriptions of her charming but vacuous hostess are found the unavoidable truths which sometimes lie behind the generally admired fictional stereotype of Southern womanhood. It is not difficult to envision Scarlett O'Hara

lamenting over similar tribulations as mistress of Tara.

From George Cary Eggleston's *A Rebel's Recollections:*

The first white person astir in the house every morning was the woman who carried the keys, mother or daughter, as the case might be. Her morning work was no light affair, and its accomplishment consumed several hours daily. To begin with she must knead the light bread with her own hands and send it to the kitchen to be baked and served hot at breakfast. She must prepare a skillet full of light rolls for the same meal, and "give out" the materials for the rest of the breakfast. Then she must see to the sweeping and garnishing of the lower rooms, passages and porches, lest the maids engaged in that task should entertain less extreme views than her own on the subject of that purity and clean-

Eastman Johnson painted his rather superficial *Old Kentucky Home* in 1859. He showed contented blacks in desultory occupations as the plantation mistress gingerly entered the nether world which existed beyond the elegance and order of her home. (*The New-York Historical Society, New York*.)

liness which constituted the house's charm and the housekeeper's crown of honor. She must write two or three notes, to be dispatched by the hands of a small Negro to her acquaintances in the neighborhood—a kind of correspondence much affected in that society . . . .

Breakfast over, the young housekeeper scalds and dries the dishes and glassware with her own hands . . . . Morning rides, backgammon, music, reading, etc., furnish amusement until one o'clock, or a little later . . . . About one the house grows quiet. The women retire to their chambers . . . .

Supper is served at eight, and the women usually retire for the night at ten or eleven.

From Harriet Martineau's *Society in America:*

Your hostess . . . has given her orders, and is now engaged in a back room, or out in the piazza behind the house, cutting out clothes for her slaves; a very laborious work in warm weather. There may be a pretense of lessons among the young people, and sometimes more than pretense if they happen to have a tutor or governess; but the probability is that their occupations are as various as their tempers . . . . Your hostess comes in at length and you sit down with her; she gratifies your curiosity about her "people," telling you how soon they burn out their shoes at the toes, and wear out their winter woollens, and tear up their summer cottons; and how impossible it is to get black women to learn to cut out clothes without waste; and how she never inquires when and where the whipping is done, as it is the overseer's business, and not hers. She has not been seated many minutes when she is called away, and returns saying how babyish these people are, and that they will not take medicine unless she gives it to them . . . .

Slave families leave their shanties and come one by one to give greetings to their owners at the "big house." The idealized depiction of noblesse oblige is titled *Plantation Christmas - "Fore de War."* (*The Museum of the Confederacy*.)

The early years of the century found adherents for the antislavery cause even in the South. In 1831, Virginia had seriously debated the end of bondage in the state, but this was also the year of Nat Turner's rebellion in Southampton County. Turner and his band murdered fifty-seven whites, including women and children, in a methodical and bloody rampage before the revolt was crushed. It was the end of Southern public debate on the issue. From then on every Southerner lived in open dread of slave uprisings and personal retribution.

John Pendleton Kennedy, a Maryland native, journeyed to the Old Dominion and described plantation life in the best terms he could summon. His attempt at objectivity deteriorated into patronization when he defined slavery as a temporary condition through which every inferior race passes on the way to its ultimate destiny. By the time war broke out Southern apologists had gone even further, formulating an anthropological doctrine holding that the black race was innately inferior to the white, and bondage their natural place in society.

From John Pendleton Kennedy's *Swallow Barn; Or, a Sojourn in the Old Dominion:*

It will be seen, that on the score of accommodation, the inmates of these [slave] dwellings were furnished according to a very primitive notion of comfort. Still, however, there were little garden-patches attached to each, where cymblings, cucumbers, sweet potatoes, water-melons, and cabbages flourished in unrestrained luxuriance. Add to this, that there were abundance of poultry domesticated about the premises, and it may be perceived that, whatever might be the inconveniences of shelter, there was no want of what, in all countries, would be considered a reasonable supply of luxuries.

Nothing more attracted my observation than the swarms of little negroes that basked on the sunny sides of these cabins, and congregated to gaze at us as we surveyed their haunts . . . and showed their slim shanks and long heels in all varieties of their grotesque natures. Their predominant love of sunshine, and their lazy, listless postures, and apparent content to be silently looking abroad, might well afford a comparison to a set of terrapins luxuriating in the genial warmth of summer, on the logs of a mill-pond.

William Ludwell Sheppard satirized black women dressed in finery imitating their "betters," in his rendering of holiday games at Richmond, Virginia, titled *The Cake Walk*. (*Valentine Museum, Richmond, Virginia*.)

From John Pendleton Kennedy's *Swallow Barn; Or a Sojourn in the Old Dominion:*

What the negro is finally capable of, in the way of civilization, I am not philosopher enough to determine. In the present stage of his existence, he presents himself to my mind as essentially parasitical in his nature. I mean that he is, in his moral constitution, a dependant upon the white race; dependant for guidance and direction even to the procurement of his most indispensable necessaries. Apart from this protection he has the helplessness of a child—without foresight, without faculty of contrivance, without thrift of any kind . . . . This helplessness may be the due and natural impression which two centuries of servitude have stamped upon the tribe. But it is not the less a present and insurmountable impediment to that most cruel of all projects—the direct, broad emancipation of these people . . . .

Remarks of a Mississippi white to Frederick Law Olmsted:

Where I used to live (Alabama) I remember when I was a boy—must ha' been about twenty years ago—folks was dreadful frightened about the niggers. I remember they built pens in the woods where they could hide and Christmas time they went and got into the pens, fraid the niggers was risin'.

From an anonymous conversation:

Little white child: "I'm English, Dutch and Irish. What are you?"

Little Negro child: "Nothin'."

From William J. Grayson's *The Hirling and the Slave:*

And yet the master's lighter rule insures
More order than the sternest code secures;
No mobs of factious workmen gather here,
No strikes we dread, no lawless riots fear;
Nuns, from their convent driven, at midnight fly,
Churches, in flames, ask vengeance from the sky,
Seditious schemes in bloody tumults end,
Parsons incite, and senators defend,
But not where slaves their easy labors ply,
Safe from the snare, beneath a master's eye;
In useful tasks engaged, employed their time,
Untempted by the demagogue to crime,
Secure they toil, uncursed their peaceful life,
With labor's hungry broils and wasteful strife,
No want to goad, no faction to deplore,
The slave escapes the perils of the poor.

In the North, there was not unity of opinion on the slavery issue, but abolitionists were becoming more vociferous as the nation entered the decade of the thirties. Fervent in the belief that the institution exemplified America's most glaring denials of liberty, their moderate appeals gave way to demands Southerners considered extremist.

The true abolitionists composed the left wing of the crusade. They wanted slavery stopped immediately, and without compensation to the former owners. Some were willing to work within the system, but others decried political action and embraced violence.

Abolitionist William Lloyd Garrison, abrasive and difficult, even to those who agreed with him, was not one to work within the system. He damned the Constitution as "a league with death and a covenant with Hell" since it protected slavery, and he constantly berated Northerners for the hypocricy of their attitudes toward blacks. The first issue of his profoundly influential newspaper, The Liberator, was published on January 1, 1831.

The first Negro slaves came to America on a Dutch trader in 1619. By the mid-1850's, the number of blacks in the South was roughly 40% of its total population. Although the Federal Constitution provided that the trade be abolished by 1808, it did not prohibit slavery itself or the sale of blacks within the country. Here slaves await sale in the Richmond market. (*Valentine Museum, Richmond, Virginia.*)

Richmond Virginia - March 3rd 53.

Slaves waiting to be sold

William Lloyd Garrison, the "Boston Firebrand," was one of the North's most dogmatic abolitionists. An intellectual and publisher of the antislavery *The Liberator*, he stood firmly opposed to any compromise with moderates on the issue of ending slavery. (*Courtesy Chicago Historical Society* .)

From William Lloyd Garrison's *The Liberator,* January 1, 1831:

. . . I shall strenuously contend for the immediate enfranchisement of our slave population. . . .

I am aware that many object to the severity of my language: but is there not cause for severity? I *will be* as *harsh* as truth, and as uncompromising as justice. On this subject I do not wish to write or speak or think with moderation. No! No! Tell a man whose house is on fire to give a moderate alarm: tell him to moderately rescue his wife from the hands of the ravisher: tell the mother to gradually extricate her babe from the fire into which it has fallen; but urge me not to moderation in a cause like the present. I am in earnest—I will not equivocate—I will not excuse—I will not retreat a single inch—AND I WILL BE HEARD . . . .

As agitation and opposition to slavery continued in the North, the eloquence of men such as Thoreau and Wendell Phillips was turned to the lecture platform.

In 1849 Thoreau had formulated his most powerful and influential essay, "Resistance to Civil Government," known today as "Civil Disobedience." He felt that no law should be of "such a nature that it requires you to be the agent of injustice to another," and that if it did it was your duty to break that law and accept the penalties. The essay was to influence John Brown, the man whose actions were the catalyst which precipitated the American Civil War.

From Wendell Phillips' speech to the Massachusetts Antislavery Society, January 27, 1853:

The public squares of half our great cities echo to the wail of families torn asunder at the auction-block; no one of our fair rivers that has not closed over the Negro seeking in death a refuge from a life too wretched to bear; thousands of fugitives skulk along our highways, afraid to tell their names, and trembling at the sight of a human being . . . . The press says, "It is all right;" and the pulpit cries, "Amen." The slave lifts up his imploring eyes, and sees in every face but ours the face of an enemy. Prove to me now that harsh rebuke, indignant denunciation, scathing sarcasm, and pitiless ridicule are wholly and always unjustifiable; else we dare not, in so desperate a case, throw away any weapon which ever broke up the crust of an ignorant prejudice, roused a slumbering conscience, shamed a proud sinner, or changed, in any way, the conduct of a human being.

From Henry David Thoreau's *"Slavery in Massachusetts,"* an address to the Antislavery Convention, July 4, 1854:

Much has been said about American slavery, but I think that we do not even yet realize what slavery is. If I were seriously to propose to Congress to make mankind into sausages, I have no doubt that most of the members would smile at my proposition, and if any believed me to be in earnest, they would think that I proposed something much worse than Congress had ever done. But if any of them will tell me that to make a man into a sausage would be much worse—would be any worse—than to make him into a slave—than it was to enact the Fugitive Slave Law—I will accuse him of foolishness, of intellectual incapacity, of making a distinction without a difference. The one is just as sensible a proposition as the other.

When Harriet Beecher Stowe's novel, *Uncle Tom's Cabin*; or *Life Among the Lowly*, was published in 1852, it touched the hearts and consciences of all who read it. From that point on it was impossible to dehumanize the problem of slavery. Wicked Simon Legree, precious Little Eva, here placing roses on kindly Uncle Tom, made the issues all too real. (*The Harry T. Peters Collection, Museum of the City of New York*.)

Phillips and Thoreau spoke largely to those already committed to the abolitionist cause, but when Harriet Beecher Stowe's novel, Uncle Tom's Cabin; or Life Among the Lowly, *burst upon the popular literary scene in 1852, it reached the masses of the uncommitted.*

Sentimental, romantic, satiric and written in the tradition of tastes molded by magazines and maidenly novels, it portrayed slavery and the slave trade at its degrading worst. Servile, docile Uncle Tom still lives today, although nearly as vilified by modern blacks as was his master, Simon Legree, during the era the book florished.

Southerners were incensed and in the North, antislavery sentiment took on new proportions. Mrs. Stowe had done more to propagandize the cause than anyone previously, and it seemed no wonder that Abraham Lincoln spoke of her as "the little woman who made this great war."

From Harriet Beecher Stowe's *Uncle Tom's Cabin; or Life Among the Lowly:*

Here is a fine bright girl, of ten years, whose mother was sold out yesterday, and who tonight cried herself to sleep when nobody was looking at her. Here, a worn old negress, whose thin arms and callous fingers tell of hard toil, waiting to be sold tomorrow as a cast-off article, for what can be got for her; and some forty or fifty others, with heads variously enveloped in blankets or articles of clothing, lie stretched around them. But, in a corner, sitting apart from the rest, are two females of a more interesting appearance than common. One of these is a respectably dressed mulatto woman between forty and fifty, with soft eyes and a gentle and pleasing physiognomy. She has on her head a high-raised turban, made of a gay red Madras handkerchief, of the first quality, and her dress is neatly fitted, and of good material, showing that she has been provided for with a careful hand. By her side, and nestling closely to her, is a young girl of fifteen, —her daughter. She is a quadroon as may be seen from her fairer complexion, though her likeness to her mother is quite descernible. She has the same soft, dark eye, with longer lashes, and her curling hair is of a luxuriant brown. She also is dressed with great neatness, and her white, delicate hands betray very little acquaintance with servile toil.

These two are to be sold tomorrow, in the same lot with the St. Clare servants; and the gentleman to whom they belong, and to whom the money for their sale is to be transmitted, is a member of a Christian church in New York, who will receive the money, and go thereafter to the sacrament of his Lord and theirs, and think no more of it.

From William J. Grayson's *The Hirling and the Slave:*

There Stowe, with prostituted pen, assails
One half her country in malignant tales;
Careless, like Trollope, whether truth she tells,
And anxious only how the libel sells,
To slander's mart she furnishes supplies,
And feeds its morbid appetite for lies
On fictions fashioned with malicious art,
The venal pencil, and malignant heart,
With fact distorted, inference unsound,
Creatures in fancy, not in nature found—
Chaste Quadroon virgins, saints of sable hue,
Martyrs, than zealous Paul more tried and true,
Demoniac masters, sentimental slaves,
Mulatto cavaliers, and Creole knaves—
Monsters each portrait drawn, each story told!
What then? The book may bring its weight in gold;
Enough! upon the crafty rule she leans,
That makes the purpose justify the means,
Concocts the venom, and, with eager gaze,
To Glasgow flies for patron, pence, and praise,
And for a slandered country finds rewards
In smiles or sneers of duchesses and lords.
For profits and applauses poor as these,
To the false tale she adds its falser Keys
Of gathered slanders—her ignoble aim,
With foes to traffic in her country's shame.

Two events were in essence to nullify earlier compromises, the Kansas-Nebraska Act which inferred that Congress could not keep slavery out of any territory, and the Dred Scott decision of the Southern-dominated Supreme Court in 1857. Scott, a slave who had sued for his freedom as a resident of a free territory, was denied any rights as a citizen by the Court led by Chief Justice Roger Taney. It meant that no black man had any rights under the Constitution, and in an auxilliary decision, the court confirmed a Kansas-Nebraska Act clause protecting the equal rights of slaveholders in any public lands.

Most people hoped that the Compromise of 1850, designed to placate Northern and Southern interests, would settle the slavery question. However the enactment only bought time for the country, perhaps enough for it ultimately to bear the strains of Civil War a decade later.

Northerners became increasingly defiant of the more stringent regulations in the compromise regarding runaway slaves. "This filthy enactment," said a livid Emerson, "was made in the nineteenth century, by people who could read and write. I will not obey it."

Dred Scott, by Louis Schultze, ca. 1880. In 1857, the Supreme Court ruled that Scott, who had sued for his liberty on the basis that he had resided in a free state, had no right to do so. He was property, not a human being with inherent human rights. *(The Missouri Historical Society, St. Louis.)*

Southerners found themselves alone in their defensiveness as slaves were emancipated abroad. Still, they reiterated their appeals, especially to the large majority of whites in the South who owned no slaves. As South Carolina Senator John C. Calhoun declared: "The two great divisions of society are not the rich and the poor, but white and black; and all the former, the poor as well as the rich, belong to the upper classes, and are respected and treated as such." No matter how low on the social and economic scale, the poor white could cling to his supposed superiority to any Negro.

Free-soilers, those who wanted no slavery in any new territory, were enraged; their Southern antagonists were satisfied. Both factions streamed to the new lands and their bloody clashes began to take on the character of a small war.

In 1858, amid the growing confusion and sporadic violence, Abraham Lincoln and Stephen Douglas were rivals for the Senate seat from Illinois. In seven small towns they debated the issues raised by the Dred Scott decision and the compromises of the previous years.

Douglas had based the success of his political career on the doctrine of popular sovereignty and had aspirations for the Presidential election in 1860. Lincoln was little known and had served only one rather undistinguished term in the House of Representatives. The contrast in the personal appearance of the two men was almost ludicrous; the "little giant," heavy set and dressed in the finest plantation style opposed to the angular and awkward Lincoln, his lankiness emphasized by his too short coatsleeves, too large trousers and stovepipe hat. Still, with his good humor and colorful stories, his facility for clear and logical argument, Lincoln was a formidable opponent for the veteran Senator.

Lincoln, committed to the principles of the Declaration of Independence, was opposed to slavery and its extension although he felt that interfering with it where it already existed would only give the Southern states ample grounds for secession.

Douglas attacked the Republicans and Lincoln personally as abolitionists in disguise, but his greatest problem was to reconcile the Dred Scott decision and his own reliance on the popular sovereignty principle, an embarrassing and dramatic predicament. The Senator's cagy answer was the formulation of the "Freeport Doctrine," which in essence supported the Taney decision, but admitted that a territorial legislature could practically nullify it by failing to pass the "police regulations" and legislation necessary to control the institution of slavery.

Douglas won the ensuing Senate race, but he lost Southern support in his bid for

From Abraham Lincoln's House Divided speech, June 16, 1858:

We are now far into the fifth year since a policy was initiated, with the avowed object, and confident promise, of putting an end to slavery agitation. Under the operation of that policy, that agitation has not only not ceased, but has continually augmented. I believe it will not cease till a crisis shall have been reached and passed. A house divided against itself cannot stand. I believe this government cannot endure permanently half slave and half free. I do not expect the Union to be dissolved. I do not expect the house to fall; but I do expect it will cease to be divided. It will become all one thing or all the other.

the Presidency. Lincoln won a national reputation for his cogent arguments and when the complex election of 1860 turned out to be a Republican victory, the ambitious and erudite lawyer from Springfield, in an era of unparalleled crisis, became the sixteenth President of the United States, succeeding James Buchanan.

Senator Stephen Douglas, the First Debate, Ottawa, Illinois, August 21, 1858:

Mr. Lincoln, following the example and lead of all the little Abolition orators, who go around and lecture in the basements of schools and churches, reads from the Declaration of Independence, that all men were created equal, and then asks how can you deprive a negro of that equality which God and the Declaration of Independence awards to him. He and they maintain that negro equality is guaranteed by the laws of God, and that it is asserted in the Declaration of Independence. If they think so, of course they have a right to say so, and so vote. I do not question Mr. Lincoln's conscientious belief that the negro was made his equal, and hence is his brother, but for my own part, I do not regard the negro as my equal, and positively deny that he is my brother or any kin to me whatever . . . .

Abraham Lincoln, the Sixth Debate, Quincy, Illinois, October 13, 1858:

We have in this nation this element of domestic slavery. It is a matter of absolute certainty that it is a disturbing element. It is the opinion of all the great men who have expressed an opinion upon it, that it is a dangerous element. We keep up a controversy in regard to it. That controversy necessarily springs from difference of opinion . . . . The Republican party think it wrong—we think it is a moral, a social and a political wrong. We think it is a wrong not confining itself merely to the persons or the states where it exists, but that it is a wrong in its tendency, to say the least, that extends itself to the existence of the whole nation. Because we think it wrong, we propose a course of policy that shall deal with it as a wrong. We deal with it as with any other wrong, in so far as we can prevent its growing any larger, and so deal with it that in the run of time there may be some promise of an end to it . . . . I suppose that in reference both to its actual existence in the nation, and to our constitutional obligations, we have no right at all to disturb it in the states where it exists, and we profess that we have no more inclination to disturb it than we have the right to do it . . . . We also oppose it as an evil so far as it seeks to spread itself. We insist on the policy that shall restrict it to its present limits. We don't suppose that in doing this we violate anything due to the actual presence of the institution, or anything due to the Constitutional guarantees thrown around it.

John Brown envisioned a massive slave uprising in the South once slaves knew that abolitionists were willing to risk violence in an effort to free them. His capture of the arsenal at Harpers Ferry in 1859 was an effort to obtain arms and assure the success of the revolt which never came. Brown himself was tried and executed for treason. (*Harpers Ferry National Historical Park*.)

Into the explosive situation in "bloody Kansas" came the former preacher, John Brown. Often depicted by artists carrying a Bible in one hand and a gun in the other, Brown was zealous, fanatic and almost monomaniacal in his dedication to ending the institution of slavery. In retaliation against pro-slavers for a raid on the town of Lawrence, Brown and his followers murdered five Kansas settlers on Pottawatomie Creek in 1856. Brown was certain there would be a slave uprising once those in bondage knew the extremes to which the abolitionists would go to free them.

On October 16, 1859, he struck at Harpers Ferry, West Virginia, with seventeen raiders and captured the Federal arsenal. There was no uprising and government troops seized Brown and his remaining followers. He was executed for treason and became a martyr in the North. But his action had struck terror in the hearts of Southerners, already horrified at the prospect of slave rebellion.

The effect of this man's single, startling action in Virginia cannot be exaggerated.

Only one event remained to seal the nation's destiny, the election of Abraham Lincoln to the Presidency of the United States.

From Henry David Thoreau's *"A Plea for Captain John Brown,"* a speech at the Concord Town Hall, October, 1859:

"All is quiet at Harper's Ferry," say the journals. What is the character of that calm which follows when the law and the slaveholder prevail? I regard this event as a touchstone designed to bring out, with glaring distinctness, the character of this government. We needed to be thus assisted to see it by the light of history. It needed to see itself. When a government puts forth its strength on the side of injustice, as ours to maintain slavery and kill the liberators of the slave, it reveals itself a merely brute force, or worse, a demoniacal force . . . . There sits a tyrant holding fettered four millions of slaves; here comes their heroic liberator. This most hypocritical and diabolical government looks up from its seat on the gasping four millions, and inquires with an assumption of innocence: "What do you assault me for? Am I not an honest man? Cease agitation on this subject, or I will make a slave of you, too, or else hang you."

Colonel Robert E. Lee ordered marines under the command of Lieutenant James E. B. Stuart
to seize the engine house at Harpers Ferry where John Brown was holding eleven hostages.
(Courtesy West Virginia Department of Natural Resources, Photo by Arnout Hyde, Jr.)

John Brown Going to His Hanging, by Horace Pippin, 1942. Brown's ill-fated scheme to free Southern blacks led to his own martyrdom in 1859. His sentiments were more tender than fanatical when, nearing his execution, he said, "This is a beautiful country. I never had the pleasure of seeing it before." *(Courtesy Pennsylvania Museum of Fine Arts, Philadelphia.)*

John Brown's last statement to the court, November 2, 1859:

This Court acknowledges, as I suppose, the validity of the law of God. I see a book kissed here which I suppose to be the Bible, or at least the New Testament. That teaches me that all things whatsoever I would that man should do to me, I should do even so to them. It teaches me, further, to "remember them that are in bonds, as bound with them." I endeavored to act up to that instruction. I say, I am yet too young to understand that God is any respector of persons. I believe that to have interfered as I have done—as I have always freely admitted I have done—in behalf of His despised poor, was

not wrong, but right. Now, if it is deemed necessary that I should forfeit my life for the furtherance of the ends of justice, and mingle my blood further with the blood of my children and with the blood of millions in this slave country whose rights are disregarded by wicked, cruel, and unjust enactments— I submit; so let it be done.

John Brown's last written statement, December 2, 1859:

I, John Brown, am not quite certain that the crimes of this guilty land will never be purged away but with blood. I had, as I now think vainly, flattered myself that without very much bloodshed it might be done.

Confederate artist Adalbert J. Volck scornfully portrayed Lincoln passing through Baltimore disguised in a Scotch cap and long cloak on the way to his inauguration. This myth of the journey was a popular one. (*The Museum of the Confederacy*.)

The election in 1860, of that "wild man from nowhere" was the catalyst which unleashed Southern fanatics who had held their secessionist sympathies only barely in check. Mississippi Senator Albert Gallatin Brown in an emotional appeal to a Southern audience stated, "The North is accumulating power, and it means to use that power to emancipate your slaves. When that is done, no pen can describe, no tongue depict, no pencil paint the horrors that will overspread this country . . . . Disunion is a fearful thing, but emancipation is worse. Better leave the Union in the open face of day, than be lighted from it at midnight by the incendiary's torch."

Very quickly, the secessionists won disunion. Between December 1860 and March 1861 which would mark Lincoln's inauguration, the seven states of the deep South seceded and formed the Confederate States of America. To lead them they called upon a Senator with an unparalleled reputation in the Congress, Jefferson Davis, who faced the almost insurmountable task of creating a new nation composed of states which were primarily concerned with protecting their individual interests. He was pitted against an established government with massive human, organizational and industrial resources at its command, led by a man about whom he knew very little.

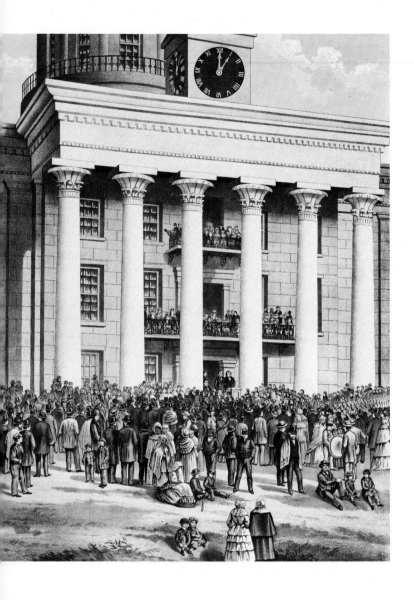

From William Howard Russell's *My Diary North and South*:

I had an opportunity of observing the President [Mr. Davis] very closely. He did not impress me as favorably as I had expected, though he is certainly a very different looking man from Mr. Lincoln. He is like a gentleman—has a slight, light figure, little exceeding middle height, and holds himself erect and straight. He was dressed in a rustic suit of slate-coloured stuff, with a black silk handkerchief round his neck; his manner is plain, and rather reserved and drastic. His head is well-formed with a fine full forehead, square and high, covered with innumerable fine lines and wrinkles. His features are regular, though the cheek-bones are too high, and the jaws too hollow to be handsome. The lips are thin, flexible, and curved, the chin square, well-defined; the nose very regular, with wide nostrils; and the eyes deep set, large and full. One seems nearly blind, and is partly covered with a film .... Wonderful to relate, he does not chew tobacco, and is neat and clean-looking, with hair trimmed and boots brushed. The expression of his face is anxious, he has a very haggard, care-worn, and paindrawn look, though no trace of anything but the utmost confidence and greatest decision could be detected in his conversation ....

From President Jefferson Davis' First Inaugural Address, February 18, 1861:

We have entered upon the career of independence, and it must be inflexibly pursued. Through many years of controversy with our late associates of the Northern States, we have vainly endeavored to secure tranquillity and obtain respect for the rights to which we were entitled. As a necessity, not a choice, we have resorted to the remedy of separation, and henceforth our energies must be directed to the conduct of our own affairs and the perpetuity of the Confederacy which we have formed. If a just perception of mutual interest shall permit us peaceably to pursue our separate political career, my most earnest desire will have been fulfilled. But if this be denied to us and the integrity of our territory and jurisdiction be assailed, it will but remain for us with firm resolve to appeal to arms and invoke the blessing of Providence on a just cause ....

It is joyous in the midst of perilous times to look around upon a people united in heart, where one purpose of high resolve animates and actuates the whole; where the sacrifices to be made are not weighed in the balance against honor and right and equality. Obstacles may retard, but they cannot long prevent, the progress of a movement sanctified by its justice and sustained by a virtuous people. Reverently let us invoke the God of our fathers to guide and protect us in our efforts to perpetuate the principles which by His blessing they were able to vindicate, establish, and transmit to their posterity. With the continuance of His favor ever gratefully acknowledged, we may hopefully look forward to success, to peace, and to prosperity.

Jefferson Davis, by John Robertson, 1863. Although he was considered cold and aloof by many, Southern delegates from the seceded states chose Davis over his more fanatical colleagues as the new President of the Confederacy.
(The Museum of the Confederacy.)

The new dome of the Federal Capitol was in the midst of construction when the inauguration of Abraham Lincoln took place on March 4, 1861. Fears for the President's life prompted the stationing of marksmen at the building's windows. *(Courtesy Chicago Historical Society.)*

From William Howard Russell's *My Diary North and South:*

The impression produced by the size of his [Mr. Lincoln's] extremities, and by his flapping and wide projecting ears, may be removed by the appearance of kindliness, sagacity, and the awkward friendliness of his face. The mouth is absolutely prodigious. The lips, straggling and extending almost from one line of black beard to the other, are only kept in order by two deep furrows from the nostril to the chin. The nose itself—a prominent organ—stands out from the face with an inquiring anxious air, as though it were sniffing for some good thing in the wind. The eyes, dark, full, and deeply set, are penetrating, but full of an expression which amounts to tenderness . . . . One would say that, although the mouth was made to enjoy a joke, it could also utter the severest sentence which the head could dictate, but that Mr. Lincoln would be . . . willing to temper justice with mercy . . . .

From President Abraham Lincoln's First Inaugural Address, March 4, 1861:

While the people retain their virtue, and vigilence, no administration, by any extreme of wickedness or folly, can very seriously injure the government, in the short space of four years.

My countrymen, one and all, think calmly and *well,* upon this whole subject. Nothing valuable can be lost by taking time. If there be an object to *hurry* any of you, in hot haste, to a step which you would never take *deliberately,* that object will be frustrated by taking time; but no good object can be frustrated by it. Such of you as are now dissatisfied, still have the old Constitution unimpaired, and, on the sensitive point, the laws of your own framing under it; while the new administration will have no immediate power, if it would, to change either. If it were admitted that you who are dissatisfied, hold the right side in the dispute, there still is no single good reason for precipitate action. Intelligence, patriotism, Christianity, and a firm reliance on Him, who has never yet forsaken this favored land, are still competent to adjust, in the best way, all our present difficulty.

In *your* hands, my dissatisfied fellow countrymen, and not in *mine,* is the momentous issue of civil war. The government will not assail *you.* You can have no conflict, without being yourselves the agressors. *You* have no oath registered in Heaven to destroy the government, while *I* shall have the most solemn one to "preserve, protect and defend" it.

I am loathe to close. We are not enemies, but friends. We must not be enemies. Though passion may have strained, it must not break our bonds of affection. The mystic chords of memory, stretching from every battle-field, and patriot grave, to every living heart and hearthstone, all over this broad land, will yet swell the chorus of the Union, when again touched, as surely they will be, by the better angels of our nature.

Abraham Lincoln, by George P. Healy, 1860. The country lawyer from Springfield, Illinois, soon proved to the nation that he would not be the tool of sophisticated Washington political professionals. *(In the collection of the Corcoran Gallery of Art.)*

There were two Federal garrisons still under Union control, Fort Sumter, on the Carolina coast and Fort Pickens at Pensacola, Florida. Major Anderson at Sumter had written the President that supplies were running low and a relief ship sent by President Buchanan in January had been turned away by gunfire. Lincoln decided to attempt reprovisioning.

From a letter of Secretary of War Simon Cameron to Major Robert Anderson, April 4, 1861:

Hoping still that you will be able to sustain yourself till the 11th. or 12th. inst. the expedition will go forward; and, finding your flag flying, will attempt to provision you, and, in case the effort is resisted, will endeavor also to reinforce you.

You will therefore hold out if possible till the arrival of the expedition.

It is not, however, the intention of the President to subject your command to any danger or hardship beyond what, in your judgment, would be usual in military life; and he has entire confidence that you will act as becomes a patriot and a soldier, under all circumstances.

Whenever, if at all, in your judgment, to save yourself and command, a capitulation becomes a necessity, you are authorized to make it.

From a letter of General Pierre Beauregard to Major Robert Anderson, April 11, 1861:

Sir: The Government of the Confederate States has hitherto forborne from any hostile demonstration against Fort Sumter, in the hope that the Government of the United States, with a view to the amicable adjustment of all questions between the two governments, and to avert the calamities of war, would voluntarily abandon it.

. . . The Confederate States can no longer delay assuming actual possession of a fortification . . . necessary to its defense and security.

I am ordered . . . to demand the evacuation of Fort Sumter . . . . All proper facilities will be afforded for the removal of yourself and command . . . to any post in the United States which you may select. The flag which you have upheld so long and with so much fortitude, under the most trying circumstances, may be saluted by you on taking it down.

From a letter of Major Robert Anderson to General Pierre Beauregard, April 11, 1861:

Sir: I have the honor to acknowledge the receipt of your communication, demanding the evacuation of this Fort, and to say in reply thereto that it is a demand with which I regret that my sense of honor and my obligations to my Government prevent my compliance . . . .

A deputation from General Beauregard followed immediately, informing Major Anderson that Southern batteries would commence firing in one hour, and at half past four, the first guns opened up on Fort Sumter. After a long and valiant attempt at defense, honorable terms of surrender were agreed upon and the Fort evacuated.

The courtesy extended by these two men in their communications would be repeated often between Union and Confederate commanders, many of whom knew each other intimately. Anderson had taught young Cadet Beauregard the uses of artillery at West Point, and Beauregard had learned his lessons well.

From a letter of Major Robert Anderson to Secretary of War Simon Cameron, April 18, 1861: [Major Anderson was writing from the steamship *Baltic* off Sandy Hook, New Jersey.]

Sir:—Having defended Fort Sumter for thirty-four hours, until the quarters were entirely burned, the main gates destroyed by fire, the gorge wall seriously injured, the magazine surrounded by flames, and its door closed from the effect of the heat, four barrels and three cartridges of powder only being available, and no provisions but pork remaining, I accepted terms of evacuation, offered by General Beauregard . . . and marched out of the fort, Sunday . . . , the 14th instant, with colors flying and drums beating, bringing away company and private property, and saluting my flag with fifty guns.

Citizens of Charleston watch the bombardment of Fort Sumter from the city's housetops. (*Valentine Museum, Richmond, Virginia.*)

John F. Weir depicted America's burgeoning industrial might in his painting *The Gun Foundry*. Massive amounts of cannon for the Federal armies rolled out of the West Point factory. (*Courtesy, Putnam County Historical Society, New York*.)

From Oliver Wendell Holmes' oration, July 4, 1863:

The first gun that spat its iron insult at Fort Sumter smote every loyal American full in the face. As when the foul witch used to torture her miniature charge, the person it represented suffered all that she inflicted on his waxen counterpart, so every buffet that fell on the smoking fortress was felt by the sovereign nation of which that was the representative . . . . Insult could go no farther, for those battered walls waved the precious symbol of all we most value in the past and most hope for in the future—the banner under which we became a nation, and which, next to the cross of the Redeemer, is the dearest object of love and honor to all who toil or march or sail beneath its waving folds of glory.

From President Abraham Lincoln's Proclamation calling the militia and convening Congress, April 15, 1861:

Whereas the laws of the United States have been for some time past, and now are opposed, and the execution thereof obstructed, in the states of South Carolina, Georgia, Alabama, Florida, Mississippi, Louisiana and Texas, by combinations too powerful to be suppressed by the ordinary course of judicial proceedings, or by the powers vested in the Marshals by law,

Now therefore, I Abraham Lincoln, President of the United States, in virtue of the power in me vested by the Constitution, and the laws, have thought fit to call forth, and hereby do call forth, the militia of the several States of the Union, to the aggregate number of seventy-five thousand, in order to suppress said combinations, and to cause the laws to be duly executed . . . .

A Nation at War

The righteous perisheth and no man layeth it to heart, and merciful men are taken away, none considering that the righteous is taken away from the evil to come.

Isaiah 57:1

In May of 1862, a young Georgian, S.G. Pryor, wrote his wife describing his initiation into the horrors of battle:

> I felt quite small in that fight the other day when the musket balls and cannon balls was flying around me as thick as hail and my best friends falling on both sides dead and mortally wounded. Oh Dear it is impossible for me to express my feelings when the fight was over & I saw what was done the tears came then free. Oh that I never could behold such a sight again to think of it among civilized people killing one another like beasts. One would think the supreme ruler would put a stop to it but we sinned as a nation and must suffer in the flesh as well as spiritually those things we can't account for.

The passionate rhetoric was long past, the fond and confident farewells from tearful wives and mothers were dim and cherished memories, the awful work of war had begun. They told Billy Yank that he was fighting to preserve the Union; they told Johnny Reb he was building a new nation, and that the devil Lincoln was out to destroy the South. But in the sound of the cannons' roar and the pitiful cries of the wounded, the rationalizations of politicians were forgotten. In battle, the purpose was simple; namely, to whip the enemy and to stay alive.

It was the Civil War, or the War Between the States, as it came to be called in the South, which proved to the world the endurance and pluck of the American soldier. He could abide cold, hunger, his own ineptitudes, personal deprivations of every sort, and jest about them. He loved to sing and to play practical jokes. He was often undisciplined, nearly always unkempt, and his frontier spirit and general boisterousness chafed at the more petty military orders. He often ignored them. But he could fight and fight he did, in the more than two thousand battles and skirmishes which have become a national poem of remembered place names: Bull Run, Fort Donelson, Antietam, Chancellorsville, Fredericksburg, Vicksburg, Gettysburg, Lookout Mountain, Chickamauga. On and on goes the list and its

A spirit of dedication to the cause prevailed following President Lincoln's call to arms. George C. Lambdin in *The Consecration, 1861,* captured those moments of sentiment and high ideals. (*Courtesy, The Indianapolis Museum of Art, James E. Roberts Fund.*)

gruesome companion, the roster of the dead and the wounded that seemingly left no home untouched.

This was a war in which the generals fought on the field, and the weary volunteer would follow a commander he respected and loved even when he led them to almost certain death. Like their subordinates, those in command also knew how to die: the audacious Nathaniel Lyon at Wilson's Creek; Stonewall Jackson, as awesome as Joshua, as daring and inventive as Lee himself, dead after Chancellorsville; Albert Sidney Johnston, a needless casualty at bloody Shiloh. The carnage of the war was indiscriminate of rank or class.

If death was indiscriminate, the Union Army was not in its complete refusal at first to allow black men to serve. To both the government and the people it was a "white man's war." An enraged Frederick Douglass said in 1862: "Colored men were good enough to fight under Washington. They are not good enough to fight under McClellan." Lincoln himself did not want to antagonize the border states by enrolling blacks and most Northerners remained deeply prejudiced against serving side by side with their "inferiors."

Therefore it was not conscience but the exigencies of war which forced a change. Whites were not as eager to enlist as the conflict became protracted, and on July 16, 1862, Congress passed the legislation which would admit the enlistment of blacks and swell the dwindling ranks. Over 200,000 served and fought valiantly for the Union effort.

Not until December 1863 would the North find, in Ulysses S. Grant, the kind of dogged and consistent military leadership which would mean certain victory. Until then successive generals would make successive attempts to take the Confederate capital of Richmond, and to destroy the Army of Northern Virginia under the brilliant command of Robert E. Lee.

It was not Lee, nor even Grant, who would be responsible for the inevitable conclusion. As the years dragged on, they took a deadly toll, not only in human life, but in that which supports it. Virginia was devastated by the ruinous battles that had raged on her soil; the Northern blockade of Confederate ports was ever tightening; and, as the lifeline of the South, the mighty Mississippi, came under total Union control, Southerners had no recourse to supplies from the west. The Confederacy was losing by attrition of manpower and supplies.

Lee described the misery of his army during the terrible winter of 1862-1863:

> The want of shoes and blankets in this army continues to cause much suffering and to impair its efficiency. In one regiment I am informed that there are only fifty men with serviceable shoes, and a brigade that recently went on picket was compelled to leave several hundred men in camp, who were unable to bear the exposure of duty, being destitute of shoes and blankets . . . . I trust that no efforts will be spared to develop our own resources of supply, as a further dependence upon those from abroad can result in nothing but increase of suffering and want . . . .

It was the beginning of the end, but the soldiers of the Army of Northern Virginia would endure. They would suffer and some of them would live to fight the yankees another day.

Right General Guide, 1861
14th "Brooklyn" Regiment,
New York State Militia
(K/S Historical Publications.)

Drum Major, 1861
1st Virginia Volunteer Infantry
(K/S Historical Publications.)

Alfred R. Waud sketched rebel soldiers taking the oath of allegiance to the Confederacy in the Senate chamber of the capitol at Richmond. Virginia had seceded in mid-April, her governor refusing to send one man to subjugate the Southern states. Colonel Robert E. Lee, who had been offered command of the Northern armies, resigned his commission in the service of the Union and returned to his native state to assume command of the forces there. (*Valentine Museum, Richmond, Virginia*.)

From Mary Ann Livermore's *My Story of the War:*

Monday dawned, April 15. Who that saw that day will ever forget . . . the voice of Abraham Lincoln calling for seventy-five thousand volunteers for three months! They were for the protection of Washington and the property of the government. All who were in arms against the country were commanded to return home in twenty days, and Congress was summoned to meet on the 4th of July.

This proclamation was like the first peal of a surcharged thunder-cloud, clearing the murky air. The South received it as a declaration of war, the North as a confession that civil war had begun; and the whole North arose as one man. . . .

Everywhere the drum and fife thrilled the air with their stirring call. Recruiting offices were opened in every city, town, and village. . . . Hastily formed companies marched to camps of rendezvous, the sunlight flashing from gun-barrel and bayonet, and the streets echoing the measured tread of soldiers. Flags floated from the roofs of houses, were flung to the breeze from chambers of commerce and boards of trade, spanned the surging streets, decorated the private parlor, glorified the schoolroom, festooned the church walls and pulpit, and blossomed everywhere. All normal habits of life were suspended, and business and pleasure alike were forgotten. . . .

From Sallie Hunt's *"Our Women in the War": The Lives They Lived, the Deaths They Died:*

One spring day in April, 1861, all Richmond was astir. Schools were broken up, and knots of excited men gathered at every street corner. Sumter had been fired upon, and Lincoln had ordered the men of Virginia to rush upon their brethren of the South and put the rebellion down. Now "the die was cast," our lot was with theirs, and come weal or woe, we would fight for independence. How merrily the sunbeams danced that day! How proud we children were of the great preparation for the illumination that night!—how few [reckoned] of the great underthrob of misery, grief and want! Every patriotic citizen had his house ablaze with a thousand lights, and the dark ones were *marked.* . . . To us it was a grand spectacle, and our hearts swelled with pride to think we could say to our tyrants: "Thus far shalt thou come, and no further."

In the spring of 1861 the battle cry of public and press alike was "On to Richmond!" Only one hundred miles from Washington lay the new Confederate capital, so invitingly near and such a tempting objective. Yet it was to be one of the most costly and elusive targets of the war.

Only reluctantly would General McDowell, in command of the green Army of the Potomac, submit to the overwhelming pressure for an immediate confrontation with the enemy beyond the river. For both Confederate and Union generals knew that the ardent, but undisciplined troops which poured into Washington and Richmond were not yet ready to do battle.

From Sara Emma Edmonds' *Nurse and Spy or Unsexed, The Female Soldier:*

The great West was stirred to its center, and began to look like a vast military camp. Recruiting offices were filled with men eager to enroll their names as defenders of their country—and women were busily engaged in preparing all the comforts that love and patriotism could suggest for those who were so soon to go forth to victory or to death, while the clash of arms and strains of martial music almost drowned the hum of industry, and war became the theme of every tongue.

About this time I witnessed the departure of the first Western troops which started for Washington. The regiments were drawn up in line—fully equipped for their journey—with their bright bayonets flashing in the morning sunlight. It was on the principal street of a pleasant little village of about a thousand inhabitants, where there was scarcely a family who had not a father, husband, son, or brother in that little band of soldiers who stood there ready to bid them farewell, perhaps for years—perhaps forever. A farewell address was delivered by the village Pastor, and a New Testament presented to each soldier, with the following inscription: "Put your trust in God—and keep your powder dry." Then came the leave-taking—but it is too painful to dwell upon—the last fond word was spoken, the last embrace given, then came the order, "march"—and amid the cheers of the citizens—with banners proudly floating, and the bands playing "The Star Spangled Banner," they moved forward on their way to the capital.

In the early summer of 1861 the horrors of war were unthought of. Uniforms were still unsullied and dreams of brave deeds and glory on the field were the orders of the day. James Walker depicted the precise drilling of a Union regiment as the company commander brought his troops smartly into line. (*The West Point Museum Collections, United States Military Academy*.)

From an editorial in the *Douglass' Monthly,*
September 1861:

Why does the Government reject the negro? Is he
not a man? Can he not wield a sword, fire a gun,
march and counter-march, and obey orders like any
other? . . . If persons so humble as we can be allowed
to speak to the President of the United States, we
should ask him if this dark and terrible hour of the
nation's extremity is a time for consulting a mere
vulgar and unnatural prejudice? . . . We would tell
him that this is no time to fight with one hand, when
both are needed; that this is no time to fight only with
your white hand, and allow your black hand to
remain tied. . . . While the Government continues
to refuse the aid of colored men, thus alienating them
from the national cause, and giving the rebels the
advantage of them, it will not deserve better fortunes that it has thus far experienced.—Men in
earnest don't fight with one hand, when they might
fight with two, and a man drowning would not
refuse to be saved even by a colored hand.

From Sallie Putnam's *Richmond During the War: Four
Years of Personal Observation:*

The services had proceeded until just at their close
in some of the churches, and in others during the
last prayer, the premonitory sound of the bell on the
Square disturbed the solemnity of the hour, and
awoke the people to a dread sense of danger—from
what source, they could not tell.

In an instant all was confusion. The men, in the
excitement, rushed pell-mell from the churches; and
the women, pale and trembling with affright, clung to
their sons and husbands, wherever they could—but
getting no response to their tearful question: "What
is the matter? What *is* the matter?"

Hasty embraces, sudden wrenchings of the hand,
tearful glances of affection, and our men rushed to
their armories, to prepare they knew not for what.
On every female face was the pale hue of dismay; but
mingled with it, the stern, unmistakable impress of
heroic resolution to yield up their hearts' most
cherished idols upon the altar of their country, if
need be. Silently, tearfully, our women wended
their way to their homes, and from every closet, the
outpourings of supplicating souls, for protection to
the loved ones, went up to the ear of the Eternal. . . .

From George Cary Eggleston's *A Rebel's Recollections:*

The unanimity of the people was simply marvel-
ous. So long as the question of secession was under
discussion, opinions were both various and violent.
The moment secession was finally determined upon,

War was still an adventure when Adjutant Robert B.
Hurt of the 55th Tennessee Infantry posed with his gleaming
and still untried weaponry. Before that adventure was over
250,000 of his comrades would be killed or fall the victims
of disease. (*The Museum of the Confederacy.*)

a revolution was wrought. There was no longer
anything to discuss, and so discussion ceased. Men
got ready for war, and delicate women with equal
spirit sent them off with smiling faces. The man who
tarried at home for ever so brief a time, after the
call to arms had been given, found it necessary to
explain himself to every woman of his acquaintance,
and no explanation was sufficient to shield him from
the social ostracism consequent upon any long-tarry-
ing. Throughout the war it was the same, and when
the war ended the men who lived to return were
greeted with sad faces by those who had cheerfully
and even joyously sent them forth to the battle.

Harper's Weekly rendered a symbolic depiction of jubilation in Virginia's capitol after the state's secession in 1861. *(Valentine Museum, Richmond, Virginia.)*

Walt Whitman, *Beat! Beat! Drums!*

Beat! beat! drums!—Blow! bugles! blow!
Through the Windows—through doors—burst like a force of ruthless men,
Into the solemn church, and scatter the congregation;
Into the school where the scholar is studying:
Leave not the bridegroom quiet—no happiness must he have now with his bride;
Nor the peaceful farmer any peace, plowing his field or gathering his grain;
So fierce you whirr and pound, you drums—so shrill you bugles blow.

Beat! beat! drums!—Blow! bugles! blow!
Make no parley—stop for no expostulation;
Mind not the timid—mind not the weeper or prayer;
Mind not the old man beseeching the young man;
Let not the child's voice be heard, nor the mother's entreaties;
Make even the trestles to shake the dead, where they lie awaiting the hearses,
So strong you thump, O terrible drums—so loud you bugles blow.

As the war opened a difficult decision faced many Union officers who suddenly found that country and home were no longer one and the same. Among these was Colonel Robert E. Lee. Offered command of the Federal forces, he refused and resigned "from a service to which I have devoted the best years of my life, and all the ability I possessed."

When Virginia seceded, Lee prepared to head the army of the Old Dominion, but was called upon by President Davis to serve as a kind of armchair advisor. Although the administrative duties galled him, he bore them with the good grace consistent with his sense of duty.

Major General McClellan's Union victory at Philippi in western Virginia put Lee back in harness again, attempting to keep the Federals from making further gains in the rugged and drenched terrain. Frustrated by ineptness and incompetency among the officers, he nevertheless decided to take the risk of facing a superior Union force at Cheat Mountain. He was unsuccessful, and by all rights should have faded into the ignominy of subordinate commands. However, like Grant, Lee had staying power, and as Grant would become the embodiment of Northern military success, Lee would become the shining symbol of all for which the South dreamed and fought.

From a letter of Colonel Robert E. Lee to his sister, Mrs. Anne Marshall, April 20, 1861:

. . . The whole South is in a state of revolution, into which Virginia, after a long struggle, has been drawn; and though I recognize no necessity for this state of things, and would have forborne and pleaded to the end for redress of grievances, real or supposed, yet in my own person I had to meet the question whether I should take part against my native state.

With all my devotion to the Union and the feeling of loyalty and duty of an American citizen, I have not been able to make up my mind to raise my hand against my relatives, my children, my home. I have therefore resigned my commission in the army, and save in defense of my native state, with the sincere hope that my poor services may never be needed, I hope I may never be called on to draw my sword. . . .

From Walter H. Taylor's *Four Years with General Lee:*

. . . I have never known a man more painstaking and thorough in all that he undertook. . . . he [Lee] seemed to address himself to the accomplishment of every task that devolved upon him in a conscientious and deliberate way, as if he himself was directly accountable to some higher power for the manner in which he performed his duty. I then discovered, too, that characteristic of him that always marked his intercourse and relations with his fellow men—scrupulous consideration for the feelings and interests of others; the more humble the station of one from whom he received appeal or request, the more he appeared to desire to meet the demand if possible or . . . to make the denial in the most considerate way, as if done with reluctance and regret. . . .

After a day's work at his office he would enjoy above all things a ride on horseback . . . and no sculpture can ever reproduce in marble or bronze the picture of manly grace and beauty that became in those days so familiar to the people in and around Richmond in the person of General Lee on his favorite horse. . . .

General Robert E. Lee quoted in Captain Robert E. Lee's *Recollections and Letters of General Robert E. Lee:* [The captain was the general's son.]

If I were an artist . . . I would draw a true picture of Traveller [Lee's famous mount]—representing his fine proportions, muscular figure, deep chest and short back, strong haunches, flat legs, small head, broad forehead, delicate ears, quick eye, small feet, and black mane and tail. Such a picture would inspire a poet, whose genius could then depict his worth and describe his endurance of toil, hunger, thirst, heat, cold, and the dangers and sufferings through which he passed. He could dilate upon his sagacity and affection, and his invariable response to every wish of his rider. He might even imagine his thoughts, through the long night marches and days of battle through which he has passed. But I am no artist; I can only say he is a Confederate gray. I purchased him in the mountains of Virginia in the autumn of 1861, and he has been my patient follower ever since—to Georgia, the Carolinas, and back to Virginia. He carried me through the Seven Days' battle around Richmond, the second Manassas, at Sharpsburg, Fredericksburg, the last day at Chancellorsville, to Pennsylvania, at Gettysburg, and back to the Rappahannock. From the commencement of the campaign in 1864 at Orange, till its close around Petersburg, the saddle was scarcely off his back, as he passed through the fire of the Wilderness, Spotsylvania, Cold Harbour, and across the James River. He was almost in daily requisition in the winter of 1864-65 on the long line of defenses from Chickahominy, north of Richmond, to Hatcher's Run, south of the Appomattox. In the campaign of 1865, he bore me from Petersburg to the final days at Appomattox Court House. . . .

General Robert E. Lee on his horse, Traveller,
an engraving from the painting by L.M.D. Guillaume.
(*The Museum of the Confederacy*.)

Dramatic recruiting posters appealed to both national and community patriotism. Volunteer companies often elected their own officers or formed under the leadership of popular home-town figures whose military skills were minimal. (*Courtesy Chicago Historical Society.*)

From Albert D. Richardson's *The Secret Service: The Field, the Dungeon, and the Escape:*

At Cannelton [Virginia, July, 1861], a hundred slaves were employed in the coal-oil works—two long, begrimed dilapidated buildings, with a few wretched houses hard by. Nobody was visible, except the Negroes. When I asked one of them: "Where are all the white people," he replied with a broad grin—"Done gone, mass'r."

A black woman, whom we encountered on the road, was asked: "Have you run away from your master?"

"Golly, no!" was the prompt answer, "mass'r run away from *me*!"

The slaves, who always heard the term "runaway" applied only to their own race, were not aware that it could have any other significance. After the war opened, its larger meaning suddenly dawned upon them. The idea of the master running away and the Negroes staying was always to them ludicrous beyond description. The extravagant lines of "Kingdom Coming" exactly depicted their feelings:

Say, darkies, hab you seen de mass'r,
  Wid de muffstach on his face,
Go 'long de road some time dis mornin',
  Like he's gwine to leave de place?

He seen de smoke way up de ribber
  Where de Linkum gunboats lay;
He took his hat and left berry sudden,
  And I s'pose he runned away.

De mass'r run, ha! ha!
  De darkey stay, ho! ho!
It must be now de kingdom comin',
  An' de year ob Jubilo!

"Dey tole us," said a group of blacks, "dat if your army cotched us, you would cut off our right feet. But, Lor! we knowed you wouldn't hurt *us*!"

At a house where we dined, the planter assuming to be loyal, one of our officers grew confidential with him, when a Negro woman managed to beckon me into a back room, and seizing my arm, very earnestly said: "I tell you, mass'r's only just putting on. He hates you all, and wants to see you killed. Soon as you have passed, he will send right to Wise's army, and tell him what you mean to do; if any of you'uns remain here behind the troops, you will be in danger. He's in a heap of trouble," she added, "but Lord, dese times just suits *me*!"

From Henry Howe's *The Times of the Rebellion in the West:*

In one of the Indiana regiments [at Garrick's Ford, West Virginia, July 13, 1861], was a Methodist preacher, said to be one of the very best shots in his regiment. During the battle, he was particularly conspicuous for the zeal with which he kept up a constant fire. The 14th Ohio Regiment, in the thick of the fight, fired an average of eleven rounds to every man, but this parson managed to get in a great deal more than that average. He fired carefully, with perfect coolness, and always after a steady aim, and the boys declare that every time, as he took down his gun, after firing he added, "And may the Lord have mercy on your soul."

From a letter of General Robert E. Lee to his wife, Mary, September 17, 1861:

. . . All the attacking parties with great labour had reached their destination, [Cheat Mountain], over mountains considered impassable to bodies of troops, notwithstanding a heavy storm that set in the day before and raged all night, in which they had to stand up till daylight. Their arms were then unserviceable, and they in poor condition for a fierce assault against artillery and superior numbers. After waiting till 10 o'clock for the assault on Cheat Mountain, which did not take place, and which was to have been the signal for the rest, they were withdrawn, and, after waiting three days in front of the enemy, hoping he would come out of his trenches, we returned to our position, [at Valley Mountain]. I can not tell you my regret and mortification at the untoward events that caused the failure of the plan. I had taken every precaution to ensure success and counted on it. But the Ruler of the Universe ruled otherwise and sent a storm to disconcert a well-laid plan, and to destroy my hopes. We are no worse off now than before, except the disclosure of our plan, against which they will guard. . . . Our poor sick, I know, suffer much. They bring it on themselves by not doing what they are told. They are worse than children, for the latter can be forced.

From Ambrose Bierce's *On a Mountain:*

Among [the dead at Cheat Mountain] was a chap belonging to my company named Abbott; it is not odd that I recollect it, for there was something unusual in the manner of Abbott's taking off. He was lying flat upon his stomach and was killed by being struck in the side by a nearly spent cannon-shot that came rolling in among us. The shot remained in him until removed. It was a solid round-shot, evidently cast in some private foundry, whose proprietor, setting the laws of thrift above those of balistics, had put his "imprint" upon it: it bore, in slightly sunken letters, the name "Abbott." That is what I was told—I was not present.

On July 16, General McDowell ordered the first Federal advance on Manassas Junction, about twenty-five miles from Washington. Waiting for him near Centerville, along the meandering creek known as Bull Run were General Pierre Beauregard, the hero of Sumter, and 32,000 rebel infantry, artillery and cavalry.

The march took the Union army two and one-half days. McDowell wrote, "They stopped every moment, to pick blackberries, or get water; they would not keep in the ranks, order as you please . . . ." Along the way Washingtonians camped to picnic and to watch the battle which would, of course, win the war.

From morning until late afternoon, it indeed seemed a Union victory. Couriers rode from the front with cheering bulletins of Federal advances. Then the yankees began to retreat and to run, in apparent terror of oncoming rebel cavalry. In panic they fled back toward Centerville, a tumbling and fear-driven mob, civilian and soldier alike. To no avail McDowell tried to rally his army. The stumbling, exhausted men found their way to the safety of the capital.

The North now knew that war was not an occasion for picnics, nor was it a game, speedily won.

General Irvin McDowell quoted in *War of the Rebellion . . . Official Records of the Union and Confederate Armies:*

The enemy was evidently disheartened and broken. But we had then been fighting since 10:30 in the morning, and it was after 3 o'clock in the afternoon. The men had been up since 2 o'clock in the morning, and had made what to those unused to such things seemed a long march before coming into action, though the longest distance gone over was not more than 9 and one half miles; and though they had 3 days' provisions served out to them the day before, many, no doubt, either did not get them or threw them away on the march or during the battle, and were therefore without food. They had done much severe fighting. Some of the regiments which had been driven from the hill in the first two attempts of the enemy to keep possession of it had become shaken, were unsteady, and had many men out of the ranks.

It was at this time that the enemy's re-inforcements came to his aid . . . . They threw themselves on the woods on our right, and opened a fire of musketry on our men, which caused them to break, and retire down the hillside. This soon degenerated into dis-

General Pierre Beauregard quoted in Robert Underwood Johnson's and Clarence Buell's *Battles and Leaders of the Civil War:*

It was now between half-past 2 and 3 o'clock; a scorching sun increased the oppression of the troops, exhausted from incessant fighting, many of them having been engaged since the morning. Fearing lest the Federal offensive should secure too firm a grip, and knowing the fatal result that might spring from any grave infraction of my line, I determined to make another effort for the recovery of the plateau, and ordered a charge of the entire line of battle, including the reserves, which at this crisis I myself led into action. The movement was made with such keeping and dash that the whole plateau was swept clear of the enemy, who were driven down the slope and across the turnpike on our right and the valley of Young's branch on our left, leaving in our final possession the Robinson and Henry houses, with most of Ricketts's and Griffin's batteries, the men of which were mostly shot down where they bravely stood by their guns.

order, for which there was no remedy. Every effort was made to rally them . . . but in vain . . . . The plain was covered with the retreating troops, and they seemed to affect those with whom they came in contact. The retreat soon became a rout, and this soon degenerated still further into a panic.

From the Charleston *Mercury,* July 25, 1861:

Overwhelmed by superior numbers, and compelled to yield before a fire that swept everything before it, General Bee rode up and down his lines, encouraging his troops, by everything that was dear to them, to stand up and repel the tide that threatened them with destruction. At last his own brigade dwindled to a mere handful, with every field officer killed or disabled. He rode up to General Jackson and said: "General, they are beating us back."

The reply was: "Sir, we'll give them the bayonet."

General Bee immediately rallied the remnant of his brigade, and his last words to them were: "There is Jackson standing like a stone wall. Let us determine to die here and we will conquer. Follow me!"

His men obeyed the call; and at the head of his column, the very moment when the battle was turning in our favor, he fell mortally wounded. General Beauregard was heard to say he had never seen such gallantry. He [General Bee] never murmured at his suffering, but seemed to be consoled by the reflection that he was doing his duty.

From Walt Whitman's *Speciman Days:*

If the Secesh officers and forces had immediately followed, and by a bold Napoleonic movement had entered Washington the first day (or even the second), they could have had things their own way and a powerful faction North to back them. One of our returning colonels expressed in public that night, amid a swarm of officers and gentlemen in a crowded room, the opinion that it was useless to fight, that the Southerners had made their title clear, and that the best course for the National Government to pursue was to desist from any further attempt at stopping them and admit them again in the lead, on the best terms they were willing to grant. Not a voice was raised against this judgment amid that large crowd of officers and gentlemen.

Below:
Quaker guns," such as these poised before Centerville, were designed to fool the enemy as to the amount and size of artillery he would face as he moved on entrenched fortifications. *(Courtesy Chicago Historical Society.)*

From Stephen Vincent Benét's *John Brown's Body:*

All night the Union army fled in retreat
Like horses scared by a shadow—a stumbling flood
Of panicky men who had been brave for a while
And might be brave again on another day
But now were merely children chased by the night
And each man tainting his neighbor with the same
Blind fear.

When men or horses begin to run
Like that, they keep on running till they tire out
Unless a strong hand masters a bridle-rein.
Here there was no hand to master, no rein to clutch,
Where the riderless horses kicked their way through the crowd
And the congressmen's carriages choked Cat Hairpin Bend.
Sykes and the regulars covered the retreat,
And a few was kept in some sort of order,
But the rest—They tried to stop them at Centerville.
McDowell and his tired staff held a haggard conference.
But before the officers could order retreat
The men were walking away.

They had fought and lost.
They were going to Washington, they were going back
To their tents and their cooking-fires and their letters from
    Susie.

McDowell lost command of the Army of the Potomac beacuse of the staggering defeat and it fell to Major General George McClellan, the egocentric but inspiring victor of the battle at Philippi which had secured Virginia's western counties for the Union. McClellan spent the remainder of the summer and fall whipping his ragtag and dispirited army into disciplined fighting shape and Confederate generals did the same as their soldiers settled in around Centerville.

In Washington the same appeals for precipitate action against the enemy were renewed, but the Union commander remained firm. Horace Greeley described the winter situation: "The loyal masses—awed by the obloquy heaped on those falsely accused of having caused the disaster at Bull Run by their ignorant impatience and precipitancy—stood in silent expectation.... First, we were waiting for reinforcements—which was most reasonable; then, for the requisite drilling and fitting for service—which was just as helpful to the rebels as to us; then for the leaves to fall—so as to facilitate military movements in a country so wooded and broken as Virginia; then, for cannon—whereof we had already more than two hundred first-rate fieldpieces in Virginia, ready for instant service; and so the long, bright autumn, and the colder but still favorable December, wore heavily away, and saw nothing of moment attempted. Even the Rebel batteries obstructing the lower Potomac

Conrad Wise Chapman sketched Confederate soldiers practicing their fencing skills. *(Valentine Museum, Richmond, Virginia.)*

were not so much as menaced—the navy laying the blame on the army; the army throwing it back on the navy—probably both right, or, rather, both wrong; but the net result was nothing done; until the daily repetition of the stereotyped telegraphic bulletin, 'All quiet on the Potomac'— which had at first been received with satisfaction; afterward with complacency; at length evoked a broad and general roar of disdainful merriment."

From a letter of Major General George McClellan to his wife, Ellen, July 30, 1861:

. . . I am getting my ideas pretty well arranged in regard to the strength of my army; it will be a very large one. I have been employed in trying to get the right kind of general officers . . . . Have been working this morning at a bill allowing me to appoint as many aides as I please from civil life and from the army. . . .

I went to the Senate to get it through, and was quite overwhelmed by the congratulations I received and the respect with which I was treated. I suppose half a dozen of the oldest made the remark I am becoming so much used to: "Why how young you look, and yet an old soldier!" It seems to strike everybody that I am very young. They give me my way in everything, full swing and unbounded confidence. All tell me that I am responsible for the fate of the nation, and that all its resources shall be placed at my disposal. It is an immense task that I have on my hands, but I believe I can accomplish it . . . . When I was in the Senate chamber to-day and found those old men flocking around me; when I afterwards stood in the library, looking over the Capitol of our great nation, and saw the crowd gathering around to stare at me, I began to feel how great the task committed to me. Oh! how sincerely I pray to God that I may be endowed with the wisdom and courage necessary to accomplish the work. Who would have thought, when we were married that I should so soon be called upon to save my country?

From George Cary Eggleston's *A Rebel's Recollections:*

. . . The men who volunteered went to war of their own accord, and were wholly unaccustomed to acting on any other than their own motion. They were hardy lovers of field sports, accustomed to out-door life, and in all physical respects excellent material of which to make an army. But they were not used to control of any sort, and were not disposed to obey anybody except for good and sufficient reason given. While actually on drill they obeyed the word of command, not so much by

Winslow Homer portrayed joyful Federals rummaging through the bounty of Christmas boxes from home in 1861. (*Valentine Museum, Richmond, Virginia.*)

reason of its being proper to obey a command, as because obedience was in that case necessary to the successful issue of a pretty performance in which they were interested. Off drill they did as they pleased, holding themselves gentlemen, and as such bound to consult only their own wills. Their officers were of themselves, chosen by election, and subject, by custom, to enforced resignation upon petition of the men. Only corporals cared sufficiently little for their position to risk any magnifying of their office by the enforcement of discipline. I make of them an honorable exception, out of regard for the sturdy corporal who, at Ashland, marched six of us (a guard detail) through the very middle of a puddle, assigning as his reason for doing so the fact that "It's plagued little authority they give us corporals, and I mean to use that little, any how."

War photographer Alexander Gardner snapped Federals "Studying the Art of War." (*Courtesy Chicago Historical Society*.)

From George Cary Eggleston's *A Rebel's Recollections:*

The drilling, of which there was literally no end, was simply funny. Maneuvers of the most utterly impossible sort were carefully taught to the men. Every amateur officer had his own pet system of tactics, and the effect of the incongruous teachings, when brought out in battalion drill, closely resembled that of the music at Mr. Bob Sawyer's party, where each guest sang the chorus to the tune he knew best.

From a letter of Major General George McClellan to his wife, Ellen, August 16, 1861:

. . . I am here in a terrible place: the enemy have from three to four times my force; the President, the old general [General Scott], cannot or will not see the true state of affairs. Most of my troops are demoralized by the defeat at Bull Run; some regiments even mutinous. I have probably stopped that; but you see my position is not pleasant . . . . I have, I believe, made the best possible disposition of the few men under my command; will quietly await events, and, if the enemy attacks, will try to make my movements as rapid and desperate as may be. If my men will only fight I think I can thrash

him, notwithstanding the disparity of numbers. As it is, I trust to God to give success to our arms, though He is not wont to aid those who refuse to aid themselves . . . . I am weary of all this. I have no ambition in the present affairs; only wish to save my country, and find the incapables around me will not permit it. They sit on the verge of the precipice, and cannot realize what they see. Their reply to everything is, Impossible! Impossible! They think nothing possible which is against their wishes . . . .

President Lincoln and the new Secretary of War, Edwin Stanton, were at loggerheads with McClellan during this period regarding the deployment of troops and the logistics of the next attempt to take Richmond, but in the West, before McClellan would strike again, came the initial major victory for the North.

In May, Captain Nathaniel Lyon had raided the camp of the secessionist-controlled Missouri state militia outside St. Louis and forced the rebels to surrender. He then proceeded to drive Governor Jackson from the capitol and moved southwest. At Wilson's Creek on August 10, far from his base of supply and outnumbered by the Confederates two to one, he met the enemy. Wielding his saber and waving his blue hat, shouting to the troops to rally, he was struck and killed by a rebel bullet. Missouri would remain in the Union, but the Confederates retained the southwestern portion of the state.

In February 1862, gunboats under the command of Flag Officer Andrew Foote pounded Fort Henry, near the Tennessee River below Paducah, Kentucky, into submission, and Brigadier General Ulysses S. Grant serving under General Henry Halleck, forced surrender on his old friend, Simon Bolivar Buckner at Fort Donelson. The call for unconditional surrender made a hero of the unknown Grant. It was the kind of news the Washington press had been waiting for, but it was not merely a propaganda victory: It gave the Federals control over a large portion of Kentucky and western Tennessee.

It was not victory without cost either. On the day Grant set out for Donelson, the air was balmy and the sweating yankees shed coats and blankets along the way. The next day, as the digging in around the Fort began, the capricious February weather turned to sleet and wind, to snow and ice. The brutal cold took its toll as wounded men froze to death without aid. Grant always remembered the nightmare of the suffering troops at Donelson.

General Nathaniel Lyon, after a last-ditch effort to rally his Union forces at Wilson's Creek, was shot from his horse. The remaining Federals fled, leaving Southwest Missouri to the Confederates. (*Missouri Historical Society, St. Louis.*)

A Currier and Ives lithograph depicted the heavy bombardment of Fort Henry by ships under the command of Flag Officer Andrew Foote, part of the Union's initial thrust at the Mississippi Valley. (*Missouri Historical Society, St. Louis.*)

From *Personal Memoirs of U.S. Grant:*

I started from Fort Henry with 15,000 men, including eight batteries and part of a regiment of cavalry, and, meeting with no obstruction to detain us, the advance arrived in front of the enemy by noon. That afternoon and the next day were spent in taking up ground to make the investment as complete as possible . . . . The greatest suffering was from want of shelter. It was midwinter and during the seige we had rain and snow, thawing and freezing alternately. It would not do to allow camp-fires except for down the hill out of sight of the enemy, and it would not do to allow many of the troops to remain there at the same time. In the march over from Fort Henry numbers of the men had thrown away their blankets and overcoats. There was therefore much discomfort and absolute suffering.

Franc B. Wilkie quoted in Frank Moore's *The Rebellion Record: A Diary of American Events:*

Friday night was one of the severest description. The men being without tents, and in many cases without fire, suffered intensely. Hundreds were frost-bitten, and from facts related to me since the surrender by some of the rebels, I have no doubt but that many of our wounded men, who fell in the fight of Friday, and were unable to walk in, were actually frozen to death. This circumstance is a terrible one, and inexpressibly shocking, but there was no help for it. During the various conflicts of Friday, the scene was constantly changed from point to point, and not again visited by our troops. Men would fall at these places, and being unable to get away, were obliged to stay where they fell. In some cases, a few of our wounded were cared for by the rebels, although they were without fire, and could give them but little valuable assistance.

From *Personal Memoirs of U.S. Grant:*

Headquarters Army in the Field,
Camp near Donelson,
February 16, 1862.

General S.B. Buckner, Confederate Army.

*Sir:—*Yours of this date, proposing armistice and appointment of Commissioners to settle terms of capitulation, is just received. No terms except an

The Confederates at Fort Donelson, under the command of Brigadier General Simon Buckner, were left with no option but unconditional surrender as Ulysses S. Grant closed in. (*Missouri Historical Society, St. Louis*.)

unconditional and immediate surrender can be accepted. I propose to move immediately upon your works.

U.S. GRANT
Brig. Gen.

To this I received the following reply:

Headquarters, Dover, Tennessee
February 16, 1862.

To Brig. Gen'l U.S. Grant, U. S. Army.

*Sir:—*The distribution of the forces under my command, incident to an unexpected change of commanders, and the overwhelming force under your command, compel me, notwithstanding the brilliant success of the Confederate arms yesterday, to accept the ungenerous and unchivalrous terms which you propose.

S.B. BUCKNER
Brig. Gen. C. S. A.

From *Personal Memoirs of U.S. Grant:*

I had been at West point three years with Buckner and afterwards served with him in the army, so that we were quite well acquainted. In the course of our conversation (during the surrender), which was very friendly, he said to me that if he had been in command I would not have got up to Donelson as easily as I did. I told him that if he had been in command I should not have tried in the way I did . . . . I had relied . . . upon their commander to allow me to come safely up to the outside of their works.

Overleaf: Business was not above exploiting human suffering for purposes of corporate aggrandizement, as in this chromolithograph captioned "Battle of Shiloh, April 16, 1862, The McCormick Machines Come Victoriously Out of Every Contest, and without a Scratch," published in 1885 by the McCormick Harvesting Machine Company. (*Courtesy Chicago Historical Society*.)

Mississippi and Alabama beckoned to Grant after Donelson's fall. He moved more deeply into the South, camping in April with 37,000 Federals at Pittsburgh Landing in southwestern Tennessee. Twenty-five thousand troops under Brigadier General Don Carlos Buell were to join him there. But at Corinth, Mississippi, about twenty-five miles from Grant, Confederate General Albert Sidney Johnston was planning a surprise. He was massing his forces with the intention of striking at the unsuspecting Grant before Buell could rendezvous. As Union troops enjoyed their breakfast on Sunday, April 6, the rebels came charging out of the woods "thicker than fleas on a dog's back."

For two days the battle, forever known as "bloody Shiloh," raged on, a battle not among seasoned troops, but of boys, many of whom did not know how to fire their rifles. The casualty list was incredible; thirteen thousand Union soldiers fell, and the Confederates lost ten thousand. Johnston sustained a wound in the leg and bled to death on the field, while rebel doctors attended the Federal wounded.

On Sunday evening Buell's reinforcements arrived, along with the troops of General Lew Wallace, and at the end of the following day's carnage, the Southerners withdrew from their position at Shiloh Church. Grant was vilified in Washington for allowing the surprise attack, and Buell given credit for the victory. There was massive pressure on Lincoln to relieve the hero of Fort Donelson, but his reply was prophetic and to the point: "I can't spare this man; he fights."

Whitelaw Reid quoted in Frank Moore's *The Rebellion Record: A Diary of American Events:*

. . . Some, particularly among our officers, were not yet out of bed. Others were dressing, others washing, others cooking, a few eating their breakfasts. Many guns were unloaded, accoutrements lying pell-mell, ammunition was ill-supplied—in short, the camps were virtually surprised—disgracefully, it might be added, unless some one can hereafter give some yet undiscovered reason to the contrary—and were taken at almost every possible disadvantage.

The first wild cries from the pickets rushing in, and the few scattering shots that preceded their arrival, aroused the regiments to a sense of their peril; an instant afterward, shells were hurtling through the tents, while, before there was time for thought of preparation, there came rushing through the woods, with lines of battle sweeping the whole fronts of the division-camps and bending down on either flank, the fine, dashing, compact columns of the enemy.

Into the just-aroused camps thronged the rebel regiments, firing sharp volleys as they came, and springing toward our laggards with the bayonet. Some were shot down as they were running, without weapons, hatless, coatless, toward the river. The searching bullets found other poor unfortunates in their tents, and there, all unheeding now, they still slumbered, while the unseen foe rushed on. Others fell, as they were disentangling themselves from the flaps that formed the doors to their tents; others as they were buckling on their accoutrements; a few, it was even said, as they were vainly trying to impress on the cruelly-exultant enemy their readiness to surrender.

Officers were wounded in their beds, and left for dead, who, through the whole two day's fearful struggle, lay there gasping in their agony, and on Monday evening were found in their gore, inside their tents, and still able to tell the tale.

From Alexander McClure's *Abraham Lincoln and Men of War-times: Some Personal Recollections of War and Politics during the Lincoln Administration:*

The first day's battle at Shiloh was a serious disaster to the Union Army commanded by Grant, who was driven from his position, which seems to have been selected without any special reference to resisting an attack from the enemy, and, although his army fought most gallantly in various separate encounters, the day closed with the field in possession of the enemy and Grant's army driven back to the river. Fortunately, the advance of Buell's army formed a junction with Grant late in the evening, and that night all of Buell's army arrived, consisting of three divisions. The two Generals arranged their plans for an offensive movement early the next morning, and, after another stubborn battle, the lost field was regained and the enemy compelled to retreat with the loss of their commander, General Albert Sidney Johnston, who had fallen early in the first day's action, and with a larger aggregate loss of killed, wounded, and missing than Grant suffered. The first reports from the Shiloh battlefield created profound alarm throughout the entire country, and the wildest exaggerations were spread in a flood tide of vituperation against Grant. It was freely charged that he had neglected his command because of dissipation, that his army had been surprised and defeated, and that it was saved from annihilation only by the timely arrival of Buell.

From *Personal Memoirs of U.S. Grant:*

During the night rain fell in torrents and our troops were exposed to the storm without shelter. I made my headquarters under a tree a few hundred yards back from the river bank. My ankle was so much swollen from the fall of my horse the Friday night preceding, and the bruise was so painful, that I could get no rest. The drenching rain would have precluded the possibility of sleep without this additional cause. Some time after midnight, growing restive under the storm and the continuous pain, I moved back to the log-house under the bank. This had been taken as a hospital, and all night wounded men were being brought in, their wounds dressed, a leg or an arm amputated as the case might require, and everything being done to save life or alleviate suffering. The sight was more unendurable than encountering the enemy's fire, and I returned to my tree in the rain.

Left: Battle-weary Confederates retreated toward Corinth, Mississippi, after the heavy fighting at Shiloh. (*Courtesy Donald S. Werner.*)

From Stephen Vincent Benét's *John Brown's Body:*

He caught Grant napping in some strange flaw of skill
Which happened once and did not happen again.
And drove his unprepared, unwatchful brigades
Back almost into the river.
                              And in the heat
Of seeing his lines go forward, he bled to death
From a wound that should not have been mortal.
                              After which,
While the broken Union stragglers under the bluff
Were still howling that they were beaten, Buell came up,
Lew Wallace came up, the knife half-sunk in the wound
Was not thrust home, the night fell the battle lagged.
The bulldog got the bone in his teeth again
The next day, reinforced, beat Beauregard back
And counted a Union victory.
                              In the books
Both sides claim victory on one day or the other
And both claims seem valid enough.
                              It only remains
To take the verdict of the various dead
In this somewhat indecisive meeting of blocks.
There were thirty-five hundred dead when the blocks had met.
But, being dead, their verdict is out of court.
They cannot puzzle the books with their testimony.

In this chromolithograph after a painting by Conrad Wise Chapman, the vicissitudes of camp life are ignored as members of the 3rd Kentucky Infantry at Corinth go about their duties. At the battle of Shiloh a month before, the rebels had lost over ten thousand. In this seemingly clean and quiet camp, disease would claim more. It was as indiscriminate as any bullet. (*Valentine Museum, Richmond, Virginia.*)

From *Personal Memoirs of U.S. Grant:*

Shiloh was the severest battle fought at the West during the war, and but few in the East equalled it for hard, determined fighting. I saw an open field . . . so covered with dead that it would have been possible to walk across the clearing in any direction, stepping on dead bodies, without a foot touching the ground.

Lincoln had set a deadline of February 22, the birthday of Washington, for McClellan to move. It passed. Finally, in mid-March, "Little Mac" began his Peninsular Campaign. From Fort Monroe his troops trudged the muddy roads to Yorktown, Virginia. McClellan, as would happen time and time again, was con-

General Thomas Jackson, who had earned his nickname, Stonewall, at Bull Run, outfoxed Union opposition in his Valley Campaign. (*The Museum of the Confederacy*.)

Johnston, in command of the Army of Northern Virginia, slipped away after a month and withdrew toward Richmond.

In a correspondence which was becoming overly familiar to both parties, McClellan again requested that President Lincoln release more divisions from the capital. Lincoln's replies were mainly in the negative. The reason the harried President was so reluctant to send enough reinforcements to satisfy the general was that the wily Stonewall Jackson and his cavalry were creating havoc in Virginia's Shenandoah Valley, and the paranoia in Washington was turning into sheer panic. Lincoln refused to leave Washington in a position he considered as grossly exposed.

The resourceful Jackson constantly outmaneuvered Union commanders such as General Nathaniel P. Banks who were desperately trying to pin him down. From March 23 to June 9, Jackson fought innumerable skirmishes, marched nearly seven hundred miles and fought five hand-to-hand engagements with the enemy. His Old Testament appearance, his brilliant blue eyes which took on a strange and mystical hue in the light of battle, made him seem bigger than life, and indeed, in the Valley Campaign, he was. On May 24, General Banks, who considered himself in a safe position at Strasburg, found that the cunning Jackson was again threatening and in a chaotic retreat he found his way back to Maryland.

founded by the misinformation supplied to him by the Northern intelligence network, headed by Allan Pinkerton, which constantly overestimated the strength of the enemy. Believing he faced too strong opposition he laid siege to the famed town where the Revolutionary War ended. Brigadier General Joe

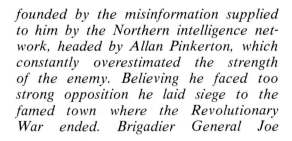

Union mortar battery and gunners faced Yorktown during McClellan's ill-fated Peninsular Campaign. Confederates withdrew before the huge mortars saw any action. (*Valentine Museum, Richmond, Virginia.*)

From a letter of President Abraham Lincoln to Major General George McClellan, April 9, 1862:

There is a curious mystery about the number of troops now with you. When I telegraphed you on the 6th, saying you had over a hundred thousand with you, I had just obtained from the Secretary of War a statement, taken, as he said, from your own returns, making 108,000 then with you and *en route* to you. You now say you will have but 85,000 when all *en route* to you shall have reached you. How can the discrepancy of 23,000 be acounted for?

I suppose the whole force which has gone forward for you is with you by this time. And if so, I think it is the precise time for you to strike a blow. By delay the enemy will relatively gain upon you— that is, he will gain faster by fortifications and reinforcements than you can by reinforcements alone. And once more let me tell you, it is indispensable to you that you strike a blow. I am powerless to help this. You will do me the justice to remember I always insisted that going down the bay in search of a field, instead of fighting at or near Manassas, was only shifting, and not surmounting, a difficulty; that we would find the same enemy and the same or equal entrenchments at either place. The country will not fail to note, is now noting, that the present hesitation to move upon an entrenched enemy is but the story of Manassas repeated.

From *McClellan's Own Story, the War for the Union:*

Referring for a moment to the President's despatch . . . it is well to recall the facts that at that time, instead of 100,000 men, I had—after deducting guards and working parties— much less than 40,000 for attack, and that the portion of the enemy's lines which he thought I had better break through at once was about the strongest of the whole, except, perhaps, the town [Yorktown] itself.

From Lord Godfrey Rathbone Benson Charnwood's *Abraham Lincoln:*

"Stonewall" Jackson's most famous campaign happened at this juncture . . . . With a small force, surrounded by other forces, each of which, if concentrated, should have outnumbered him, he caught each in turn at a disadvantage, inflicted on them several damaging blows, and put the startled President and Secretary of War in fear for the safety of Washington. There seemed to be no one available who could immediately be charged with the supreme command of these three Northern forces, unless McDowell could have been spared from where he was; so Lincoln with Stanton's help took upon himself to ensure the co-operation of their three commanders by orders from Washington. His self-reliance had now begun to reach its full stature; his military good sense in comparison with McClellan's was proving greater than he had supposed, and he had probably not discovered its limitations . . . . Jackson, having successfully kept McDowell from McClellan, had before the end of June escaped safely southward . . . .

At Hampton Roads, Virginia, in March 1862, the first battle of the ironclads forever changed the history of naval warfare. The Confederates had refurbish-

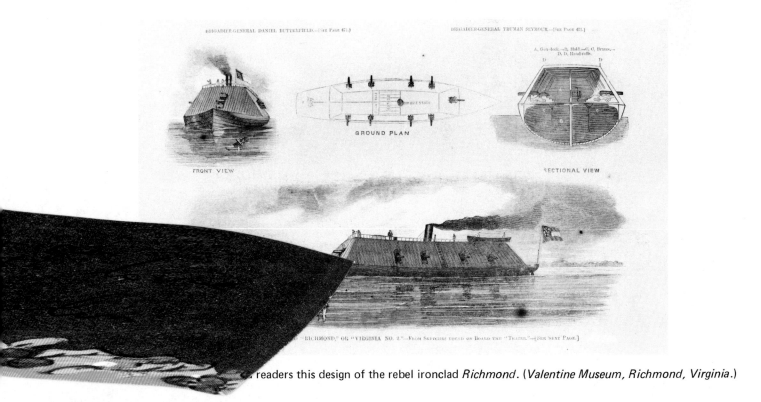

FRONT VIEW

GROUND PLAN

SECTIONAL VIEW

... readers this design of the rebel ironclad *Richmond*. (*Valentine Museum, Richmond, Virginia.*)

ed the old U.S.S. Merrimac *and renamed her the* Virginia. *In her first dramatic encounter on March 8, she sank the* Congress *and the* Cumberland, *and drove the* Minnesota *aground. Washington was again panic-stricken, but Secretary of the Navy Gideon Welles had faith in a newly commissioned ship, and in its Swedish-born designer, John Ericsson. In January, the iron-bulwarked* Monitor, *with a revolving gun turret, was launched from New York. On the morning of March 9, she met and conquered the* Merrimac. *Washingtonians could stop peering out of their windows to see if the Confederate vessel was steaming up the Potomac.*

From a letter of engineer Alban G. Stimers on board the *Monitor* to Captain John Ericsson, March 9, 1862:

After a stormy passage, which proved us to be the finest sea-boat I was ever in, we fought the *Merrimac* for more than three hours this forenoon, and sent her back to Norfolk in a sinking condition. Iron-clad against iron-clad. We manoeuvred about the bay here, and went at each other with mutual fierceness. I consider that both ships were well fought; we were struck twenty-two times: pilot-house twice, turret nine times, side-armor eight times, deck three times . . . . She tried to run us down and sink us as she did the *Cumberland* yesterday, but she got the worst of it. Her bow passed over our deck, and our sharp upper-edged side cut through the light iron shoe upon her stem and well into her oak. She will not try that again. She gave a tremendous thump, but did not injure us in the least. We are just able to find the point of contact.

From Lucius E. Chittenden's *Recollections of President Lincoln and His Administration:*

It was evident, from the general excitement, that news had been received from the James River. As I entered the room some one was saying, "Would it not be fortunate if the *Monitor* should sink her?" "It would be nothing more than I have expected," calmly observed President Lincoln. "If she does not, something else will. Many providential things are happening in this war, and this may be one of them. The loss of two good ships is an expensive lesson, but it will teach us all the value of ironclads. I have not believed at any time during the last twenty-four hours that the *Merrimac* would go right on destroying right and left without any obstruction. Since we knew that the *Monitor* had got there, I have felt that she was the vessel we wanted." I then learned that the *Monitor* had arrived at Fortress Monroe on Saturday evening; without waiting for any preparation, she had steamed up to Newport News, and laid herself alongside the grounded *Minnesota*. The *Merrimac* had made her appearance shortly after daylight; Captain Worden had promptly advanced to make her acquaintance, and had ever since been sticking to her closer than a brother. It was also reported that the two fighters had ever since been pounding each other terrifically, and that the *Monitor* as yet showed no signs of weakness. Time passes quickly in such an excitement. Very soon came a message that evoked cheers from everybody. Its substance was that the *Merrimac* had withdrawn, and was again steaming for Norfolk. Even this news, which stirred the enthusiasm of every one else, so that all burst into a long-continued volley of applause, did not seem to elate the President. "I am glad the *Monitor* has done herself credit for Worden's sake—for all our sakes," was all he said. He then walked slowly to the White House.

Battle of the Ironclads Monitor *and* Merrimac, *March 9, 1862*, by William Torgerson, 1877. News of the Confederate *Merrimac* and her destructive capabilities sent tremors of fear through *Washington*. Navy Captain John Ericsson plotted her defeat in his design of the Federal ship *Monitor*, which engaged the *Merrimac* for four hours on the morning of March 9. Ericsson's ship left the naval duel unscathed, while the Confederate vessel fled. (*Courtesy Chicago Historical Society*.)

The strategy to gain control of the Mississippi and its tributaries, thus putting a stranglehold on Southern commerce and lines of supply, was moving ahead and with great success. On April 24, Flag Officer David G. Farragut took the queen city of the South, New Orleans. The citizens of that most cosmopolitan and colorful harbor hated the yankees with a passion and the famed Southern gentility simply didn't exist when it came to dealing with the invaders.

It was most unfortunate then, that the pompous and unscrupulous Benjamin Butler was sent to command the occupying forces. By the end of his administration, the residents were calling him "Beast" and "Spoon" Butler, the former because of his infamous General Order No. 28, which as much as called the ladies of New Orleans whores, and the latter because of his alleged theft of private property for personal gain, including some sterling silver spoons. Jefferson Davis was so incensed at Butler's order regarding the women, he considered him a criminal and said that if captured he should be hanged.

Flag Officer David Farragut battled Confederate vessels for five days before the capture of the port of New Orleans. He received the navy's first commission as rear admiral for his efforts toward subduing the city. (*Courtesy Chicago Historical Society*.)

George W. Cable quoted in Robert Underwood Johnson's and Clarence Buell's *Battles and Leaders of the Civil War:*

What a gathering! The riff-raff of the wharves, the town, the gutters. Such women—such wrecks of women! And all the juvenile rag-tag. The lower steamboat landing, well covered with sugar, rice, and molasses, was being rifled. The men smashed; the women scooped up the smashings. The river was overflowing the top of the levee. A rainstorm began to threaten. "Are the Yankee ships in sight?" I asked of an idler. He pointed out the tops of their naked masts as they showed up across the huge bend of the river. They were engaging the batteries at Camp Chalmette—the old field of Jackson's renown. Presently that was over. Ah, me! I see them now as they come slowly round Slaughterhouse Point into full view, silent, grim, and terrible; black with men, heavy with deadly portent; the long-banished Stars and Stripes flying against the frowning sky. Oh, for the *Mississippi!* the *Mississippi!* Just then she came down upon them. But how? Drifting helplessly, a mass of flames.

The crowds on the levee howled and screamed with rage. The swarming decks answered never a word; but one old tar on the *Hartford,* standing with lanyard in hand beside a great pivot-gun, so

plain to view that you could see him smile, silently patted its big black breech and blandly grinned.

And now the rain came down in sheets. About one or two o'clock in the afternoon (as I remember), I being again in the store with but one door ajar, came a roar of shoutings and imprecations and crowding feet down Common street. "Hurrah for Jeff Davis! Hurrah for Jeff Davis! Shoot them! Kill them! Hang them!" I locked the door on the outside, and ran to the front of the mob, bawling with the rest, "Hurrah for Jeff Davis!" About every third man there had a weapon out. Two officers of the United States Navy were walking abreast, unguarded and alone, looking not to right or left, never frowning, never flinching, while the mob screamed in their ears, shook cocked pistols in their faces, cursed and crowded, and gnashed upon them. So through the gates of death those two men walked to the City Hall to demand the town's surrender. It was one of the bravest deeds I ever saw done.

From Stephen Vincent Benét's *John Brown's Body:*

New Orleans is taken, the fangs of the forts drawn out,
The ambiguous Butler wins ambiguous fame
By issuing orders stating that any lady
Who insults a Union soldier in uniform
Shall be treated as a streetwalker plying her trade.
The orders are read and hated. The insults stop
But the ladies remember Butler for fifty years
And make a fabulous devil with pasteboard horns
—"Beast" Butler, the fiend who pilfered the silver spoons—
From a slightly-tarnished, crude-minded, vain politician
Who loved his wife and ached to be a great man.
You were not wise with the ladies, Benjamin Butler,
It has been disproved that you stole New Orleans spoons
But the story will chime at the ribs of your name and stain
    it,
Ghost-silver, clinking against the ribs of a ghost,
As long as the ladies have tongues.

                Napoleon was wiser
But he could not silence one ugly, clever DeStaël.
Make war on the men—the ladies have too-long memories.

General Benjamin Butler was a favorite target of Confederate satirist Adalbert Volck, who probably did this caricature. As military governor of New Orleans, Butler was under heavy criticism for his General Order No. 28, directed at the ladies of that city. (*Courtesy Chicago Historical Society*.)

From Edward A. Pollard's *The Second Year of the War:*

It would occupy many pages to detail what the people of New Orleans suffered at the hands of the invaders whom they had so easily admitted into their city, in insult, wrongs, confiscation of property, seizure of private dwellings, and brazen robbery. The Yankee officers, from colonel to lieutenant, as the caprice of each might dictate, seized and took possession of gentlemen's houses, broke into their winerooms, forced open the wardrobes of ladies and gentlemen, and either used or sent away from the city the clothing of whole families. Some of the private residences of respectable citizens were appropriated to the vilest uses, the officials who had engaged them making them the private shops of the most infamous female characters.

But while Butler was thus apparently occupied with the oppression of rebels, he was too much of a Yankee to be lost to the opportunity of making his pecuniary fortune out of the exigencies which he had created. The banker and broker of the corrupt operations in which he was engaged was his own brother, who bought confiscated property, shipped large consignments from New Orleans, to be paid for in cotton, and speculated largely in powder, saltpeter, muskets, and other war material sold to the Confederacy, surreptitiously sent out from the city and covered by permits for provisions. Of the trade in provisions for cotton, Butler received his share of the gains, while the robbery was covered up by the pretence of consumption in New Orleans "to prevent starvation," or by reported actual issue to troops. The Yankee general did not hesitate to deal in the very life-blood of his own soldiers.

Major General Benjamin Butler's General Order No. 28 to the City of New Orleans, May 15, 1862:

As the officers and soldiers of the United States have been subject to repeated insults from the women (calling themselves ladies) of New Orleans, in return for the most scrupulous noninterference and courtesy on our part, it is ordered that hereafter when any female shall, by word, gesture or movement, insult or show contempt for any officer or soldier of the United States, she shall be regarded and held liable to be treated as a woman of the town plying her avocation.

A delaying action fought by Major General James Longstreet's Confederate infantry at Williamsburg, Virginia, allowed Johnston to move for Richmond ahead of McClellan. It was another cruel battle fought in the seemingly interminable pelting rain, which the soldiers were beginning to accept as normal weather for Virginia. But by June the yankee commander and around 105,000 troops were resting outside Richmond.

The next skirmish, known as the Battle of Seven Pines or Fair Oaks, was a draw, but it was also a turning point for Confederate fortunes. Joe Johnston was wounded and in his place as commander of the Army of Northern Virginia Jefferson Davis appointed the eagle of the South, Robert E. Lee. He was to inspire in his troops the kind of devotion that exists only between a superior and dedicated commander and his men. He would

men. *The battles they fought in the week which ended with July 1 were ever after known as the Seven Days': on the Chickahominy, to Mechanicsville, Gaines' Mills, Savage Station; at White Oak Swamp and on to Malvern Hill—the grim contest took its awful toll, and immortality was bestowed upon unfamiliar place names on the ravaged map of Virginia.*

Lee had won. Richmond breathed a sigh of relief. McClellan, again repulsed, recouped at Harrison's Landing on the James River.

From Thomas W. Hyde's *Following the Greek Cross or, Memories of the Sixth Army Corps:*

Well, up we started [at Williamsburg], and the long line of sabre bayonets came down together as if one man swayed them as we crossed the crest, and with a roar of cheers the 7th Maine dashed on. It was an ecstacy of excitement for a moment; but the foe, breathless from their long tug over the heavy ground, seemed to dissolve all at once into a quivering and disintegrating mass and to scatter in all directions. Upon this we halted and opened fire, and the view of it through the smoke was pitiful. They were falling everywhere; white handkerchiefs were held up in token of surrender; no bullets were coming our way except from a clump of a few trees in front of our left. Here a group of men, led by an officer whose horse had just fallen, were trying to keep up the unequal fight, when McK, the crack shot of Company D, ran forward a little and sent a bullet crashing through his brain. This was Lieutenant-Colonel J. C. Bradburn of the 5th North Carolina, and at his fall all opposition ceased. We gathered in some three hundred prisoners before dark. Then the rain came, though there is nothing specially remarkable about that, for it was always coming down.

remold the Army of Northern Virginia and keep the yankees guessing all the way to Appomattox Court House.

Lee was well entrenched around Richmond and determined to drive the hesitant McClellan from the outskirts of the capital. Quickly joined by the battle-wearied forces of Jackson, who were used to long marches on short rations, ("He druv us like Hell." said one proud but disgruntled soldier), Lee commanded about 35,000

From a letter of Major General George McClellan to his wife, Ellen, May 8, 1862:

I have ordered up headquarters and the accompanying paraphernalia at once, so I hope to get within a few miles of my tooth-brush in a day or two. It is not very pleasant, this going entirely without baggage, but it could not be helped. I find that the results of my operations are beginning to be apparent. The rebels are evacuating Norfolk, I learn. Your two letters of Sunday and Monday reached me last night. It would have been easy for me to have sacrificed 10,000 lives in taking Yorktown, and I presume the world would have thought it more brilliant. I am content with what I have done. The battle of Williamsburg was more bloody. Had I reached the field three hours earlier I could have gained far greater results and have saved a thousand lives. It is, perhaps, well as it is, for officers and men feel that I saved the day . . . .

From George Alfred Townsend's *Campaigns of a Non-Combatant, And His Romaunt Abroad during the War:*

The lanterns hanging around the room streamed fitfully upon the red eyes, and half-naked figures. All were looking up, and saying, in pleading monotone: "Is that you, doctor?" Men with their arms in slings went restlessly up and down, smarting with fever. Those who were wounded in the lower extremities, body, or head, lay upon their backs, tossing even in sleep. They listened peevishly to the wind whistling through the chinks of the barn. They followed one with their rolling eyes. They turned away from the lantern, for it seemed to sear them.

Soldiers sat by the severely wounded, laving their sores with water. In many wounds the balls still remained, and the discolored flesh was swollen unnaturally. There were some who had been shot in the bowels, and now and then they were frightfully convulsed, breaking into shrieks and shouts. Some of them iterated a single word, as, "doctor," or "help," or "God," or "oh!" commencing with a loud spasmodic cry, and continuing the same word till it died away in cadence. The act of calling seemed to lull the pain. Many were unconscious and lethargic, moving their fingers and lips mechanically, but never more to open their eyes upon the light; they were already going through the valley of the shadow.

I think, still, with a shudder, of the faces of those who were told mercifully that they could not live. The unutterable agony; the plea for somebody on whom to call; the longing eyes that poured out prayers; the looking on mortal as if its resources were infinite; the fearful looking to the immortal as if it were so far off, so implacable, that the dying appeal would be in vain; the open lips, through which one could almost look at the quaking heart below; the ghastliness of brow and tangled hair; the closing pangs; the awful *quietus* . . . .

From J.F.C. Fuller's *Grant and Lee: A study in Personality and Generalship:*

That his [Lee's] example did influence his army is beyond doubt—it sanctified it and him; yet its discipline remained beneath contempt. Towards it he acted like a soft-hearted father; he was its exalted leader, its high priest, but not its general. "Colonel," he said to an officer who begged for a visit, "a dirty camp gives me nausea. If you say your camps are clean, I will go." A normal general would not have avoided dirty camps, but would have sought them out, so that the officers in charge might suffer for their uncleanliness. But Lee was not a normal general; in place of the hot word he relied upon the half-disguised censure. He was always tolerant, even when tolerance was little short of criminal. "His one great aim and endeavor," writes Colonel Taylor, "was to secure success for the cause in which he was enlisted; all else was made subordinate to this." The cause was God's: who was he then to judge the soldiers of the Almighty?

From George Alfred Townsend's *Campaigns of a Non-Combatant, And His Romaunt Abroad during the War:*

In the misty dawn [at Savage Station] I saw the maimed still lying on the ground, wrapped in relics of blankets, and in one of the outhouses a grim embalmer stood amid a family of nude corpses. He dealt with the bodies of high officers only; for, said he: "I used to be glad to prepare private soldiers. They were wuth a five-dollar bill apiece. But, Lord bless you, a colonel pays a hundred, and a brigadier-general two hundred. There's lots of them now, and I have cut the acquaintance of everything below a major. I might," he added, "as a great favor, do a captain, but he must pay a major's price. I insist upon that! Such windfalls don't come every day. There won't be another such killing for a century."

From a letter of Major General George McClellan to his wife, Ellen, July 1, 1862:

The whole army is here; worn out and war-worn, after a week of daily battles. I have still very great confidence in them, and they in me. The dear fellows cheer me as of old as they march to certain death, and I feel prouder of them than ever.

Rebel soldiers advanced to seize guns abandoned by Union forces at Gaines' Mills in Alfred R. Waud's drawing. Lee had broken McClellan's supply line during the battle there on June 27, 1862. (*The Museum of the Confederacy*.)

From Lord Godfrey Rathbone Benson Charnwood's
Abraham Lincoln:

McClellan was slowly but steadily nearing Richmond. From June 26 to July 2, there took place a series of engagements between Lee and McClellan, or rather the commanders under him, known as the Seven Days' Battles. The fortunes of the fighting varied greatly, but the upshot is that, though the corps on McClellan's left won a strong position not far from Richmond, the sudden approach of Jackson's forces upon McClellan's right flank, which began on the twenty-sixth, placed him in what appears to have been, as he himself thought it, a situation of great danger. Lee is said to have "read McClellan like an open book," playing upon his

caution, which made him, while his subordinates fought, more anxious to secure their retreat than to seize upon any advantage they gained. But Lee's reading deceived him in one respect. He had counted upon McClellan's retreating, but thought he would retreat under difficulties right down the Peninsula to his original base and be thoroughly cut up on the way. But on July 2, McClellan with great skill withdrew his whole army to Harrison's Landing far up the James estuary, having effected with the Navy a complete transference of his base. Here his army lay in a position of security; they might yet threaten Richmond, and McClellan's soldiers still believed in him. But the South was led by a great commander and had now learned to give him unbounded confidence; there was some excuse for a panic in Wall Street, and every reason for dejection in the North.

In Washington they had had enough of "Little Mac's" excuses, and Lincoln brought the ponderous, "by-the-book" Henry W. Halleck from the west to become general in chief. With him came arrogant General John Pope. Quickly the new commander of the Army of the Potomac alienated the dispirited troops by reminding them that in the western theater, the Federals were used to seeing the backs of their enemy. Pope's mission was another attack on Richmond. When he met the Machiavellian Jackson at Cedar Mountain and was surprised by an attack on his left flank from Longstreet near the site of the old battle of Bull Run, the bewildered Pope suffered an ignominious defeat. It was the second for Union forces in two months. The Confederate star was rising. Lincoln gave the army back to McClellan. It indeed seemed that only he could renew their esprit.

From the *Diary of Gideon Welles, Secretary of the Navy under Lincoln and Johnson:*

September 2, Tuesday. At Cabinet Meeting all but Seward were present . . . . Stanton said, in a suppressed voice, trembling with excitement, he was informed McClellan had been ordered to take command of the forces in Washington. General surprise was expressed. When the President came in and heard the subject matter of our conversation, he said he had done what seemed to him best and would be responsible for what he had done to the country. Halleck had agreed to it. McClellan knows this whole ground; he is a good engineer, all admit; there is no better organizer; he can be trusted to act on the defensive; but he is troubled with the "slows," and good for nothing for an onward movement. Much was said. There was a more disturbed and desponding feeling than I have ever witnessed in council; the President was greatly distressed. There was a general conversation as regarded the infirmities of McClellan, but it was claimed, by Blair and the President, he had beyond any officer the confidence of the army. Though deficient in the positive qualities which are necessary for an energetic commander, his organizing powers could be made temporarily available till the troops were rallied.

From George Alfred Townsend's *Campaigns of a Non-Combatant, And His Romaunt Abroad during the War:*

After the Confederates retired from Manassas Junction the vicinity of Warrenton was a sort of neutral ground. At one time the Southern cavalry would ride through the main street, and the next day a body of mounted Federals would pounce upon the town, the inhabitants, meanwhile, being apprehensive of a sabre combat in the heart of the place . . . .

There was some female society in Warrenton, but the blue-coats engrossed it all. The young women were ardent partisans, but also very pretty; and treason somehow heightened their beauty. Disloyalty is always pardonable in a woman, and these ladies appreciated the fact. They refused to walk under Federal flags, and stopped their ears when the bands played national music; but every evening they walked through the main street, arm-in-arm with dashing lieutenants and captains. Many flirtations ensued, and a great deal of gossip was elicited. In the end, some of the misses fell out among themselves, and hated each other more than the common enemy. I overheard a young lady talking in a low tone one evening to a captain in the Ninth New York regiment.

"If you knew my brother," she said, "I am sure you would not fire upon *him.*"

Virginia was ravaged, and in a bold move which he would repeat at Gettysburg, Lee decided to move North. He felt, and with justification, that it would be a tactic which would rouse the increasing anti-war sentiment in the North, and allow his depleted supplies to be restocked from foraging in the less devastated Northern countryside. Unfortunately, McClellan had come into possession of Lee's orders, and pursued, although as usual not quickly enough, to repel the invasion. The armies met at Sharpsburg, Maryland, on Antietam Creek. Three battles were fought on the day of September 17, the bloodiest day of the war. The Confederates lost 10,500 out of 40,000. Northern casualties were 12,000, as McClellan used half of his 87,000 troops. Lee's broken army recrossed the Potomac the following day and again McClellan did not pursue.

It seemed the pattern would go on and on. The appeals, the demands, from Washington, to move, to win and to have a victory which would be decisive in ending the lengthening .and costly stalemate existing between the two armies. McClellan was again removed, this time permanently, and into his place as commander of the Army of the Potomac, came Major General Ambrose Burnside.

General McClellan receives a rousing cheer from his troops. Although "Little Mac" caused much consternation in Washington for his lack of boldness in pursuit of the enemy, the spirit he was able to instill in battle-weary men was unequalled by any commander of the Army of the Potomac. (*National Park Service*.)

September 17, 1862, was the bloodiest day of the war. In that day's fighting Confederates and Federals lost nearly 24,000 men. Mathew Brady's photograph, taken after the carnage at Antietam Creek, shows the unburied body of a young rebel soldier next to the fresh grave of one of his Federal opponents. (*Courtesy Chicago Historical Society.*)

From a letter of Major General George McClellan to his wife, Ellen, September 18, 1862:

We fought yesterday a terrible battle (Antietam) against the entire rebel army. The battle continued fourteen hours and was terrific; the fighting on both sides was superb. The general result was in our favor; that is to say, we gained a great deal of ground and held it. It was a success, but whether a decided victory depends upon what occurs to-day. I hope that God has given us a great success. It is all in His hands, and there I am content to leave it. The spectacle yesterday was the grandest I could conceive of; nothing could be more sublime. Those in whose judgment I rely tell me that I fought the battle splendidly and that it was a masterpiece of art. I

am well-nigh tired out by anxiety and want of sleep. God has been good in sparing the lives of all my staff.

From a letter of Major General George McClellan to his wife, Ellen, September 20, 1862:

. . . Am glad to say that I am much better to-day; for, to tell you the truth, I have been under the weather since the battle. The want of rest, and anxiety, brought on my old disease [malaria]. The battle of Wednesday *was* a terrible one. I presume the loss will prove not less than 10,000 on each side. Our victory was complete, and the disorganized rebel army has rapidly returned to Virginia, its dreams of "invading Pennsylvania" dissipated for

Ambrose Burnside, in his own opinion, was not fit to command the huge Army of the Potomac. After the debacle at Fredericksburg, Washington agreed. (*Courtesy Chicago Historical Society*.)

ever. I feel some little pride in having, with a beaten and demoralized army, defeated Lee so utterly and saved the North so completely. Well, one of these days history will, I trust, do me justice in deciding that it was not my fault that the campaign of the Peninsula was not successful . . . . Since I left Washington, Stanton has again asserted that *I*, not Pope, lost the battle of Manassas No. 2! . . . I am tired of fighting against such disadvantages, and feel that it is now time for the country to come to my help and remove these difficulties from my path. If my countrymen will not open their eyes and assist themselves they must pardon me if I decline longer to pursue the thankless avocation of serving them.

From *McClellan's Own Story, the War for the Union:*

I read the [dismissal] papers with a smile, immediately turned to Burnside, and said: "Well, Burnside, I turn the command over to you."

They soon retired, Burnside having begged me to remain for a few days with the army, and I having consented to do so, though I wished to leave the next morning.

Before we broke up from the Maryland side of the Potomac I had said to Burnside that, as he was second in rank in the army, I wished him to be as near me as possible on the march, and that he must keep himself informed of the condition of affairs. I took especial pains during the march to have him constantly informed of what I was doing, the positions of the various corps, etc., and he ought to have been able to take the reins in his hands without a day's delay.

The order depriving me of the command created an immense deal of deep feeling in the army—so much so that many were in favor of my refusing to obey the order, and of marching upon Washington to take possession of the government. My chief purpose in remaining with the army as long as I did after being relieved was to calm this feeling, in which I succeeded.

I will not attempt to describe my own feelings nor the scenes attending my farewell to the army. They are beyond my powers of description. What words, in truth, could convey to the mind such a scene— thousands of brave men, who under my very eye had changed from raw recruits to veterans of many fields, shedding tears like children in their ranks, as they bade good-by to the general who had just led them to victory after the defeats they had seen under another leader? Could they have foreseen the future their feelings would not have been less intense!

Although the water in Antietam Creek was shallow enough for wading through in most places, Major General Burnside, in an attempt to attack Lee's right flank, was determined to take this bridge. He succeeded, but sustained heavy losses in the face of firm rebel resistance. (*Missouri Historical Society, St. Louis.*)

The battle at Antietam had been a Union victory and President Lincoln took the occasion to announce his preliminary Emancipation Proclamation. It warned the South that if they did not return to the Union within one hundred days, all slaves in the rebellious states would be considered forever free. On New Year's day of 1863, he signed the final pronouncement, which, in literal terms, only freed the bonded in areas over which he had no legal control.

However, the moral impact in the United States and abroad was staggering. The Federal government had aligned itself irrevocably on the side of justice for all men, set the machinery in motion for passage of the Thirteenth Amendment and precluded European intervention on the side of the Confederacy in the war.

From President Abraham Lincoln's Emancipation Proclamation:

And by virtue of the power, and for the purpose aforesaid, I do order and declare that all persons held as slaves within said designated states, and parts of states, are, and henceforward shall be free ....

And I hereby enjoin upon the people so declared to be free to abstain from all violence, unless in necessary self-defense; and I recommend to them that, in all cases when allowed, they labor faithfull for reasonable wages.

And I further declare and make known, that such persons of suitable condition, will be received into the armed service of the United States to garrison forts, positions, stations, and other places, and to man vessels of all sorts in said service.

And upon this act, sincerely believed to be an act of justice, warranted by the Constitution, upon military necessity, I invoke the considerate judgement of all mankind, and the gracious favor of Almighty God ....

From John Nicolay's and John Hay's *Abraham Lincoln, A History:*

Vast as were its consequences, the act itself was only the simplest and briefest formality. It could in no wise be made sensational or dramatic .... No ceremony was made or attempted of this final official signing. The afternoon was well advanced when Mr.

Lincoln went back from his New Year's greetings with his right hand so fatigued that it was an effort to hold the pen. There was no special convocation of the Cabinet or of prominent officials. Those who were in the house came to the Executive Office merely from the personal impulse of curiosity joined to momentary convenience. His signature was attached to one of the greatest and most beneficent military decrees of history in the presence of less than a dozen persons; after which it was carried to the Department of State to be attested by the great seal and deposited among the archives of the government.

From the New York *Tribune,* March 28, 1863:

Facts are beginning to dispel prejudices. Enemies of the negro race, who have persistently denied the capacity and doubted the courage of the Blacks, are unanswerably confuted by the good conduct and gallant deeds of the men whom they persecute and slander. From many quarters comes evidence of the swiftly approaching success which is to crown what is still by some persons deemed to be the experi-

ment of arming whom the Proclamation of Freedom liberates.

From Abraham Lincoln's Annual Message to Congress, December 8, 1863:

Of those who were slaves at the beginning of the rebellion, full one hundred thousand are now in the United States military service, about one-half of which number actually bear arms in the ranks; thus giving the double advantage of taking so much labor from the insurgent cause, and supplying the places which otherwise must be filled with so many white men. So far as tested, it is difficult to say they are not as good soldiers as any. No servile insurrection, or tendency to violence or cruelty, has marked the measures of emancipation and arming the blacks. These measures have been much discussed in foreign countries, and contemporary with such discussion the tone of public sentiment there is much improved. At home the same measures have been fully discussed, supported, criticised, and denounced, and the annual elections following are highly encouraging to those whose official duty it is to bear the country through this great trial. Thus we have the new reckoning. The crisis which threatened to divide the friends of the Union is past.

President Lincoln's Emancipation Proclamation, which freed blacks in the rebel states, made him a living hero to the thousands in bondage who immediately began to desert shanty and plantation. *(Library of Congress.)*

Above: Dead horses and overturned wagons littered roads after the defeat at Fredericksburg. Said Lee, "It is well that war is so terrible, we should grow too fond of it." (*Courtesy Chicago Historical Society*.) Right: Conrad Wise Chapman painted a dishevelled picket manning his tree-stump post in 1863. (*Valentine Museum, Richmond, Virginia*.)

The heavily whiskered, imposing Burn-side had told Lincoln, "I am not competent to command such a large army," and at Fredericksburg in December, he proved it.

It was a slaughter for the Union, as they tried to take Lee's impregnable defensive position above the town. Again the screams of the wounded, the desperate calls for water, the agony of irreparable injury, the curses and the prayers for release. It would be the end of waste for awhile as winter took over and shattered armies retired to brace for another spring.

General Robert E. Lee quoted in Captain Robert E. Lee's *Recollections and Letters of General Robert E. Lee:*

I had supposed they were just preparing for battle, and was saving our men for the conflict. Their hosts crown the hill and plain beyond the river, and their numbers to me are unknown. Still I felt the confidence we could stand the shock, and was anxious for the blow that is to fall on some point, and was prepared to meet it here. Yesterday evening I had my suspicions that they might return during the night, but could not believe they would relinquish their hopes after all their boasting and preparation, and when I say that the latter is equal to the former you will have some idea of the magnitude. This morning they were all safe on the north side of the Rappahannock. They went as they came—in the night. They suffered heavily as far as the battle went,

but it did not go far enough to satisfy me. Our loss was comparatively slight, and I think will not exceed two thousand. The contest will have now to be renewed, but on what field I cannot say.

From *The Soldiers and Sailors Half-Dime Tales of the Late Rebellion:*

"Hi, Yank! is that the Sixth Corps picket-line over there?" inquired a Confederate on the Rappahannock, one day, after we had fallen back from in front [of Fredericksburg] after the battle in December, 1862.

"Yes," answered the boy in blue, grumblingly, for he hadn't forgotten the thrashing yet. "Yes, of course it is; what of it?"

"Why, nothing particular, only I know somebody in it. What regiment is that on picket?"

"The ____st Pennsylvania."

"You don't day so; is Company H on post?"

"Yes, I belong to Company H."

"Well, won't you tell Harry B_____, if he is alive, to come down to the edge of the river, his brother wants to see him?"

"Certainly; what regiment?"

"Eight Alabama."

So Harry went down and through, contrary to orders, to the rebel side of the river and had a talk with his brother. Returning, after a while, to his own side, he went "on post" opposite to him and watched him as closely as if he were some stranger rebel. Truly, queer events grew out of this war.

As Confederate troops under Stonewall Jackson marched through Frederick, Maryland, in 1862, one of the war's most famous legends was born. The rebels began to fire on the Union flag waved from the window of Dame Barbara Frietchie's home. In Whittier's words, " 'Shoot, if you must, this old grey head, / but spare your country's flag!' she said." *(Library of Congress.)*

From John Greenleaf Whittier's *Barbara Frietchie:*

Up from the meadows rich with corn,
Clear in the cool September morn,

The clustered spires of Frederick stand
Green-walled by the hills of Maryland.

Round about them orchards sweep,
Apple and peach tree fruited deep,

Fair as the garden of the Lord
To the eyes of the famished rebel horde,

On that pleasant morn of the early fall
When Lee marched over the mountain wall;

Over the mountains winding down,
Horse and foot, into Frederick town.

Forty flags with their silver stars,
Forty flags with their crimson bars,

Flapped in the morning wind: the sun
Of noon looked down, and saw not one.

Up rose old Barbara Frietchie then,
Bowed with her fourscore years and ten;

Bravest of all in Frederick town,
She took up the flag the men hauled down.

In her attic window the staff she set,
To show that one heart was loyal yet.

Up the street came the rebel tread,
Stonewall Jackson riding ahead.

Under his slouched hat left and right
He glanced; the old flag met his sight.

"Halt!"—the dust-brown ranks stood fast.
"Fire!"—out blazed the rifle-blast.

It shivered the window, pane and sash;
It rent the banner with seam and gash.

Quick, as it fell, from the broken staff
Dame Barbara snatched the silken scarf.

She leaned far out on the window-sill,
And shook it forth with a royal will.

"Shoot, if you must, this old gray head,
But spare your country's flag," she said.

The next major engagement in the East would come under the leadership of "fighting Joe" Hooker who assumed command after the resignation of Burnside. At the end of April 1863, with a force vastly superior to that of the enemy, the well-

Field artist Edwin Forbes witnessed this tedious scene of straining horses struggling to pull a heavy cannon through the mud and rain at Spotsylvania Court House in 1864. Foul weather beset both armies throughout the lengthy conflict, confounding logistics and adding much to the suffering of both the soldiers and their hard-pressed animals. *(Library of Congress.)*

organized Hooker faced the rebels at Chancellorsville, near a heavy and dark forest known as the Wilderness. It was to be the redoubtable Lee's greatest day but it would cost him dearly, taking the life of his firm friend and comrade-in-arms, Stonewall Jackson.

Hooker was ebullient and overly optimistic: "The rebel army is now the legitimate property of the Army of the Potomac," he said in anticipatory elation. It was not to be so. In a bold move Lee split his small army into three parts, while he alone with only 12,000 men held against the main body of 73,000 Federals. Jackson, in one of his audacious marches across the Union front, outflanked Hooker on the right and deluded the hapless general into thinking he was simply retreating. As the yankee soldiers ate their supper that evening, Jackson's intrepid force spilled out of the forest and drove the Federals back to Chancellorsville.

It was dark as the stalwart general rode out with the hope of enlarging the victory. A nervous North Carolina regiment opened fire on what they took to be Union cavalry. Jackson was shot three times in the arm. Amputation followed, and, sever- *al days later, pneumonia. It was the end for one of the South's most gallant and brilliant men. The star of the Confederacy would begin to wane in the dawn of Union endurance.*

From Captain Robert E. Lee's *Recollections and Letters of General Robert E. Lee:*

During this winter, which was a very severe one, the sufferings of General Lee's soldiers on account of insufficient shelter and clothing, the scant rations for man and beast, the increasing destitution throughout the country, and his inability to better these conditions, bore heavily upon him. But he was bright and cheerful to those around him, never complaining of any one nor about anything, and often indulging in his quaint humour, especially with the younger officers, as when he remarked to one of them, who complained of the tough biscuit at breakfast:

You ought not to mind that; they will stick by you the longer!"

His headquarters continued all the winter at the same place, and with stove and fire-places in the tents, the General and his military family managed to keep fairly comfortable.

The Mud March, by an unknown artist. General Burnside's men plod through the January mud of the Rappanhannock River in their retreat from the battle of Fredericksburg. (*The West Point Museum Collections, United States Military Academy*.)

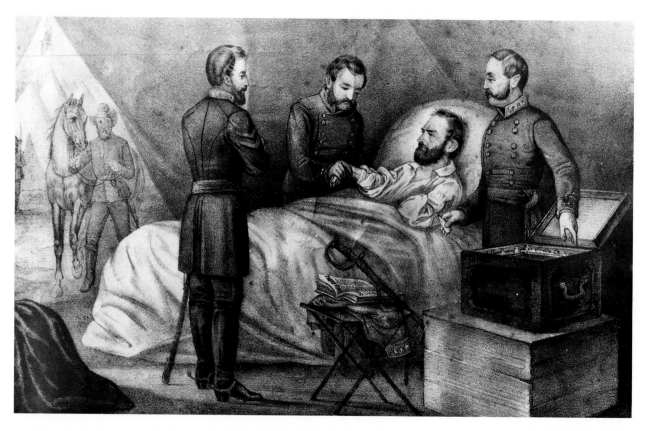

Stonewall Jackson, wounded at Chancellorsville, suffered the amputation of his left arm. A few days later he succumbed to pneumonia. The Confederacy had lost an irreplaceable general. (*The Museum of the Confederacy*.)

From Captain Robert E. Lee's *Recollections and Letters of General Robert E. Lee:*

The dreary winter gradually passed away. Toward the last of April, the two armies, which had been opposite each other for four months, began to move, and, about the first of May, the greatest of General Lee's battles was fought. My command was on the extreme left, and, as Hooker crossed the river, we followed a raiding party of the enemy's cavalry over toward the James River above Richmond; so I did not see my father at any time during the several days' fighting. The joy of our victory at Chancellorsville was saddened by the death of "Stonewall" Jackson. His loss was the heaviest blow the army of Northern Virginia ever sustained. To Jackson's note telling him he was wounded, my father replied:

"I cannot express my regret at the occurrence. Could I have directed events, I should have chosen for the good of the country to have been disabled in your stead. I congratulate you on the victory, which is due to your skill and energy."

Jackson said, when this was read to him,

"Better that ten Jacksons should fall than one Lee."

Afterward when it was reported that Jackson was doing well, General Lee playfully sent him word:

"You are better off than I am, for while you have only lost your *left,* I have lost my *right* arm."

Then, hearing that he was worse, he said:

"Tell him that I am praying for him as I believe I have never prayed for myself."

After his death, General Lee writes to my mother, on May 11th:

". . . In addition to the deaths of officers and friends consequent upon the late battles, you will see that we have to mourn the loss of the great and good Jackson. Any victory would be dear at such a price. His remains go to Richmond to-day. I know not how to replace him. God's will be done! I trust He will raise up some one in his place."

Jones, in his Memoirs, says: "To one of his officers, after Jackson's death, he [General Lee] said: 'I had such implicit confidence in Jackson's skill and energy that I never troubled myself to give him detailed instructions. The most general suggestions were all that he needed.'"

At dawn on May 2, 1863, General Lee and Stonewall Jackson met for the final time. (*The Museum of the Confederacy*.)

From Noah Brooks' *Washington in Lincoln's Time:*

I was at the White House on Wednesday, May 6, and the President, who seemed anxious and harassed beyond any power of description, said that while still without any positive information as to the result of the fighting at Chancellorsville, he was certain in his own mind that "Hooker had been licked." He was only then wondering whether Hooker would be able to recover himself and renew the fight. The President asked me to go into the room then occupied by his friend Dr. Henry, who was a guest in the house, saying possibly we might get some news later on.

In an hour or so, while the doctor and I sat talking, say about three o'clock in the afternoon, the door opened, and Lincoln came into the room. I shall never forget that picture of despair. He held a telegram in his hand, and as he closed the door and came toward us, I mechanically noticed that his face, usually sallow, was ashen in hue. The paper on the wall behind him was of the tint known as "French gray," and even in that moment of sorrow and dread expectation I vaguely took in the thought that the complexion of the anguished President's visage was almost exactly like that of the wall. He gave me the telegram, and in a voice trembling with emotion, said, "Read it—news from the army." The dispatch was from General Butterfield, Hooker's Chief of Staff, addressed to the War Department, and was to the effect that the army had been withdrawn from the south side of the Rappahannock, and was then "safely encamped" in its former position. The appearance of the President, as I read aloud these fateful words, was piteous. Never, as long as I knew him, did he seem to be so broken, so dispirited, and so ghostlike. Clasping his hands behind his back, he walked up and down the room, saying, "My God! My God! What will the country say! What will the country say!"

Hooker was full of plans to strike at Richmond again in the summer of 1863. Washington had tired of repetitive promises from successive commanders to destroy the Confederate capital and Lincoln's stinging retort to the general was "I think Lee's army and not Richmond, is your true objective point."

Lee had decided on another bold move into the North. His army was badly in need of food and supplies the depleted and ravished Virginia could no longer provide. Through the Shenandoah, the scene of Jackson's early triumph, into Maryland and Pennsylvania moved the Army of Northern Virginia. Hooker's army followed, but before the great battle at Gettysburg, he graciously resigned, leaving command to the tempestuous Major General George G. Meade, who had served long and ably on the eastern front.

The first day's fighting on July 1 found the bluecoats drawn back to Cemetery Ridge and Cemetery Hill. On July 2, the rebel attack was valiant, but the North stood firm. On the third, Lee ordered an

Last charge of the Maryland Infantry at Gettysburg, July 3, 1863. (*The Museum of the Confederacy*.)

attack on the center of Meade's line at the Ridge. General Longstreet would be reinforced by George E. Pickett's three rebel brigades. The encounter would forever be known as "Pickett's charge," an engagement unparalleled for bravery, daring and response to order as his men marched toward certain death amidst the smoke and the roar of the flaming Federal repulse.

The assault failed; less than half of the fifteen thousand who marched so bravely forward made it back to their lines. Lee told Pickett . . . "This has been my fight and upon my shoulders rests the blame."

The broken Confederate army, with its trains of ambulance wagons carrying the screaming wounded for whom the jostling was agony, made its way home again. Meade did not follow soon enough; Lincoln told him: "Your golden opportunity is gone."

From Carl Sandburg's *Abraham Lincoln, the War Years:*

Before starting his men on their charge to the Union center, Pickett handed Longstreet a letter to a girl in Richmond he was to marry if he lived. Longstreet had ordered Pickett to go forward and Pickett had penciled on the back of the envelope, "If Old Peter's [Longstreet's] nod means death, good-by, and God bless you, little one!" An officer held out a flask of whiskey to Pickett; "Take a drink with me; in an hour you'll be in hell or glory." And Pickett said No; he had promised "the little girl" he wouldn't.

Across the long rise of open ground, with the blue flag of Virginia floating ahead, over field and meadow Pickett's 15,000 marched steadily and smoothly, almost as if on a drill ground. Solid shot, grape and canister, from the Union artillery plowed through them, and later a wild rain of rifle bullets. Seven-eighths of a mile they marched in the open sunlight, every man a target for the Union marksmen behind stone fences and breastworks. They obeyed orders; Uncle Robert had said they would go anywhere and do anything.

As men fell their places were filled, the ranks closed up. As officers tumbled off horses it was taken as expected in battle.

Perhaps half who started reached the Union lines surmounting Cemetery Ridge.

Then came cold steel, the bayonet, the clubbed musket. The strongest and last line of the enemy was reached. "The Confederate battle flag waved over his defenses," said a Confederate major, "and the fighting over the wall became hand to hand, but more than half having already fallen, our line was too weak to rout the enemy."

Meade rode up white-faced to hear it was a repulse and cried, "Thank God!" Lee commented; "They deserved success as far as it can be deserved by human valor and fortitude. More may have been required of them than they were able to perform." To one of his colonels, Lee said, "This has been a sad day for us, a sad day, but we cannot expect always to gain victories."

As a heavy rainfall came on the night of July 4, Lee ordered a retreat toward the Potomac.

From *The Reminiscences of Carl Schurz:*

The wounded—many thousands of them—were carried to the farmsteads behind our lines. The houses, the barns, the sheds, and the open barnyards were crowded with the moaning and wailing human beings, and still an unceasing procession of stretchers and ambulances was coming in from all sides to augment the number of the sufferers. A heavy rain set in during the day—the usual rain after a battle—and large numbers had to remain unprotected in the open, there being no room left under roof. I saw long rows of men lying under the eaves of the buildings, the water pouring down upon their bodies in streams. Most of the operating tables were placed in the open where the light was best, some of them partially protected against the rain by tarpaulins or blankets stretched upon poles.

There stood the surgeons, their sleeves rolled up to the elbows, their bare arms as well as their linen aprons smeared with blood, their knives not seldom held between their teeth, while they were helping a patient on or off the table, or had their hands otherwise occupied; around them pools of blood and amputated arms or legs in heaps, sometimes more than man-high. Antiseptic methods were still unknown at that time. As a wounded man was lifted on the table, often shrieking with pain as the attendants handled him, the surgeon quickly examined the wound and resolved upon cutting off the injured limb. Some ether was administered and the body put in position in a moment. The surgeon snatched his knife from between his teeth, where it had been while his hands were busy, wiped it rapidly once or twice across his bloodstained apron, and the cutting began. The operation accomplished, the surgeon would look around with a deep sigh, and then— "next!"

The massive Philippoteaux Cyclorama at Gettysburg renders the final moments of Pickett's charge at the point of breakthrough. General Armistead falls fatally wounded. (*Eastern National Park and Monument Association.*)

92

At the dedication of the National Cemetery at Gettysburg, President Lincoln delivered his stirring defense of democracy.

In mid-November President Lincoln journeyed to Gettysburg for the dedication of the battlefield as a national cemetery, where the soldiers who had fallen on both sides would be buried.

He had been asked to make "a few appropriate remarks," although the main speaker of the day was to be the famous educator and orator, Edward Everett.

Everett's speech took two hours to deliver. The President's consisted of ten sentences and took only five minutes, but the eloquence of his few brief words lives to this day as perhaps the most stirring definition of democratic principle ever formulated.

President Abraham Lincoln's Gettysburg Address:

Fourscore and seven years ago our fathers brought forth on this continent a new nation, conceived in liberty, and dedicated to the proposition that all men are created equal.

Now we are engaged in a great civil war, testing whether that nation, or any nation so conceived and so dedicated, can long endure. We are met on a great battlefield of that war. We have come to dedicate a portion of that field as a final resting-place for those who here gave their lives that that nation might live. It is altogether fitting and proper that we should do this.

But in a larger sense, we cannot dedicate—we cannot consecrate—we cannot hallow—this ground. The brave men, living and dead, who struggled here, have consecrated it far above our poor power to add or detract. The world will little note nor long remember what we say here, but it can never forget what they did here. It is for us, the living, rather, to be dedicated here to the unfinished work which they who fought here have thus far so nobly advanced. It is rather for us to be here dedicated to the great task remaining before us—that from these honored dead we take increased devotion to that cause for which they gave the last full measure of devotion; that we here highly resolve that these dead shall not have died in vain; that this nation, under God, shall have a new birth of freedom; and that government of the people, by the people, for the people, shall not perish from the earth.

From Carl Sandburg's *Abraham Lincoln, The War Years:*

He had stood that day, the world's foremost spokesman of popular government, saying that democracy was yet worth fighting for. He had spoken as one in mist who might head on deeper yet into mist. He incarnated the assurances and pretenses of popular government, implied that it could and might perish from the earth. What he meant by "a new birth of freedom" for the nation could have a thousand interpretations. The taller riddles of democracy stood up out of the address. It had the dream touch of vast and furious events epitomized for any foreteller to read what was to come. He did not assume that the drafted soldiers, substitutes, and bounty-paid privates had died willingly under Lee's shot and shell, in deliberate consecration of themselves to the Union cause. His cadences sang the ancient song that where there is freedom men have fought and sacrificed for it, and that freedom is worth men's dying for. For the first time since he became President he had on a dramatic occasion declaimed, howsoever it might be read, Jefferson's proposition which had been a slogan of the Revolutionary War—"All men are created equal"—leaving no other inference than that he regarded the Negro slave as a man. His outwardly smooth sentences were inside of them gnarled and tough with the enigmas of the American experiment.

From Stephen Vincent Benét's *John Brown's Body:*

You took a carriage to that battlefield.
Now, I suppose, you take a motor-bus,
But then, it was a carriage—and you ate
Fried chicken out of wrappings of waxed paper,
While the slow guide buzzed on about the war
And the enormous, curdled summer clouds
Piled up like giant cream puffs in the blue.
The carriage smelt of axle-grease and leather
And the old horse nodded a sleepy head

Adorned with a straw hat. His ears stuck through it.
It was the middle of hay-fever summer
And it was hot. And you could stand and look
All the way down from Cemetery Ridge,
Much as it was, except for monuments
And startling groups of monumental men
Bursting in bronze and marble from the ground,
And all the curious names upon the gravestones. . . .

So peaceable it was, so calm and hot,
So tidy and great-skied.
                              No men had fought
There but enormous, monumental men
Who bled neat streams of uncorrupting bronze,
Even at the Round Tops, even by Pickett's boulder,
Where the bronze, open book could still be read
By visitors and sparrows and the wind:
And the wind came, the wind moved in the grass,
Saying . . . while the long light . . . and all so calm . . .
    "Pickett came
    And the South came
    And the end came,
    And the grass comes
    And the wind blows
    On the bronze book
    On the bronze men
    On the grown grass,
    And the wind says
    'Long ago
    Long
    Ago.' "

Then it was time to buy a paperweight
With flags upon it in decalcomania
And hope you wouldn't break it, driving home.

Citizens parade toward Cemetery Hill for the dedicatory ceremonies, November 19, 1863. (*Courtesy Chicago Historical Society*.)

95

War Spirit at Home, Celebrating the Victory at Vicksburg, by Lilly M. Spencer. These cherubic Northern infants romping in gay dishabille provided a marked contrast to the children of Vicksburg who had been subsisting on mule meat, peas and even less during the long weeks of General Grant's siege of the Mississippi city. *(Collection of The Newark Museum.)*

Union forces had controlled the Mississippi as far south as the heavily fortified Confederate city of Vicksburg and as far north as Port Hudson, Louisiana. To complete the stranglehold on Southern supply lines from the west, it was necessary as President Lincoln said that "the Father of Waters flows again unvexed to the sea."

Vicksburg was the real stronghold; its giant batteries high on the bluffs of the eastern shore commanded a large stretch of the river and repeated assaults by navy gunboats had been unsuccessful in subduing the city. Attempts by the Union army had also failed.

Grant, with around twenty thousand under his command, approached Vicksburg in May 1863 and began a siege. He surrounded the community, cutting it off from reinforcements, food and ammunition, while the navy continued its heavy bombardment. The city became a mass of rubble and its citizens took to living in caves for refuge from the constant shelling. One resident described the terrifying situation: "We are utterly cut off from the world, surrounded by a circle of fire. Would it be wise like the scorpion to sting ourselves to death? . . . People do nothing but eat what they can get, sleep when they can, and dodge the shells. . . . At all the caves I could see . . . people were sitting, eating their poor suppers at the cave doors, ready to plunge in again. . . . I think the dogs and cats must be killed or starved, we don't see any more pitiful animals prowling around."

Pickets trading between the lines were sketched by Edwin Forbes. *(Library of Congress.)*

On the fourth of July, Lieutenant General John Pemberton, in charge of the garrison, surrendered unconditionally his thirty thousand remaining troops, massive amounts of arms and the Confederate colors. Shortly after, Port Hudson fell to the Federals. The great river belonged to the Union.

From Mary Ann Loughborough's *My Cave Life in Vicksburg, with letters of trial and travel:*

We were now swiftly nearing the end of our siege life: the rations had nearly all been given out. For the last few days I had been sick. . . . My little one had swung in her hammock, reduced in strength, with a low fever flushing in her face. . . . A soldier brought up, one morning, a little jaybird, as a plaything for the child. After playing with it for a short time, she turned wearily away. "Miss Mary," said the servant, "she's hungry; let me make her some soup from the bird." At first I refused: the poor little plaything should not die; then, as I thought of the child, I half consented. With the utmost haste, the servant disappeared; and the next time she appeared, it was with a cup of soup, and a little plate, on which lay the white meat of the poor little bird.

On Saturday a painful calm prevailed: there had been a truce proclaimed; and so long had the constant firing been kept up, that the stillness now was absolutely oppressive. . . . I put on my bonnet and sallied forth beyond the terrace, for the first time since I entered. . . .

From *Personal Memoirs of U.S. Grant:*

During the siege there had been a good deal of friendly sparring between the soldiers of the two armies, on picket and where the lines were close together. All the rebels were known as "Johnnies," all Union troops as "Yanks." Often "Johnny" would call: "Well, Yank, when are you coming into town?" The reply was sometimes: "we propose to celebrate the 4th of July there." Sometimes it would be: "we always treat our prisoners with kindness and do not want to hurt them"; or, "We are holding you as prisoners of war while you are feeding yourselves."

The Vicksburg paper, which we received regularly through the courtesy of the rebel pickets, said prior to the 4th, in speaking of the "Yankee" boast that they would take dinner in Vicksburg that day, that the best receipt for cooking a rabbit was "First ketch your rabbit." The last number was issued on the 4th and announced that we had "caught our rabbit."

From a letter of Private John Brobst, twenty-fifth Wisconsin regiment, to Mary Englesby, July 5, 1863: [John Brobst and Mary Englesby began their correspondence as friends, fell in love through their letters and were married after the war.]

Friend Mary, I now seat myself to let you all know what kind of a Fourth we had. You folks up there had a more sociable time, perhaps, than we had, but I know you could not be half as happy as we were. We had the unspeakable pleasure of planting our glorious old flag in Vicksburg at four o'clock on the morning of the Fourth. There was pleasure and the right kind of pleasure. At 4 o'clock in the morning of the Fourth the rebels took down their flag and ran up a white one that was a surrender. Then they came out on the breastworks and stacked their arms and fell back and our men took possession and went out and took down the white flag, and the stars and stripes, our flag, that floats so proudly over the southern Gibraltar is 36 feet long. It is the greatest victory of the war.

The war in the East was over for the remainder of 1863. Both armies had suffered badly, but the Confederates would find it more and more difficult to recoup.

In the West, General William S. Rosecrans, with about 60,000 Union troops left Chattanooga in search of Confederate General Braxton Bragg, who with 47,000 in his command provided one of the main defenses of the Deep South and its essential railroad links. The two armies met at Chickamauga Creek, near Chattanooga, in a desperate battle on September 19 and 20. In a move involving incredible logistics by rail, Longstreet joined Bragg and cut the Union line. He had come all the way from Virginia, a distance of some 800 miles, over tracks in dangerous disrepair and on outmoded and decrepit cars of every sort and variety.

Rosecrans retreated to Chattanooga, but Major General George Thomas fought a superior delaying action which earned him the nickname, "Rock of Chickamauga."

Bragg laid siege to the Tennessee city where Rosecrans was encamped. But then, by mid-October, Grant and reinforcements arrived. Hooker and Sherman joined him. While Union soldiers within the city were near starvation, the contentious Grant immediately set about destroying Confederate strongholds. There were new names in the papers at Washington—Lookout Mountain, Missionary Ridge—and they bore the sweet sounds of victory.

Southerners fought on when nearly everything pointed to defeat of the cause, and Lee wrote about the Army of Northern Virginia, " . . . never forget it in your prayers. It is preparing for a great struggle, but I pray and trust that the great God, mighty to deliver, will spread over it His almighty arms, and drive its enemies before it."

It was as noble a plea as it was futile, for in the late winter of 1863, President Lincoln had decided that he had found his general, that only Grant was persistent and driving enough to conclude the cause in favor of the Union. He summoned him to Washington in March and placed him in command of all the armies of the United States.

From George Cary Eggleston's *A Rebel's Recollections:*

Did the Southerners really think themselves a match for ten times their own numbers? I know the reader wants to ask this question, because almost everybody I talk to on the subject asks it in one shape or another. In answer let me say, I think a few of the more enthusiastic women, cherishing a blind faith in the righteousness of their cause, and believing, in spite of historical precedent, that wars always end with strict regard to the laws of poetic justice, did think something of the sort; and I am certain that all the stump speakers . . . held a like faith most de-

Thomas Nast captured this defense of a Union battery at the battle of Chickamauga, September 19, 1863. (*Missouri Historical Society, St. Louis.*)

General William Tecumseh Sherman
(*Courtesy Donald S. Werner.*)

voutly. But with these exceptions I never saw any Southerner who hoped for any but well-fought-for success. It was not a question of success or defeat with them at all. They thought they saw their duty plainly, and they did it without regard to the consequences.

From William Franklin Gore Shanks' story in the *New York Herald,* September 27, 1863:

Thomas still remained on the field [at Chickamauga], with remnants of his glorious old corps; and the man who had the day before, in equal contest, defeated the boastful chivalry of Long-

street, now bent all his energies, with an unequal force, to cover the retreat and save the flying army from absolute destruction.

. . . But this abandonment of the field by the centre and right enabled the enemy to do with Thomas' right what he had signally failed, at frightful cost, to do with his left, and soon the rebels were pushing forward . . . doubling them up and pushing them back upon Brannan and Reynolds. . . .

The raid had begun at twelve o'clock; the stand of Thomas was made in half an hour, and the repulse and check of the enemy had been effected in a desperate engagement along the whole of this little line of not over fifteen minutes' duration.

Imagine this line—a thread without supports— the whole force to the front line—a force not over 20,000—and no one who saw it and who writes of it will put it at so much—and you have in your mind's eye the heroic corps which saved the whole army. And imagine the black lines of a powerful enemy marching upon it flank and front, and all the time pressing it closely in front and flank. . . .

General Thomas, near the centre of the army, was engaged, about one o'clock . . . watching a heavy cloud of dust in his rear, in such a direction that it might be General Granger with reinforcements, or it might be the enemy. . . .

. . . In a few minutes . . . emerged . . . the red, white and blue crescent-shaped battle flag of Gordon Granger. . . . At a quarter-past one, Steadman first, and Gordon Granger afterwards, had wrung the hand of the statue Thomas, who had gone all through the terrible scenes of the last two days' battle to be melted and moved at this hour. . . .

Winslow Homer's delightful lithographs of *Life in Camp* were issued in color prints the size of playing cards and sold to the public in sets. (*The Metropolitan Museum of Art, Harris Brisbane Dick Fund, 1947.*)

From *The War of the Rebellion... Official Records of the Union and Confederate Armies:*

The reconnaissance [to the top of Lookout Mountain] was made as directed, and having ascertained that the enemy had evacuated during the night, General Hooker was then directed to move on the Rossville road with the troops under his command

About noon, General Sherman becoming heavily engaged by the enemy, they having massed a strong force in his front, orders were given for General Baird to march his division within supporting distance of General Sherman. Moving his command promptly in the direction indicated, he was placed in position to the left of Wood's division of Granger's corps.

. . . The whole line then advanced against the breastworks, and soon became warmly engaged with the enemy's skirmishers; these, giving way, retired upon their reserves, posted within their works. Our troops advancing steadily in a continuous line, the enemy, seized with panic, abandoned the works at the foot of the hill and retreated precipitately to the crest, where they were closely followed by our troops, who, apparently inspired by the impulse of victory, carried the hill simultaneously at six different points, and so closely upon the heels of the enemy that many of them were taken prisoners in the trenches. We captured all their cannon and ammunition before they could be removed or destroyed.

After halting for a few moments to reorganize the troops, who had become somewhat scattered in the assault of the hill, General Sheridan pushed forward in pursuit, and drove those in his front who escaped capture across Chickamauga Creek. Generals Wood and Baird, being obstinately resisted by re-inforcements from the enemy's extreme right, continued fighting until darkness set in, slowly but steadily driving the enemy before them. In moving upon Rossville, General Hooker encountered Stewart's division and other troops. Finding his left flank threatened, Stewart attempted to escape by retreating toward Graysville, but some of his force, finding their retreat threatened from that quarter, retired in disorder toward their right, along the crest of the ridge, when they were met by another portion of General Hooker's command, and were driven by these troops in the face of Johnson's division of Palmer's corps, by whom they were nearly all made prisoners.

From *Memoirs of General W. T. Sherman:*

. . . I never saw the rear of an army engaged in battle but I feared that some calamity had happened at the front—the apparent confusion, broken wagons, crippled horses, men lying about dead and maimed, parties hastening to and fro in seeming disorder, and a general apprehension of something dreadful about to ensue; all these signs, however, lessened as I neared the front, and there the contrast was complete—perfect order, men and horses full of confidence, and it was not unusual for general hilarity, laughing, and cheering. Although cannon might be firing, the musketry clattering, and the enemy's shot hitting close, there reigned a general feeling of strength and security that bore a marked contrast to the bloody signs that had drifted rapidly to the rear; therefore, for comfort and safety, I surely would rather be at the front than the rear line of battle. So also on the march, the head of a column moves on steadily, while the rear is alternately halting and then rushing forward to close up the gap; and all sorts of rumors, especially the worst, float back to the rear. Old troops invariably deem it a special privilege to be in the front—to be at the "head of column"—because experience has taught them that it is the easiest and most comfortable place, and danger only adds zest and stimulus to this fact.

The hardest task in war is to lie in support of some position or battery, under fire without the privilege of returning it; or to guard some train left in the rear, within hearing but out of danger; or to provide for the wounded and dead of some corps which is too busy ahead to care for its own.

To be at the head of a strong column of troops, in the execution of some task that requires brain, is the highest pleasure of war—a grim one and terrible, but which leaves on the mind and memory the strongest mark; to detect the weak point of an enemy's line; to break through with vehemence and thus lead to victory; or to discover some key-point and hold it with tenacity; or to do some other distinct act which is afterward recognized as the real cause of success. These all become matters that are never forgotten. Other great difficulties, experienced by every general, are to measure truly the thousand-and-one reports that come to him in the midst of conflict; to preserve a clear and well-defined purpose at every instant of time, and to cause all efforts to converge to that end.

Behind the Lines

If, as it has often been remarked that "War is the result of a nation's sins"— then the sins of this nation must have been very great, and the atonement is truly one of the most painful mortality.

From the introduction to the autograph album of an unknown prisoner of war at Johnson's Island, Lake Erie, October 20, 1864

The "painful mortality" of war extended beyond the battlefield, where swift death did not allow speculations on the philosophical implications of human waste. Perhaps none understood it so well as those who survived battle only to languish, to suffer and to die in the prisons and hospitals of both North and South.

At the opening of hostilities, the Union and Confederate governments were woefully ill-prepared to handle the massive casualties from disease and battlefield wounds. Even the best medical schools graduated doctors after a four-or five-month course. The age of quackery and the widespread use of nostrums (whose main ingredient was often alcohol), peddled by itinerant self-styled "doctors," was in full fashion. Many medical men who found their way to the battlefields had never seen an operation, and professional literature was scarce.

Medical examining boards were organized to pass on the qualifications of those who desired appointments as assistant surgeons and these often came under heavy criticism. Phoebe Yates Pember, a supervisor and matron in Richmond's Chimborazo General Hospital, asserted that the board in that city "rejected good practitioners and gave appointments to apothecary boys."

Early in the war, the situation was most depressing. While there were still the problems of organizing the general hospitals to handle the sick and wounded transferred from the battlefields, organizing the logistics of such transportation, procuring necessary supplies, and arranging for adequate field hospitals: raw recruits were already pouring into camps by the thousands, and proper sanitation was as impossible to maintain as military discipline. Typhoid, dysentery and pneumonia took deadly tolls in both armies. Insects and lice (graybacks) carried disease from one soldier to another. Mosquitoes brought malaria. Hardly anyone escaped diarrhea and nothing was known of antiseptics and sterile techniques.

Still, under the Confederate Surgeon General, Samuel Preston Moore, the medical department did work as efficiently as possible under outstanding handicaps. He promoted the writing and wide distribution of publications helpful to the doctors in the field and encouraged the preparation of medicines derived from plants native to the South, especially important in the last years of the war when the blockade made it virtually impossible to get medical supplies from Europe.

In 1862, the Confederate government approved an act which would allow women to serve in the hospitals. Patient care had previously been entrusted to male volunteers, or to those temporarily removed from active duty. They had little or no knowledge of their work and even less disposition to perform it.

Sergeant, 1861
Hampton's Legion,
South Carolina Volunteers
(K/S Historical Publications.)

Private, 1863
42nd Pennsylvania,
Volunteer Infantry, "Bucktails"
(K/S Historical Publications.)

A Union officer confronts tattered rebels in Winslow Homer's *Prisoners from the Front.* In the latter days of the war, General Lee's troops were badly clothed and fed. These men symbolized the condition into which the proud army was falling. They did not lack the spirit to fight, only the means. (*The Metropolitan Museum of Art, gift of Mrs. Frank B. Porter, 1922.*)

In the North, women were also assuming a new role. Initially, there were no women nurses in the military hospitals, and city hospital patients were administered to by badly paid, uneducated denizens of the lowest classes. Florence Nightingale's selfless work in the Crimean War of 1853-1856 was fresh in people's minds, and Elizabeth Blackwell had become America's first woman doctor, one with a campaign for sanitary reform. She was well aware of the contribution which could be made by adequately trained and devoted nurses. A meeting at the Cooper Union in New York City, attended by the wealthiest and most elegant women of New York society and inspired by Dr. Blackwell, formed the Women's Central Association of Relief to deal with the care of the soldiers and to make some effort toward the proper training of nurses. Other similar groups were initiated throughout the North, and finally the movement was centralized as the United States Sanitary Commission, serving as an adjunct (often an unwelcome one) to the regular army medical department.

Secretary of War Simon Cameron gave the venerable but aging reformer Dorothea Dix the position of Superintendent of Nurses. Miss Dix wanted no nonsense: "No women under thirty need apply to serve in government hospitals. All nurses are required to be plain looking women. Their dresses must be brown or black with no adornments. No hoop skirts."

Women of all classes applied, finding ingenious ways to circumvent Miss Dix's restrictions, and throughout the war, not only in general

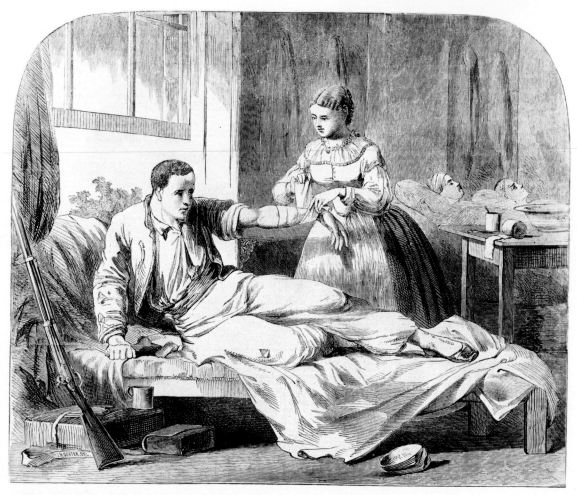

As the war raged on, American women proved their worth and hardiness as they relinquished traditional domestic duties to care for the wounded. *(Library of Congress.)*

and private hospitals, but on the field, they served with the same fearlessness as the soldiers they nursed.

The care received in hospitals varied greatly, the worst, by the nature of war, being on the field and in the prisons. The dedication of personnel, the availability of medical supplies, clothing and adequate sanitary facilities meant the difference between life or death.

In the South, as the Union's General Sherman pushed toward the sea, Confederate hospitals faced the exigencies of moving the sick and wounded at a moment's notice and the lack of cooperation of the Quartermaster Corps, who could not, or would not, meet the crucial needs of their three million sick and wounded. When it was over, disease had taken the lives of 150,000 Confederate soldiers, three-quarters of their total mortalities. The Union had lost over 100,000 on the field and twice as many to sickness. Said one Confederate doctor, "We did not the best we would, but the best we could."

Of all the lingering recriminations which are the inevitable aftermath of war, those concerning the treatment of prisoners are the most bitter, and this war was no exception. While Northerners pointed with wrath to Andersonville Prison in Georgia where fully one-third of those confined died, Southerners cited Elmira, New York, where inspectors found two thousand cases of scurvy and ill-equipped hospitals overflowing with those waiting for release from life. If mortality was high on the field and in general hospitals, it was increased to the point of morbidity in prison stockades, barracks and open camps.

Previous to the establishment of the stockades at Camp Sumter (named Andersonville by its inmates), a sweet stream of the purest

New York women worked at the Cooper Union Headquarters for the Women's Central Association of Relief. Their efforts resulted in better nursing for Union soldiers throughout the war. (*Museum of the City of New York*.)

drinking water flowed through the center of the proposed enclosure. Within weeks of the arrival of the first contingents, it was a stagnant open sewer, fouling the very air with its pestilential odors. The same condition developed rapidly at Elmira.

The goal of any captured man was to stay well. Very few achieved it. There were desperate sufferings caused by lack of shelter and sufficient wood for fires. In some camps disease was rampant from overcrowding, poor sanitary facilities and the crude habits of the inmates who refused to dig or use latrines. At Johnson's Island, Ohio, on Lake Erie, the rebels, unused to Northern winters were plagued by frostbite and pneumonia. Andersonville was literally a prison hospital, with thirty thousand crowded into its twenty-seven acres, many of the men arriving already emaciated from previous confinement at Richmond's Belle Isle. As the war progressed, drugs, including much needed quinine and opium, were not available in Southern prisons and scurvy took its deadly toll on both sides because of bad food, and sometimes very little even of that.

As always, things went better for those who had money, or knew how to make it, through gambling, the sale of hand-crafted jewelry, liquor and foodstuffs, by robbery or outright murder of those too weak to defend themselves. Through barter with guards or other prisoners, purchases from the camp sutler, those who had something to trade could get additional wood, food, blankets, or any of the other items necessary to their "comfort."

Northern prisons, seem, in general, to have had sufficient and varied rations until the spring of 1864, when some no longer received coffee and restrictions were placed on the amount of food which could be sent in by relatives and relief organizations. This action was apparently taken by the Federal government in retaliation for the increasing reports of severe food deficiencies among Union prisoners. In any case, it caused one rebel at Johnson's Island to remark, "Rats are found to be very good for food, and every night many are captured and slain."

Monotony was a constant problem if you were relatively well and could afford to be bored. Soldiers played cards, gambled, held races between the ubiquitous lice and cracked the ever-present graybacks. Johnson's Island had a circulating library and at Point Lookout, Maryland, the Aeolian Glee Club was organized. In terms of conversation, the inmates never tired of discussing escape or exchange, and the hope of it kept them going.

As for escape, some prisons made it impossible by their location, as at Johnson's Island and Point Lookout on Chesapeake Bay. At Libby, in Richmond, anyone who poked his head out the window was a dead man; at Andersonville and others a narrow open space and a fence marked the "deadline." To step over it, or to be suspected of surpassing the boundary meant instant doom. In addition, if prisoners did manage to escape their Georgia confinement, usually by tunneling, they were far from any Union lines, and Commandant Henry Wirz's bloodhounds were on the trail immediately. Of over thirty thousand confined there, only 329 escaped.

Survivors of the camps accused their captors of inhumane and even brutal treatment. Wirz paid with his life at the end of the war for his intentional maliciousness and callous disregard in providing even the most basic needs of the men.

A crude field hospital at the site of Antietam battlefield. (*The Museum of the Confederacy*.)

From Sylvia Dannett's *Noble Women of the North:*

Through the system of Sanitary Commission depots, hospital transports, hospital cars, diet kitchens, and relief stations and by the quick effective movements of agents in the field, such as lifting the soldiers from the battlefields onto stretchers and ambulances, plying them with restoratives, placing them in clean cots, clothing them with new uniforms, the Sanitary Commission often preserved the wounded until adequate medical and nursing care could take over. In this way the Sanitary Commission assumed the major role it was to hold throughout the war—that of getting medical and sanitary supplies to the men at the front to the seats of immediate battle far in advance of the Medical Department.

Within one week of the Battle of Antietam, the Sanitary Commission had distributed through its agents on the field enormous supplies of dry goods, medicine, first aid material, and food, as well as bottles of wine and cordials. It had succeeded in transporting from the medical purveyor's office in New York to the depot at Frederick, four thousand sets of hospital clothing and one hundred twenty bales of blankets. The women of the country were stirred anew by the gravity of the situation and the great need for their services in the field.

Georgeanna Woolsey quoted in Sylvia Dannett's *Noble Women of the North:*

No one knows, who did not watch the thing from the beginning, how much opposition, how much ill-will, how much unfeeling want of thought, these women nurses endured. Hardly a surgeon of whom I can think, received or treated them with even common courtesy. Government had decided that women should be employed, and the army surgeons—unable, therefore, to close the hospitals against them—determined to make their lives so unbearable that they should be forced in self-defence to leave. It seemed a matter of cool calculation, just how much ill-mannered opposition would be requisite to break up the system . . . .

None of [the army nurses] were strong-minded. Some of them were women of the truest refinement and culture; and day after day they quietly and patiently worked, doing, by order of the surgeon, things which not one of those gentlemen would have dared to ask of a woman whose male relative stood able and ready to defend her and report him. I have seen small white hands scrubbing floors, washing windows, and performing all menial offices. I have known women, delicately cared for at home, half-fed in hospitals, hard-worked day and night, and given, when sleep must be had, a wretched closet just large enough for a camp bed to stand in. I have known surgeons who purposely and ingeniously arranged these inconveniences with the avowed intention of driving away all women from their hospitals.

These annoyances could not have been endured by the nurses but for the knowledge that they were pioneers, who were, if possible, to gain standing ground for others—who must create the position they wished to occupy. This, and the infinite satisfaction of seeing from day to day sick and dying men comforted in their weary and dark hours, comforted as they never would have been but for these brave women, was enough to carry them through all and even more than they endured . . . .

When the war began, among the many subjects on which our minds presented an entire blank was that sublime, unfathomed mystery—"Professional Etiquette." Out of the army, in practice which calls itself "civil," the etiquette of the profession is a cold spectre, whose presence is felt everywhere, if not seen; but in the Medical Department of the Army, it was an absolute Bogie, which stood continually in one's path, which showed its narrow, ugly face in camps and in hospitals, in offices and in wards; which put its cold paw on private benevolence, whenever benevolence was fool enough to permit it; which kept shirts from ragged men, and broth from hungry ones; an evil Regular Army Bogie, which in full knowledge of empty kitchens and "exhausted funds," quietly asserted that it had need of nothing, and politely bowed Philanthropy out into the cold.

From Sylvia Dannett's *Noble Women of the North:*

Young doctors, many unskilled and without sufficient training, flocked to the army from medical schools and hospitals. They were frequently called upon to perform operations in the field hospitals with no preparation other than a quick course in military surgery at the outbreak of the War. A small pocket text, *A Handbook of Operative Surgery,* had been hurried to press and was in such demand that it went into twenty editions. The book was carefully illustrated and briefly explained the most common type of operations . . . . There were strict rules concerning amputations, for example: "In army practice on the field, amputations when necessary ought to be primary . . . therefore amputate with as little delay as possible."

So the women of the North went to war, and against the long-held prejudices of their husbands, they served on transports and in the field, dodging bullets like any recruit, and helping wherever they found the need. Young ladies of fashion, of delicate breeding and impeccable educations, without hoopskirts, became immune to the most gory scenes of battle and operating room and performed their services with all the refinements of nineteenth-century Christian charity.

Lousia May Alcott, best known for her novel, Little Women, *actually only gained literary success after publication of* Hospital Sketches, *which told of her experiences as a Union nurse.*

Union soldiers engage in an ambulance drill. It sometimes took days to gather the wounded from the field of battle. If they still lived, ambulance wagons took them to hosptial facilities behind the lines. (*Courtesy Chicago Historical Society.*)

From Louisa May Alcott's *Hospital Sketches:*

The sight of several stretchers, each with its legless, armless, or desperately wounded occupant, entering my ward, admonished me that I was there to work. . . . Forty beds were prepared, many already tenanted by tired men who fell down anywhere, and drowsed till the smell of food aroused them. Round the great stove was gathered the dreariest group I ever saw—ragged, gaunt and pale, mud to the knees, with bloody bandages untouched since put on days before; many bundled up in blankets, coats being lost or useless; and all wearing that disheartened look which proclaimed defeat . . . . Presently, Miss Blank . . . put basin, sponge, towels, and a block of brown soap into my hands, with these appalling directions:

"Come, my dear, begin to wash as fast as you can. Tell them to take off socks, coats and shirts, scrub them well, put on clean shirts, and the attendants will finish them off, and lay them in bed."

If she had requested me to shave them all, or dance a hornpipe on the stove funnel, I should have been less staggered; but to scrub some dozen men at a moment's notice was really—really—. However, there was no time for nonsense, and, having resolved when I came to do everything I was bid, I . . . clutched my soap manfully, and, assuming a business-like air, made a dab at the first dirty specimen I saw . . . .

From Sylvia Dannett's *Noble Women of the North:*

On a foggy Saturday morning, Burnside's men charged the Rebels on Marye's Heights [at Fredericksburg]. As the General observed, there was "enough bloodshed to satisfy any reasonable man." Charge after charge was made until sheets of flame covered the enemy stronghold as the boys in blue marched to their death. The butchery finally ended at nightfall, and 12,500 Union boys were killed or maimed. Some burned to death in long dry grass that had been set afire by cannons. Others died of exposure in the bitter cold. The President's heart was heavy at the news . . . .

Dorothea Dix sent several nurses on board the Government transport steamer *Rockland* . . . to look after the wounded en route to Washington hospitals after Fredericksburg. Those who were not wounded from battle soon became ill after being dragged up the Rappahannock by Ambrose Burnside who is known to posterity not for his deeds but for the sideburns he inspired.

The nurses often had to leave the transports, going in the ambulances to pick up the wounded, carrying food and drink to those who must wait longer. Now and then a nurse was forced to spend a night in the ambulance on the battlefield, very near the enemy. No one dared to make a fire or light a match. One intrepid girl wrote later that she "drank water from holes made by the horses' feet in the mud; it tasted good and sweet."

Belle Reynolds quoted in Sylvia Dannett's *Noble Women of the North:*

And that operating table! These scenes come up before me now with all the vividness of reality . . . one by one, they would take from different parts of the hospital a poor fellow, lay him out on those bloody boards, and administer chloroform; but before insensibility, the operation would begin, and in the midst of shrieks, curses, and wild laughs, the surgeon would wield over his wretched victim the glittering knife and saw; and soon the severed and ghastly limb, white as snow and spattered with blood, would fall upon the floor—one more added to the terrible pile . . . .

At night I lived over the horrors of the field hospital and the amputating table. If I but closed my eyes, I saw such horrible sights that I would spring from my bed; and not until fairly awakened could I be convinced of my remoteness from the sickening scene. Those groans were in my ears; I saw again the quivering limbs, the spouting arteries, and the pinched and ghastly faces of the sufferers.

Prejudice toward women entering the service on any basis was even stronger in the South, where, as elsewhere, it was considered one step above prostitution. However, as it became obvious to the surgeons of the medical department that the ministrations of women to the wounded lowered the mortality rate, the policy was changed.

Kate Cumming, against the extreme disapprobation of family and friends, was one of the first to leave for the front. She received her initiation into the wards in Corinth, Mississippi, at the Tishomingo Hotel, which, like many other private buildings, served as an auxilliary hospital.

From Kate Cumming's *A Journal of Hospital Life in the Confederate Army of Tennessee from the Battle of Shiloh to the end of the War:*

Mrs. Ogden tried to prepare me for the scenes I should witness upon entering the wards. But Alas! nothing that I had ever heard or read had given me the faintest idea of the horrors witnessed here . . . . Certainly, none of the glories of the war were pre-

Howard's Grove Hospital, near Richmond, painted by an unknown rebel soldier. (*Courtesy Chicago Historical Society.*)

sented here. But I must not say that; for if uncomplaining endurance is glory, we had plenty of it. If it is that which makes the hero, here they were by scores. Gray-haired men—men in the pride of manhood—beardless boys—Federals and all, mutilated in every imaginable way, lying on the floor, just as they were taken from the battlefield . . . . O, if the authors of this cruel and unnatural war could but see what I saw there, they would try and put a stop to it! To think, that it is man who is working all this woe upon his fellow-man. What can be in the minds of our enemies . . . . May God forgive them, for surely they know not what they do.

This was no time for recrimination; there was work to do; so I went at it to do what I could. If I were to live a hundred years, I should never forget the poor sufferers' gratitude; for every little thing, done for them—a little water to drink, or the bathing of their wounds—seemed to afford them the greatest relief.

The Federal prisoners are receiving the same attention as our own men; they are lying side by side . . . . Before I went in, I thought I would be polite, and say as little as possible to them; but when I saw them laughing, and apparently indifferent to the woe which they had been instrumental in bringing upon us, I could not help being indignant; and when one of them told me he was from Iowa, and that was generally called out of the world, I told him that was where I wished him, and all like him, so that they might not trouble us any more . . . .

From Phoebe Yates Pember's *A Southern Woman's Story:*

The duty which of all others pressed most heavily upon me and which I never did perform voluntarily was that of telling a man he could not live, when he was perhaps unconscious that there was any danger apprehended from his wound. The idea of death so seldom occurs when disease and suffering have not wasted the frame and destroyed the vital energies, that there is but little opening or encouragement to commence such a subject unless the patient suspects the result ever so slightly. In many cases too, the yearning for life was so strong that to destroy the hope was beyond human power. Life was for him a furlough, family and friends once more around him; a future was all he wanted, and he considered it cheaply purchased if only for a month by the endurance of any wound, however painful or wearisome.

There were long discussions among those responsible during the war, as to the advisability of the frequent amputations on the field, and often when a hearty, fine-looking man in the prime of life would be brought in minus an arm or leg, I would feel as if it might have been saved, but experience taught me the wisdom of prompt measures. Poor food and great exposure had thinned the blood and broken down the system so entirely that secondary amputations performed in the hospital almost invariably resulted in death, after the second year of the war. The blood lost on the battlefield when the wound was first received would enfeeble the already impaired system and render it incapable of further endurance . . . .

The only cases [secondary amputations] under my observation that survived were two Irishmen, and it was really so difficult to kill an Irishman that there was little cause for boasting on the part of the officiating surgeons . . . .

From H. H. Cunningham's *Doctors in Gray: The Confederate Medical Service:*

Some of the disadvantages under which Confederate medical officers worked was set forth concisely by one of their number: "The surgeon-general issued some valuable and useful publications, but we had no 'Medical and Surgical History of the Confederate States'; we had scarcely a journal; we had no 'Army Medical Museum'; we had no men of science and leisure to produce original work, or to record, classify and arrange the rich and abundant material gathered in the departments of either medicine or surgery . . . ."

Neither, it might be added, did they have blood plasma, x-rays, antibiotics, vitamin concentrates, vaccine to prevent typhoid fever and tetanus, and other products of recent medical and surgical research considered so essential today to the military medical officer. Nor did they have in the latter part of the war . . . patients whose physical condition was favorably influenced by a confident mental outlook. The men became less and less sanguine as the war entered its final stages, and the surgeons' task was rendered more difficult by the ensuing mental depression . . . .

"A Hospital Catechism" From *Southern Punch,* August 27, 1863:

For the use of medical surgeons of the C.S.A.

QUESTION. What is the first duty of a physician who has lost his practice at home?

ANSWER. To join the service.

QUESTION. What is the first duty of a young man who has graduated in medicine, or passed through one course of lectures at some medical school?

ANSWER. To join the service.

QUESTION. How do most physicians get into the service?

ANSWER. Through family influence or political favoritism.

QUESTION. What is the second duty of an M.S. [Medical Surgeon]?

ANSWER. To physic soldiers according to the rules of defunct writers, such as Cullen, Brown & Co., without regard to constitutional idiosyncracies, or climatic influence.

QUESTION. What is the third duty of an M.S.?

ANSWER. To cut, slash, and saw off as many arms and legs as possible in one day.

QUESTION. Is it the duty of an M.S. to exert all his skill and exhaust all the remedies of his command in endeavoring to save a limb?

ANSWER. No. The way to dispatch business is by resorting to immediate amputation.

QUESTION. Should an M.S. ever consult, in doubtful cases, with private physicians of acknowledged ability?

ANSWER. It is a waste of time to do so, and it would interfere with digestion, social pleasures and position.

QUESTION. Should an M.S. pause to consider that the injudicious amputation of limbs deprives the Confederacy of many valuable soldiers?

ANSWER. By no means. John Hunter boasted that he had dissected several thousand human bodies. An M.S. should boast of his array of amputated arms and legs as proof conclusive of his scientific attainments.

Conscripts often complained about the qualifications and methods of the medical boards of examiners. *Southern Punch* ran this devastating cartoon showing a bewildered draftee at the mercy of his "doctors." If the young man was found to have a pulse, and if he was breathing, he would probably be deemed fit for active service. (*The Museum of the Confederacy*.)

QUESTION. What is the fourth duty of an M.S.?

ANSWER. To keep disabled soldiers in the hospitals until they either die, or will die very soon.

QUESTION. When is a disabled soldier discharged, if ever?

ANSWER. Just as he is about to "shuffle off this mortal coil."

QUESTION. What should the soldier's diet in a hospital be?

ANSWER. Meat that is oderiferous; bread, that a squirrel cannot get its teeth into.

QUESTION. What is the fifth duty of an M.S.?

ANSWER. To feast on fish, sirloin steaks, chicken, etc., and drink the best liquor.

Field surgeons attend the wounded during an enemy engagement. While such immediacy of care was vitally important to the injured, it seems almost brutally inadequate in comparison to modern standards and techniques. (*Library of Congress.*)

From Sophronia Bucklin's *In Hospital and Camp:*

About the amputating tent lay large piles of human flesh—legs, arms, feet, and hands. They were strewn promiscuously about—often a single one lying under our very feet, white and bloody—the stiffened members seeming to be clutching ofttimes at our clothing . . . .

Death met us on every hand. It was a time of intense excitement. Scenes of fresh horror rose up before us each day. Tales of suffering were told, which elsewhere would have well-nigh frozen the blood with horror. We grew callous to the sight of blood, and great gashed lips opened under our untrembling hands . . . .

A soldier came to me one day, when I was on the field, requesting me to dress his wound, which was in his side. He had been struck by a piece of shell, and the cavity was deep and wide enough to insert a pint bowl. This cavity was absolutely filled with worms; not the little slender maggots from which a woman's hand is wont to shrink in nervous terror, but great blackheaded worms, which had grown on the living flesh, and surfeiting of the banquet some of them crawled into his hair, and over his torn clothing.

While I was endeavoring to clear them from the wound, one of the surgeons came around, and paused to watch me at work. "That is too hard for you; I will assist you some," he said, and taking the can of chloroform—which always accompanied us on our rounds, the contents serving our purpose instead of fire in causing the strips of adhesive plaster to remain over the wounds—he poured the entire con-

Mrs. Charlotte Greenhow, shown with her daughter during her imprisonment in Washington's Old Capitol Prison, continued sending information to the Confederate staff under General Beauregard. It was she who informed Beauregard of McDowell's advance on Manassas in July 1861. (*The Museum of the Confederacy*.)

tents of the can into the mass of creeping life, which for a moment fought the contest with the fiery fluid and then straightened out.

Women were doing other unusual things in the war, and as spies they often excelled the men. Mrs. Rose O'Neal Greenhow, a socially prominent Washington matron, is credited with supplying General Beauregard with the first news of the Federal advance on Manassas in July 1861. Detective Allan Pinkerton soon had her placed under arrest and put under military guard at her home. She was then transferred to the Old Capitol Prison and confined there until April of the following year. Even

while imprisoned Mrs. Greenhow corresponded with Beauregard's staff.

Sara Emma Edmonds played the part of Franklin Thompson for two years during the war on the side of the Union. Her sex was never known to anyone in the military.

Another famous Confederate was Belle Boyd, who worked in the area of West Virginia, gathering vital information from the Federal officers and relaying it to the rebels. Several times she was captured and released, surviving to lecture on her experiences and to write them in Belle Boyd in Camp and Prison.

From Rose O'Neal Greenhow's *My Imprisonment and the First Year of Abolition Rule in Washington:*

On Friday, August 23, 1861, . . . I was arrested by two men, one in citizen's clothes and the other in the dress of an officer of the United States Army. This latter was called Major Allen, and was the chief of the detective police of the city. They . . . asked "Is this Mrs. Greenhow?" I answered "Yes. Who are you and what do you want?" "I come to arrest you"— "By what authority?" The man Allen, or Pinkerton (for he had several aliases) said: "By sufficient authority." I said: "Let me see your warrant." He mumbled something about verbal authority from the War and State Department and then followed me into the house. By this time the house had become filled with men, and men also surrounded it outside like bees from a hive. An indiscriminate search now commenced throughout my house . . . .

As the evening advanced I was ordered upstairs accompanied by my friend, Miss Mackall, a heavy guard of detectives being stationed in the room with us. I was never alone for a moment. Wherever I went a detective followed me. If I wished to lie down he was seated a few paces from my bed. If I desired to change my dress or anything else, it was obliged to be done with open doors, and a man peering in at me . . . .

The work of examining my papers commenced. I had no reason to fear the consequences from the papers which had as yet fallen into their hands. I had a right to my own political opinions. I am a Southern woman, born with revolutionary blood in my veins, Freedom of speech and of thought were my birthright, guaranteed, signed and sealed by the blood of our fathers.

The search went on . . . I was, however, all the more anxious to be free from the sight of my captors for a few moments; so feigning the pretext of change of dress etc. as the day was intensely hot, after great difficulty and thanks to the slow movements of these agents of evil, I was allowed to go to my chamber and I then resolved to destroy some important papers which I had in my pocket, even at the expense of my life. (The papers were my cipher, with which I corresponded with my friends at Manassas.) Happily I succeeded without such a painful sacrifice . . . .

One morning I started all alone for a five-mile ride to an isolated farmhouse . . . report said was well supplied with all the articles of which I was in search . . . .

I rode up to the house and dismounted, hitched my horse to a post at the door, and proceeded to ring the bell. A tall stately lady made her appearance, and invited me in with much apparent courtesy . . . .

She invited me into another room, while she prepared the articles which she proposed to let me have, but I declined, giving as an excuse that I preferred to sit where I could see whether my horse remained quiet. I watched all her movements narrowly, not daring to turn my eyes aside for a single moment . . . . Could it be she was meditating the best mode of attack, or was she expecting someone to come, and trying to detain me until their arrival? Thoughts like these passed through my mind in quick succession . . . .

In a few moments she came to the door, but did not offer to assist me or to hold the basket, or anything, but stood looking at me most maliciously, I thought . . . . I had scarcely gone a rod when she discharged a pistol at me; by some intuitive movement I threw myself forward on my horse's neck and the ball passed over my head. I turned my horse in a twinkling, and grasped my revolver. She was in the act of firing the second time, but was so excited that the bullet went wide of its mark . . . . I did not wish to kill the wretch, but did intend to wound her. When she saw that two could play at this game, she dropped her pistol and threw up her hands imploringly. I took deliberate aim at one of her hands, and sent the ball through the palm of her left hand. She fell to the ground in an instant with a loud shriek. I dismounted, and took the pistol which lay beside her, and placing it in my belt, proceeded to take care of her ladyship in the following manner: I unfastened the end of my halter-strap, tied it painfully tight around her right wrist, and remounting my horse, I started, and brought the lady to consciousness by dragging her by the wrist two or three rods along the ground . . . I presented a pistol, and told her that if she uttered another word or scream she was a dead woman. In that way I succeeded in keeping her from alarming anyone who might be within calling distance, and so made my way toward McClellan's headquarters.

From Sarah Emma Edmonds' *The Female Spy of the Union Army: My Thrilling Adventures, Experiences, and Escapes of a Woman:*

I was often sent out to procure supplies for the hospitals, butter, eggs, milk, chickens, etc., and in my rambles I used to meet with many interesting adventures . . . .

Belle Boyd quoted in *Stories of Our Soldiers: . . . Collected from the Series Written Especially for the* Boston Journal:

There was a young Federal officer at our house who I knew had the countersign. He fell in love with me, and I was engaged to him to be married, but I had always refused to kiss him good night.

As a Confederate agent, Belle Boyd supplied Stonewall Jackson with information during his Valley Campaign. After the war she married a Union officer who had followed her to England to propose. (*The Museum of the Confederacy*.)

the route not even that, and here and there rough, hard climbs up the stony beds of the brooks, with stiffish ledges and rocky barriers to leap in the gloomy and precipitous ravines and gorges.

I found Jackson and delivered my dispatches. Coming back in the gray of the morning I was overtaken by a thunder storm. I dared not stop, so kept straight on, wet to the skin, 'mid the gloom of the storm and the blinding glare of the lightning.

In one vivid flash there stood revealed the Federal guard with rifle poised.

"Who comes there?" rang out his challenge.

For the moment I forgot the countersign, when luckily kind fate produced the corporal standing close beside the sentry. The friendly lightning gave him a glimpse of me.

Said he, "Let the boy pass; I know him."

I was awfully glad he thought he did, and dashed by the picket with a lightened heart . . . .

One reason for the deplorable conditions in hospitals and prisons was the inflationary spiral caused by the tremendous cost of carrying on the war. Those on the homefront suffered many deprivations as wages in the North did not keep up with the rising cost of goods. Southern currency became practically worthless and the blockade cut off nearly all European supplies.

Richmond experienced a bread riot in the spring of 1863, and President Davis was speaking of the culinary merits of eating rats, although through the years of crisis the President and Mrs. Davis continued to give lavish and sumptuous parties, equal to those of Washington society.

The poorer women of the South tended their farms by themselves or with the few remaining slaves they owned or with the help they could hire. They made their own clothes, wore underwear of homespun, gathered roots and herbs for medicines. All were required to surrender one-tenth of their produce to the Confederate government, but many seemed to make the sacrifice readily.

Amid all the surrounding disaster and despoilation, nothing could dim the unsuppressed gaiety of young Esther Alden as she attended her first party at Fort Sumter, encircled by dashing Confederate officers. As Natasha Rostov in Tolstoy's novel, War and Peace, *had blithely danced the evening away in the arms of Prince André, oblivious to the impending carnage of Napoleon's invasion, the guns of the block-*

I wanted his papers, and so this night when he pressed me for a kiss I saw these papers sticking from his pocket. Here was the opportunity, and have them I must. I kissed him and at the same time deftly removed the packet of letters. He never missed them until long after I had gone.

So you see it was the kiss of Judas after all.

Fortune favored me. Those papers were more valuable than I had imagined.

In the garb of a boy I mounted my horse that evening and started on my journey. It was not a moonlight night, though the stars were out at the commencement of my weird journey, but soon became obscured.

Ah, that was a wild ride that we took—Fleeta and I. I will never forget it. With only a general conception of the way, oftentimes I got off my course. At the best, there was only a bridle path. For much of

Esther Alden quoted in Sallie Hunt's *"Our Women in the War": the Lives They Lived; the Deaths They Died:*

...It is too delightful to be at home! In spite of the war every one is so bright and cheerful, and the men are so charming and look so nice in their uniforms. We see a great many of them, and I have been to a most delightful dance in Fort Sumter. The night was lovely and we went down in rowing boats. It was a strange scene, cannon balls piled in every direction, sentinels pacing the ramparts, and within the case-mates pretty, well-dressed women, and handsome well-bred men dancing, as though unconscious that we were actually under the guns of the blockading fleet. It was my first party, and the strange charm of the situation wove a spell around me; every man seemed to me a hero—not only a possible but an actual hero! One looks at a man so differently when you think he may be killed to-morrow! Men whom up to this time I have thought dull and commonplace that night seemed charming. I had a rude awakening as we rowed back to the city. When we came abreast of Fort Ripley, the sentinel halted us demanding the countersign, the oarsmen stopped, but Gen. R., who was steering the boat, ordered them to row on. Three times the sentinel spoke and then he fired. The ball passed over the boat and Gen. R. ordered his men to row up to the fort, called the officer of the day, and ordered the sentinel put under arrest! Of course I knew nothing about it, but it seemed to me frightfully unjust, and I was so indignant that I found it hard to keep quiet until we got home.

From a letter of Agnes _____ to Sara Rice Pryor, January 7, 1863:

Do you realize the fact that we shall soon be with-out a stitch of clothes? There is not a bonnet for sale in Richmond. Some of the girls smuggle them, which I for one consider in the worst possible taste, to say the least. We have no right at this time to dress better than our neighbors, and besides, the soldiers need every cent of our money. Do you remember in Washington my pearl-gray silk bonnet, trimmed inside with lilies of the valley? I have ripped it up, washed and ironed it, dyed the lilies blue (they are bluebells now), and it is very becoming. All the girls intend to plait hats next summer when the wheat ripens, for they have no blocks on which to press the coalscuttle bonnets, and after all when our blockade is raised we may find they are not at all worn, while hats are hats and never go out of fashion. The country girls made them last summer and pressed the crowns over

bowls and tin pails. I could make lovely flowers if I had materials.

It seems rather volatile to discuss such things while our dear country is in such peril. Heaven knows I would costume myself in coffee-bags if that would help, but having no coffee, where could I get the bags?...

I attended Mrs. Davis's last reception. There was a crowd, all in evening dress. You see, as we don't often wear our evening gowns, they are still quite passable. I wore the gray silk with eleven flounces ... and by the bye, who do you think was at the battle of Williamsburg, on General McClellan's staff? The Prince de Joinville who drank the rose wine with you at the Baron de Limbourg's reception to the Japs. Doesn't it all seem so long ago—so far away? The Prince de Joinville escorted me to one of the President's levees—don't you remember?—and now I attend another President's levee and hear him calmly telling people that rats, if fat, are as good as squirrels, and that we can never afford mule meat. It would be too expensive, but the time may come when rats will be in demand.

From Parthenia Antoinette Hague's *A Blockaded Family: Life in Southern Alabama during the Civil War:*

The woods, as well as being the great storehouse for all our dyestuffs, were also our drug stores. The berries of the dogwood tree were taken for quinine, as they contained the alkaloid properties of cinchona and Peruvian bark. A soothing and efficacious cordial for dysentery and similar ailments was made from blackberry roots; but ripe persimmons, when made into a cordial, were thought to be far superior to blackberry roots. An extract of the barks of the wild cherry, dogwood, poplar, and wahoo trees were used for chills and agues. For coughs and all lung diseases a syrup made with the leaves and roots of the mullein plant, globe flower, and wild-cherry tree bark was thought to be infallible. Of course the castor-bean plant was gathered in the wild state in the forest, for making castor oil.

Many also cultivated a few rows of poppies in their gardens to make opium, from which our laudanum was created; and this at times was very needful. The manner of extracting opium from poppies was of necessity crude. The heads or bulbs of the poppies were plucked when ripe, the capsules pierced with a large-sized sewing needle, and the bulbs placed in some small vessel (a cup or saucer would answer) for the opium gum to exude and to become inspissated by evaporation. The soporific influence of this drug was not excelled by that of the imported articles . . . .

One of our most difficult tasks was to find a good substitute for coffee. This palatable drink, if not a

An etching by Adalbert Volck depicted Southern women industriously engaged in making clothes for the boys in the army. (*The Museum of the Confederacy.*)

real necessary of life, is almost indispensable to the enjoyment of a good meal, and some Southerners took it three times a day. Coffee soon rose to thirty dollars per pound; from that it went to sixty and seventy dollars per pound. Good workmen received thirty dollars per day; so it took two days' hard labor to buy one pound of coffee, and scarcely any could be had even at that fabulous price. Some imagined themselves much better in health for the absence of coffee, and wondered why they had ever used it at all, and declared it good for nothing any way; but "Sour grapes" would be the reply for such as they. Others saved a few handfuls of coffee, and used it on very important occasions, and then only as an extract . . . for flavoring substitutes for coffee.

From *The Printer*, New York, July, 1864:

We have "gone through the mill," and "know whereof we speak," and are satisfied that no family embracing four children can exist in comfort on less than the following:

One bag of flour	$1.40
Small measure of potatoes, daily, at 13¢ per day	.91
One quarter of a pound of tea	.32
One pound of coffee (mixed or adulterate— can't afford better)	.35
Three and a half pounds of sugar	.80
Meats for the week	$3.00
Two bushels of coal	$1.20
Four pounds of butter	$1.60
Two pounds of lard	.38
Kerosene	.20
Soap, starch, pepper, salt, vinegar, etc.	.75
Vegetables	.50
Dried apples (to promote the health of children)	.25
Sundries	.44
Rent	$4.00
Total	$16.10

. . . The average wages of all branches of printers in this city is sixteen dollars per week—the average family consists of the number stated. How, then, are these families to subsist, if . . . every dollar is consumed for food and house-rent? Wearing apparel has trebled in price, and not one dollar is left from the weekly wage to procure a supply. Every workman's family is short of house-linens, underclothing, shoes, etc.; and the fortunate printer that has more than one suit to his back, or whose wife can boast of more than a change of calicoes, can scarcely be found.

From George Cary Eggleston's *A Rebel's Recollections:*

I am sometimes asked at what time prices attained their highest point in the Confederacy, and I find that memory fails to answer the question satisfactorily . . . . The financial condition got steadily worse to the end. I believe the highest price, relatively, I ever saw paid, was for a pair of boots. A cavalry officer, entering a little country store, found there one pair of boots that fitted him. He inquired the price. "Two hundred dollars," said the merchant. A five hundred dollar bill was offered, but the merchant, having no

A company of Negro soldiers liberated their Southern brethen from a North Carolina plantation. Such groups would then come under the protection of the army.
(Library of Congress.)

smaller bills, could not change it. "Never mind," said the cavalier, "I'll take the boots anyhow. Keep the change. I never let a little matter of three hundred dollars stand in the way of a trade."

That was on the day before Lee's surrender, but it would not have been an impossible occurrence at any time during the preceding year. The money was of so little value that we parted with it gladly whenever it would purchase anything at all desirable. I cheerfully paid five dollars for a little salt, at Petersburg, in August, 1864, and . . . drank my last two dollars in a half-pint of cider.

While those at home were surviving on the scraps of a ravaged economy, the prisoners in the 150 military compounds of North and South were damning the parsimony of their jailers, and writing their day by day accounts of prison life. George Darby was an extremely daring young man and succeeded in escaping from his Confederate captors many times, but never made it back far enough from Richmond to reach yankee lines. He served time both in Libby and at Belle Isle.

His friend Private Golden, whose story is included in Darby's own book, was confined at Salisbury, in western North Carolina and also at Belle Isle. Private Golden's reminiscences, also written long after his captivity, show that the burden of his experience would never be forgotten. At Salisbury, 17,500 of his fellows lie buried.

From George Darby's *Incidents and Adventures in Rebeldom:*

. . . From the middle of the year 1864 until the collapse of the rebellion, I say on, and after, the date last named, were the darkest and most desperate days of the Southern Confederacy . . . . Oh! how I thank heaven to-day as I remember and seem to see again, the comrades of my prison life, with emaciated forms, sunken cheeks and eyes, eyes which were wont to sparkle and glow with life's loves and ambitions, now glazing in death's slow oncoming tide, and I seem to hear again the voice once strong and musical as the spheres, now weak and sepulchral as though it issued from the tomb, as its last cadence dies away in a feeble cry for bread. As I remember these things my heart swells with gratitude when I remember also that Jehovah hath said "Vengeance is Mine! I will repay, saith the Lord!" It was not until after the regime of starvation was inaugurated by the rebel government as a course of treatment of the prisoners of war, that the other barbarities which I have enumerated were put into practice, so that those of our comrades who were prisoners during the earlier period of the war scarcely know what breathing holes of hell these later prisons were. Here it was that imprisonment for a few months meant death sure and certain, graduated solely on the power of constitutional endurance of the individual prisoner. May God forgive those worse than red-handed murders . . . , but I believe I never can.

Private C.H. Golden quoted in George Darby's *Incidents and Adventures in Rebeldom:*

Belle Isle is a small island in the James River, which, as viewed from a little distance, has enough pretentions of beauty to justify its name. A portion of the island consists of a bluff covered with trees; but the part used as a prison pen was low, sandy and barren, without a tree to protect it from the rays of the sun. The Belle Isle prison pen was an inclosure of some four or five acres, surrounded by an earthwork several feet high, with a ditch on either side. On the edge of the outer ditch guards were stationed all around the enclosure at intervals of forty feet. The interior of the enclosure had some resemblance at a distance to an encampment, a number of low tents being set in regular rows. Close inspection revealed the fact that the tents were old, rotten and torn and at best could have sheltered only a small percentage of the prisoners. Within these low tents were huddled from fourteen to sixteen thousand men at one time, not housed up in walls nor buried in dungeons, but simply turned into the field like so many animals, to find shelter when and how they might. So crowded were they that if each man had lain down on the ground, occupying the generous allotment of a "hospital grave," say seven feet by two, the whole area of the enclosure would have been covered. Here thousands of us lay from the 18th of August, 1864, until the 8th of October, with naught but the sky for a covering and sand for a bed. When the hot glare of the summer sun fell upon the oozing morasses of the James, covering its stagnant pools with green slime, we prayed in vain for some shelter from the sickening heat of day, and torrents of rain at night, that our fevered bodies might be dipped in the stream beyond. But no, we were forced to broil and bake under the tropical rays of a midday sun, or huddled together like cattle throughout the livelong night in the pourdown storm. Some of us burrowed in the sand, while others scooped out a shallow ditch long enough and wide enough to receive their bodies, and covering it with brush, made a temporary refuge. When the rain descended they were forced to abandon this haven of rest.

From George Darby's *Incidents and Adventures in Rebeldom:*

As food [at Belle Isle Prison] is the all-absorbing thought by day and the theme of dreams by night to starving men, it is proper to give a description of the quality and quantity of the grub, for to call it food would be to misname it, (even if it were designed for hogs). It would be almost impossible to give [a des-

Prisoners at Belle Isle on the James River could look toward the Confederate Capitol building in Richmond (left center) and know with certainty they were in the very heart of rebel territory. (*Valentine Museum, Richmond, Virginia.*)

cription to] one who did not have an opportunity of seeing the rations which were furnished us, as prisoners of war at our country retreat on Belle Isle, and at the Hotel de Libby in the city. For breakfast we had a piece of cornbread about two inches square, or one slice of wheat bread, (usually sour), and one pint of coffee (so-called), made from parched rye. For dinner we had absolutely nothing. For supper we were served the same amount of bread, and of the same quality, and either a pint of rye coffee or instead thereof a pint of pea soup, or one tablespoonful of boiled rice, or two ounces of rotten bacon or beef. This constituted the entire bill of fare at the two hostelries named. The variety consisted alone in the fact that if you got coffee you did not get soup, and if you got soup you did not get rice, and if you got rice, you did not get meat. They never made the unpardonable mistake of serving any two of the articles named at any one meal. The peas used in making soup were of a variety known in the South as "Nigger peas" and were invariably bug-eaten. The soup was flavored with a bit of the kind of pork of which I have spoken; it was necessary to skim the bugs off before the soup could be swallowed, as they arose to the surface in great quantities. In regard to the bacon furnished, if the human mind can conceive of anything really loathsome, that bacon would stand for its representa-

tive; if a bit of the rind were lifted it would reveal a squirming mass of maggots and worms, or if it were cooked, there they would lie in grim and greasy rows, rigid in death. The beef supply consisted of shin bones and heads from which the tongues were invariably extracted, and the eyes left in, and sometimes the cud would be found sticking between the jaws. When the meat was served an ox eye was a full ration of meat for one prisoner, and the poor starved men would trim and gnaw them until they had the appearance of large glass marbles. On Christmas and New Years, and holidays, we were given nothing whatever to eat. One day when we were to be counted, I saw a rebel give a prisoner a quart of peas, and surmising that they had been given to him as a reward for "informing," I concluded to watch him. I did so. The poor fellow being so near starved gulped them, as a hog might have done, without chewing, but very soon his famished stomach revolted, and threw them up, when one of his comrades carefully picked them up from the ground where they had fallen and ate them. "Oh, the rarity of Christian charity under the sun!" What a commentary upon Christian progress! After more than eighteen hundred years of zealous teaching and preaching, here was a Christian man starved by Christian men until he was reduced to the miserable extremity of eating vomit like a dog.

121

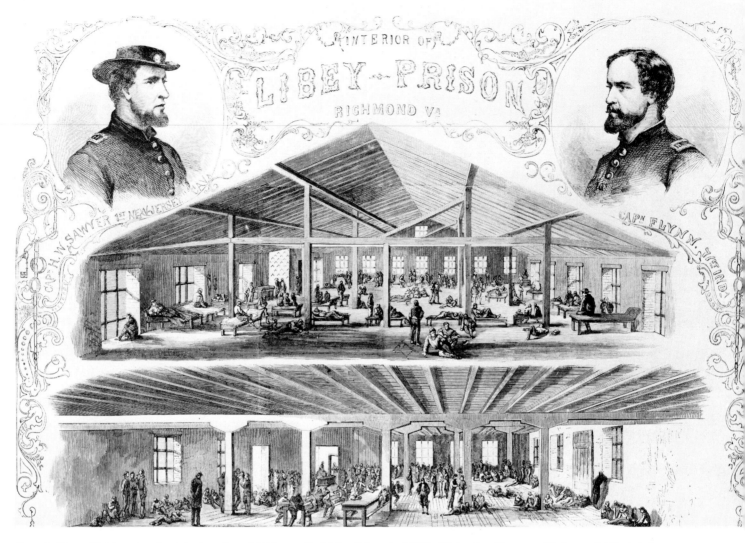

Captain Harry Wrigley sketched the interior of Richmond's Libby Prison in 1863. *(Valentine Museum, Richmond, Virginia.)*

Libby Prison in Richmond was generally supposed to be a transfer point, but it, too, was subject to the inevitable overcrowding, bad diet, and had its despised commander, Brigadier General John Winder. "We look upon his visits to the prison office as an inevitable roughening of our confinement," explained Lieutenant William Harris.

Libby gives one illustration of the different treatment afforded to officers and enlisted men, the latter of whom were confined to the upper and drafty floors of the old warehouse, and subsisted on lesser rations, possibly because they lacked the money for purchase of adaquate food.

From F.F. Cavada's *Libby Life: Experiences of a Prisoner of War:*

Now for the Libby itself. It stands close by the Lynchburg canal, and in full view from the river. It is a capacious warehouse, built of brick and roofed with tin. It was a busy place previous to the Rebellion; barrels and bales obstructed the stone sidewalk which surrounds the building on all four of its sides. . . . There is something about it indicative of the grave, and, indeed, it *is* a sort of unnatural tomb, whose pale, wan inhabitants gaze vacantly out through the barred windows on the passer-by, as if they were peering from the mysterious precincts of another world.

The building has a front of about one hundred and forty feet, with a depth of about one hundred and five. There are nine rooms, each one hundred and two feet long by forty-five wide. The height of ceilings from the floor, is about seven feet; except in the upper story, which is better ventilated owing to the pitch of the roof. At each end of these rooms are five windows.

Nothing but bread has, as yet, been issued to us, half a loaf twice a day, per man. This must be washed down with James River water, drawn from a hydrant over the wash-trough. Tomorrow, we are to be indulged with the luxury of bacon-soup.

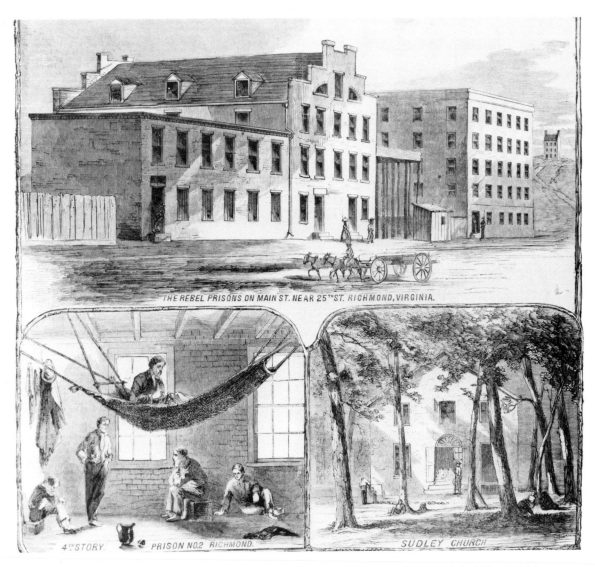

THE REBEL PRISONS ON MAIN ST. NEAR 25.™ ST. RICHMOND, VIRGINIA.

4.™ STORY.   PRISON NO.2 RICHMOND.   SUDLEY CHURCH.

James Gillette, a prisoner in Richmond, made a detailed drawing of some of the city's buildings which were pressed into service as jails for the flood of yankee captives. (*Valentine Museum, Richmond, Virginia.*)

There are some filthy blankets hanging about the room; they have been used time and again by the many who have preceded us; they are soiled, worn, and filled with vermin, but we are recommended to help ourselves in time; if we do so with reluctance and profound disgust it is because we are now more particular than we will be by-and-by.

We have tasted of the promised soup; it is boiled water sprinkled with rice, and seasoned with the rank juices of stale bacon; we must shut our eyes to eat it; the bacon, I have no doubt, might have walked into the pot of its own accord. It is brought up to us in wooden buckets, and we eat it, in most cases without spoons, out of tin cups . . . .

From William C. Harris' *Prison-Life in the Tobacco Warehouse at Richmond:*

Although in October [1862] the treatment of the officers has improved, that of the privates remains the same. Two thousand eight hundred and thirty-eight have been confined in Richmond since the commencement of hostilities; and their condition in the upper stories of the warehouse is harrowing to the sternest heart. With the floor for a bed, without straw, many without pantaloons, all with scant raiment, but few with blankets, whilst the keen air of mid-winter pierces through the ill-protected building—receiving half the ration of food allowed in the Federal army, covered with vermin, starved and shivering—they are crowded together in herds. Regardless of life, dead to the dictates of humanity, their jailers see them die daily—apparently without sympathy, evidently without attempting to prevent mortality.

At ten o'clock they are furnished with breakfast, consisting of a small piece of cold beef and five ounces of bread; at seven P.M. they receive about a half-pint of soup and five ounces of bread, with rice occasionally in lieu of meat. They receive but two meals per day, and those of the poorest quality. The rice is often wormy; the meat is cooked two days before consumed, and lies exposed in a trough in the yard, becoming covered with dust and ashes, and the

Patriotic drawings by Union prisoners often found their way into *Harper's Weekly* and made good propaganda for the war effort. M. Nevin revealed that even in their anguish and boredom, the men still remembered what they fought and suffered for. (*Valentine Museum, Richmond, Virginia.*)

juice being extracted by making soup for one meal before the meat is served, dry and hard, for the next.

For two weeks the men have not been able to procure water or brooms with which to scrub the floor, and the dirt and bones are swept into one corner: it cannot be thrown from the window, the sentinel having orders to shoot any one who approaches it.

Seven Federal prisoners have been shot dead by the sentinels for inadvertently leaning from the windows.

They have been known to hunt for bone from the pile of filth, and gnaw eagerly upon it. There being but one hydrant in the yard, for the use of five hundred and fifty men, they are kept waiting for hours in line before being able to reach it; and the same buckets used for distributing meat and soup are furnished them for washing their bodies and clothes.

Every day, from early morning until late at night, emaciated soldiers may be seen waiting longingly for the surplus bread and meat from the officers' table. It is a scene of piteous sadness when a steward brings forth a pan of food to distribute among them.

As he appears, every soldier's eye glares with a hungry look, arms are reached forth beyond the sentry's musket, and each man jostles with his neighbor for a crust of bread, and crunches his share with eager, ravenous haste.

From William C. Harris' *Prison-Life in the Tobacco Warehouse at Richmond:*

The Hon. Mr. Faulkner, released by the United States government in exchange for the Hon. Mr. Ely, M.C., of Rochester, N.Y., visited us [in] 1861. We were solicitous of his unprejudiced opinion regarding the comparative treatment of Federal and Confederate prisoners of war . . . .

He passed through the officers' floor, greeting us with much cordiality and evident sympathy. His recent arrival from France, brief residence in "Secessia," with his "wheelbarrow experience" in Fort Warren, had, no doubt, mellowed the bitterness of his Southern heart, as we were thoroughly impressed with his kindness . . . and the interest he evinced in the details of our imprisonment and treatment.

After examination of our quarters, he said, "But little difference existed between them and those of the Confederate prisoners at Fort Warren, excepting in out-door exercise, which was imperatively needed, and he hoped, would soon be allowed us.

After conversing socially for a short time, he was passing from the building, when an officer suggested that probably he was desirous of visiting the quarters of the privates. He remarked that he had just passed through them. Upon being informed of his error—that those he was now in belonged to the officers—he appeared much astonished, and desired to be shown those of the privates.

He was led into the upper stories, and evinced surprise and pity at the condition and treatment of our soldiers.

During his visit to our warehouse, he expressed the following opinions:—

"That United States officers in Richmond received treatment similar to that of the Confederate privates in the North.

"That United States privates were treated much worse than Confederate privates were in the North.

"That the privateers North received every comfort possible under the circumstances.

"That the Federal hostages in Richmond . . . were treated far worse than the privateers . . . in the North."

George Darby, while a prisoner at Libby served as an assistant in Richmond General Hospital Number Twenty-one, and as such saw much of the "dead house," a common and gruesome Civil War hospital and prison adjunct.

From George Darby's *Incidents and Adventures in Rebeldom:*

As no clothing was allowed to remain on a corpse, Sawyer removed the ragged habiliments from Barman's body, and covering it with a sheet, he and I carried it to a building across the way used as a dead house. Oh, my God! what a horrible sight was here presented to our view. I cannot think of it even to this day without a thrill of horror, for there on the floor lay sixteen corpses, perfect skeletons, stark naked, with eyes, noses and mouths all eaten away by the rats. The eyeless sockets, missing nose and grinning teeth of these poor bodies made such a scene of gruesome, horrible reality as was never conceived of even by the morbid imagination of a Dante . . . .

The dead-cart was purposely allowed to make but one trip each twenty-four hours, so that those dying after the cart-man had made his round could be left in the dead house to fatten the rats until the next day. These rats, . . . from long usage had become adepts in their gastly work, and attacked only the eyes, nose and lips of their victims until these had been exhausted, and as the supply of new corpses was always equal to the demand, they fed on these dainties constantly. Now this hideous mutilation could have been prevented by having the cart conveying the dead make two trips daily, and allowing the bodies of those dying after the last trip to lie on the cots until the following morning or until the cart came around again; but this you see would not have so fully gratified the rebel desire to heap indignities upon the Yankee dead. The rat-eaten dead were thrown indiscriminately into the cart, like so many logs of wood, a tarpaulin was stretched over them and they were hauled out through the streets of Christian Richmond and consigned to a ditch and slightly covered with earth, and left there unrecorded and unknown, to molder back to dust; and thus was their identity effectually obliterated.

This was the fate of every Union soldier who died at General Hospital No. 21 at Richmond, Va., during my sojourn there, which covered . . . several months.

At the time of his release from Andersonville Prison, E.W. McIntosh of the 14th Illinois Infantry, purportedly weighed sixty-five pounds and suffered from scurvy and gangrene. (*Courtesy Chicago Historical Society.*)

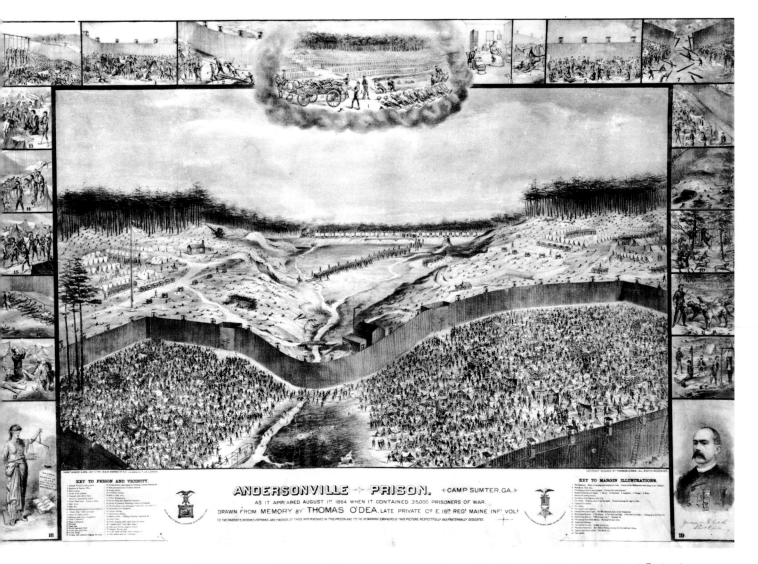

Andersonville Prison in Georgia became the focal point of Northern wrath over Southern treatment of captured Federals. Within its twenty-six acres were confined upwards of 32,000 Union prisoners. (*Missouri Historical Society, St. Louis.*)

Andersonville was the most infamous of Southern prisons and when Private Prescott Tracy was within its confines, conditions were at their worst. Its superintendent, Henry Wirz, was tried and executed after the war and within sight of the United States Capitol. General Winder was dead, but those above him, responsible for the choice of the campsite, the incredible overcrowding, the lack of food and medical supplies, went free.

The only source of drinking water for the men at that time was a fetid stream which ran only ankle deep, befouled with human offal and debris. Then, in the late summer of 1864, a downpour opened a new spring near the west deadline. Andersonville is now a park and those who come there to wonder that the horrors ever existed can drink freely from a stream which still flows there.

From Prescott Tracy's deposition on Andersonville quoted in *Narrative of the Privations and Sufferings of United States Officers and Privates While Prisoners of War in the Hands of Rebel Authorities:*

On entering the Stockade Prison we found it crowded with twenty-eight thousand of our fellow-soldiers. By *crowded* I mean that it was difficult to move in any direction without jostling and being jostled. This prison is an open space . . . without trees or shelter of any kind . . . . The fence is made of upright trunks of trees, about twenty feet high, near the top of which are small platforms, where the guards are stationed. Twenty feet inside and parallel to the fence is a light railing, forming the "deadline," beyond which the projection of a foot or finger is sure to bring the deadly bullet of the sentinel.

Through the ground . . . runs or rather creeps a stream . . . varying from five to six feet in width, the water about ankle deep, and near the middle of the enclosure, spreading out into a swamp of about six acres . . . . Before entering this enclosure, the stream, or more properly sewer, passes through the camp of the guards, receiving from this source, and others farther up, a large amount of the vilest material . . . . The water is of a dark color, and an ordinary glass would collect a thick sediment. This was our only drinking and cooking water. It was our custom to filter it as best we could; through our remnants of haversacks, shirts and blouses . . . .

. . . The rebel authorities never removed any filth. There was seldom any visitation by the officers in charge. Two surgeons were at one time sent by President Davis to inspect the camp, but a walk through a small section gave them all the information they desired, and we never saw them again . . . .

From Prescott Tracy's deposition on Andersonville quoted in *Narrative of the Privations and Sufferings of United States Officers and Privates While Prisoners of War in the Hands of Rebel Authorities:*

The "deadline" bullet . . . spared no offender. One poor fellow, just from Sherman's army—his name was Roberts—was trying to wash his face near the "deadline" railing, when he slipped . . . and fell with his head just outside the fatal border. We shouted to him, but it was too late—"another guard would have a furlough," the men said. It was a common belief among our men, arising from statements made by the guard, that General Winder, in command, issued an order that anyone of the guards who should shoot a Yankee outside of the "deadline" should have a month's furlough, but there probably was no truth in this. About two a day were thus shot, some being cases of suicide, brought on by mental depression or physical misery, the poor fellows throwing themselves, or madly rushing outside the "line."

A southeast view of the Andersonville stockade, taken in August 1864, shows the infamous prison at the height of its overcrowding. The fetid stream which flowed through the center of the compound was the only source of drinking water. It was also a garbage dump and latrine for thousands of men. (*Courtesy Chicago Historical Society.*)

While John T. Omenhausser was a prisoner at Point Lookout camp in Maryland, he made a series of lively watercolors depicting Northern prison life. *Catching Rats — Cooking Rats* recorded one occupation in a camp where over twenty thousand Confederates were held at one time, and the only shelters were tents. (*The Maryland Historical Society, Baltimore*.)

From Prescott Tracy's deposition on Andersonville quoted in *Narrative of the Privations and Sufferings of United States Officers and Privates While Prisoners of War in the Hands of Rebel Authorities:*

Some few weeks before being released, I was ordered to act as clerk in the hospital. This consists simply of a few scattered trees and . . . tents, and is in [the] charge of Dr. White, an excellent and considerate man, with very limited means, but doing all in his power for his patients . . . . I have seen one hundred and fifty bodies waiting passage to the "dead house," to be buried with those who died in the hospital. The average of deaths through the earlier months was thirty a day: at the time I left, the average was over one hundred and thirty, and one day the record showed one hundred and forty-six.

The proportion of deaths from starvation . . . I cannot state; but to the best of my knowledge, information and belief, there were scores every month. We could, at any time, point out many for whom such a fate was inevitable, as they lay or feebly walked, mere skeletons . . . . For example: in some cases the inner edges of the two bones of the arms, between the elbow and the wrist, with the intermediate blood vessels, were plainly visible when held toward the light. . . .

The number in camp when I left was nearly thirty-five thousand, and daily increasing. The number in hospital was about five thousand. . . .

From Stephen Vincent Benet's *John Brown's Body:*

. . . The triple stockade of Andersonville the damned,
Where men corrupted like flies in their own dung
And the gangrened sick were black with smoke and their filth.
There were thirty thousand Federal soldiers there
Before the end of the war.
        A man called Wirz,
A Swiss, half brute, half fool, and wholly a clod,
Commanded that camp of spectres.
                One reads what he did
And longs to hang him higher than Haman hung.
And then one reads what he said when he was tried
After the war—and sees the long, heavy face,
The dull fly buzzing stupidly in the trap,
The ignorant lead of the voice, saying and saying,
"Why, I did what I could, I was ordered to keep the jail.
Yes, I set up deadlines, sometimes chased men with dogs,
Put men in torturing stocks, killed this one and that,
Let the camp corrupt till it tainted the very guards
Who came there with mortal sickness.
But they were prisoners, they were dangerous men,
If a hundred died a day—how was it my fault?
I did my duty. I always reported the deaths.
I don't see what I did different from other people.
I fought well at Seven Pines and was badly wounded.
I have witnesses here to tell you I'm a good man
And that I was really kind. I don't understand.
I'm old. I'm sick. You're going to hang me. Why?"

Henry Wirz, commander of the prison at Andersonville, was publicly hung on November 10, 1865. Officially, he had been tried and convicted on charges of conspiracy to destroy the lives of prisoners in his charge. (*Courtesy Chicago Historical Society*.)

Albert Moyer, a Pennsylvania private, painted an idyllic view of Camp Douglas Prison, near Chicago, formerly a volunteer training center. (*Courtesy Chicago Historical Society*.)

The sentimental poems of a Dixie prisoner at Johnson's Island on Lake Erie in Ohio enjoyed a wide circulation throughout the camp. He signed himself simply "Asa Heartz."

No One Writes to Me:

The list is called, and one by one
The anxious crowd now melts away,
I linger still, and wonder why
No letter comes for me to-day.
Are all my friends in Dixie dead?
Or would they all forgotten be?
What have I done, what have I said,
That no one writes a line to me?
  It's mighty queer!
I watch the mails each weary day,
With anxious eyes the list o'er run,
I envy him whose name is called,
But love him more who gets not one.
For I can sympathize with him,
And feel how keen his grief must be,
Since I'm an exile from my home,
And no one writes a line to me,
  I do declare!
Within a quiet, happy home,
Far, far in Dixie's sunny clime,
There dwells a quiet happy maid,
Who wrote to me in by-gone time.
Now, others from their loved ones hear
In tender letters, loving, free,
Yet here I've been this half a year,
And no one writes a line to me,
  We're not estranged!
Will no one write me, just a line,
To say, that I'm remembered yet?
You can not guess how much delight
I'd feel could I a letter get.
Could I but hear from some kind friend
Whose face I ne'er again may see.
Will some one now my anguish end—
If some one doesn't write to me,
  I'll—get exchanged!

From *The Raving Foe, The Civil War Diary of Major James T. Poe, C.S.A.:*

. . . We get plenty to eat here [Johnson's Island] such as it is, viz, loaf bread, beef, pork, coffee, sugar and sometimes dried beans. We get very tired of being confined to one diet. If the question was asked what we will have tomorrow for dinner we can easily tell for we know that it will be the same old diet. There are men in prison here that live in Ky. and Tenn. and Mo. that are inside of the enemies' lines. They write to their families and if they want money their friends send it to them. This way they can get vegetables from the sellers of all kinds, such as Irish potatoes, radishes, beets, onions, green beans, cucumbers, strawberries and raspberries. In fact, a man that has money can buy anything he wants, can live as well here as if at home. But the poor prisoner that has no money here lives hard and the greater portion of prisoners here are without means . . . .

There are about 11 hundred prisoners here, mostly officers, this being the 31st and last day of July, 1862. The men in this prison devote their time in many ways, some by reading the papers, some by reading the Bible, some by reading history, tracts, or novels. We get papers every day by paying 5¢ for one. Some devote their time by gaming at all kinds of games, card playing of every description, some by playing marbles, pitching dollars, playing ball in many ways. Others devote their time in making fancy sticks, fancy pipes, watch chains, fob chains, cuff buttons, sleeve buttons, bracelets, and, in fact, there are men here making almost any and everything that can possibly be made of Girtipurture, (Note—presumably a type of wood, common to the area) shell, wood and so forth. There are men here that wash every day from morning till night. They wash for 5¢ and iron for 10¢ a garment. Those that have no means wash and cook their victuals themselves.

News from Home, by William Ludwell Sheppard.
(The Museum of the Confederacy.)

Henry Dickinson of the Second Virginia Cavalry endured captivity in several Northern prisons for over a year. He was a lawyer, a literate writer and a gentleman of the old school and in the first entry of his diary, made on Morris Island, south of the entrance to Charleston Harbor, he spoke not only for himself, but for others who put their daily lives as captives of the yankees on record: "Being on Morris Island today without books to read, hungry, and finding it impossible to mingle freely with my friends in their small tents, or to exercise in the streets by reason of the heat; having no comfort or enjoyment (unless it be a comfort to ponder over the cruelties of the United States Government),. . . I have concluded to spend some of my time in jotting down my impressions of prison life as I have seen it, concluding that it may not be uninteresting to my home folks and friends who have never tasted the sweets of imprisonment."

Captain Dickinson was one of the last rebel prisoners to take the oath of allegiance to the Federal government, and did so only at the persuasion of his father after the capture of Jefferson Davis.

W.H. Morgan, member of a volunteer company known as the Clifton Grays, also served at Morris Island and, in a light vein, introduced his reminiscences in the following manner: "The old sailor spins his yarns of the adventures and perils of the deep; the old fisherman will sometimes tell a big fish tail, and the old soldier is wont to join in with the rest and tell of his life in camp and field."

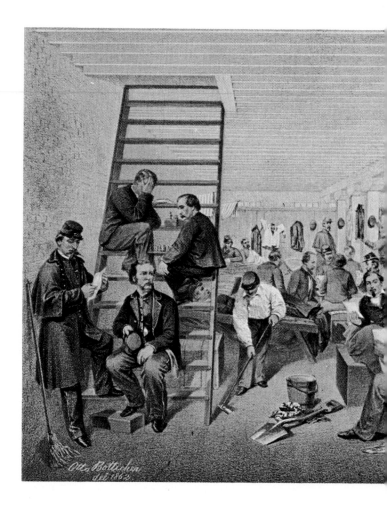

From W.H. Morgan's *Personal Reminiscences of the War of 1861-1865:*

While here [at Morris Island Prison] the rations were scant and sorry. For breakfast, we had three crackers, sometimes two, and sometimes only one and a half, and a very small piece of bacon, about two ounces; towards the last, five crackers per day were issued. For dinner, we had soup made of some kind of dried peas, about one pint, very unpalatable—for supper, a pint of very thin mush or rice. The mush was made of stale cornmeal, full of worms. One prisoner picked out and counted 125 small, black-headed worms from a cup of this mush. I would pick out worms a while, and then eat the stuff a while, then pick out more worms until all were gone. Some just devoured worms and all, saying they could not afford to loose that much of their rations; that if the worms could stand it, they could. The detestable Yankee lieutenant-colonel would sometimes come into the camp while we were devouring the mush and worms and with a contemptible sneer and Yankee nasal twang, say: "You fellows need fresh meat to keep off scurvy, so I give it to you in your mush."

From the *Diary of Captain Henry C. Dickinson, C.S.A.:*

The amount of clothing, food, etc., received by us from friends was very considerable. Boxes were generally sent by express and received by, or rather issued to, us twice each week. The box was always broken open in presence of the crowd and thoroughly examined. All cans of fruit were cut open to find whiskey, and so with bottles. The clothing was thoroughly searched for money, contraband letters, etc., and if more than a bare supply of any article was received it was at once confiscated. A good hat, or good shirts, or fine pants, generally fell to the lion's share, on the plea that they were not needed by the owner. If any article of clothing was delivered,

Libby Prison, after the drawing by Otto Botticher, 1862. More than one thousand men were later crowded into the stuffy rooms of the former tobacco warehouse which became Richmond's infamous Libby Prison. *(Courtesy Chicago Historical Society.)*

the owner was compelled to shed off his old clothes then and there . . . .

From the *Diary of Captain Henry C. Dickinson, C.S.A.:*

The medical department within the barracks was under the control of a doctor who was known to some of the officers as a carpenter in north Mississippi at the inception of the war; therefore his skill was more than questionable. He prescribed and administered medicine through a hole in the wall, having a few of the most common remedies for diseases of prisoners. He was obstinate and would allow no suggestions. For neuralgia he gave rhubarb . . . and he gave many other like prescriptions which proved his utter incompetency. He came to the hole in the wall once each day. If a man were seized with cramp-colic or stricture, or stone in the bladder (as my mess-mate once was), he must suffer and bear it till the doctor's hour. But for some opium I found, my mess-mate would have died. The sick were never moved from the barracks until the ravages of disease necessitated the use of a litter. They were then taken to a hospital on the island, which was clean and well

kept, but convalescence drove the patient back to the barracks to get food.

From the *Diary of Captain Henry C. Dickinson, C.S.A.:*

Some females visited the fort [at Morris Island] today and took a look at the "Rebs." As our sink is in full view, of course they see that, too. The colonel had the band out for their edification, and also sounded the alarm to show them how quickly his men and officers rally. This is all well done, but, if we chose to take this place, the rally would be about one minute after the fort was ours. However, if we take the place what shall we do with it? The land batteries can batter it down in six hours or storm us out in a few days. We can't get away.

Today they are putting up iron grates at each end of our quarters to prevent us from surprising the Yanks at night. They evidently suspect us and keep almost in line of battle hourly. If we once despair of exchange they had better look out. We will not stay in prison four long, dreary years, and old Abe's re-election means that.

135

Northern prisons had their own horror stories. When the head of the United States Sanitary Commission came to inspect Camp Douglas, he found such a disgusting situation in regard to unpoliced grounds, foul latrines, standing water and "soil reeking with miasmatic accretions," that it was "enough to drive a sanitarian mad." (*Courtesy Chicago Historical Society*.)

Private C.W. Jones of the Twenty-fourth Virginia Cavalry was captured in December 1863 after an engagement with General Sheridan at Charles City, Virginia. Young, resourceful and not above a swindle here and there, he fared quite well until his release from Point Lookout Prison on Maryland's Chesapeake Bay.

Luther Hopkins' descriptions of the camp life he shared with Jones show a man much more dejected by what he saw happening around him. His lethargic attitude, common to many in long confinement, was often the difference between mortality or survival under barely subsistence standards.

Luther Hopkins quoted in Edwin W. Beitzell's
Point Lookout Prison Camp for Confederates:

The food, while good, was very scant. Breakfast consisted of coffee and a loaf of bread, the latter under ordinary circumstances, with vegetables and other food, would probably suffice for two meals. This loaf was given us at breakfast, and if we ate it all then we went without bread for dinner. If there was any left over we took it to our tents, laid it on the ground, and saved it for the next meal.

The dinners consisted of a tin cup of soup (generally bean or other vegetable), a small piece of meat on a tin plate, on which a little vinegar was poured to prevent scurvy. My recollection is we had no other meal, but my mind is not perfectly clear on this point. I do know, however, that we were always hungry, and the chief topic of conversation was the sumptuous meals we had sat down to in other days. . . . We were told that the short rations were given us in retaliation for the scanty food supplied to their soldiers in Southern prisons. . . .

Many of the prisoners had a peculiar affliction of the eyes caused, perhaps, by the glare from the white tents, the sand and the reflection from the water. There was nothing green to be seen anywhere, consequently many of the prisoners became blind for a

At Point Lookout Prison for Confederates, on Maryland's Chesapeake Bay, the mortality rate did not approach that at Andersonville. However, nearly four thousand inmates died within a period of twenty-two months. *(National Archives Photo.)*

portion of the 24 hours. Just as the sun was sinking behind the fence they would become totally blind, and had to be led by someone. As morning light came the blindness would disappear.

Some of the prisoners who were mechanics or artisans got work outside, but I believe they got no pay except full rations and the privilege of bringing things into camp, such as blocks of wood and pieces of metal. Out of these were manufactured a great many interesting little articles, small steam locomotives, wooden fans, rings from rubber buttons set with gold and silver, and sometimes gems. One ingenious fellow built a small distillery and made whiskey from potato rinds and whatever refuse he could pick up, and got drunk on the product.

All about the camp were boards on which these manufactured articles were exposed for sale. A cracker would buy a chew of tobacco. The tobacco was cut up into chews and half chews. The crackers were brought in by the men who went out to work. I cannot recall all the curious things that were exposed for sale within the camp. . . .

C. W. Jones quoted in Edwin W. Beitzell's
Point Lookout Prison Camp for Confederates:

The various occupations, the scheming, the tricking, the hustling for grub, the flanking and pointing to the goal for hardtack and pickled pork, and trading for rations, were the issues, which required no oratory, no preaching, but chicanery and trickery. My strong forte was molasses taffy and corn mush, with black strap syrup. Whenever I could collect enough of the material together I could fry flap jacks so thin you could read through them, and dilute the molasses so that it would run on a board. My price for a palatable dish was five hardtacks and a chew of tobacco. By pushing my trade I would soon collect enough hardtack and tobacco to last me a week, with careful economy. In one interesting instance an old soldier from Tennessee came straggling along with an old army blanket for his whole suit, probably a Gettysburg relic. Reinforced with "greybacks," he spied my tempting outlay. His ravenous appetite allured him to my stand. He invested his last cracker and chew of tobacco, and settled himself down for a delightful repast, and I shall never forget his disappointment when he had finished. "Well," said he, "I was an overseer before the war, in Tennessee. I have patrolled it, I have log-rolled, horse-swapped, volunteered in the war, was in the battle of Gettysburg, been through all the war up to prison, been hungry, cold and done many things: but you have put the confoundest swindle on me that I have ever experienced in all my days from boyhood to the present time, and I hope the good Lord may have mercy on you from now until this war is over."

C. W. Jones quoted in Edwin W. Beitzell's
Point Lookout Prison Camp for Confederates:

My long stay in prison and the hardships educated me in a great many things especially now to manipulate little tricks to get extra rations. I had been in prison so long that I had almost adopted the prison for home, but, as the old adage goes "the darkest hour is just before day." I was strolling up the street one morning, near where a large bulletin board was used for registering names of those who had letters or boxes sent them, and my attention was called to the following lines in large letters at the top of the board: "All prisoners who were captured on (a certain date) must report to headquarters on (a certain date) to be paroled."

This was in the latter part of February 1864, and after nearly two years of suffering and torment we were at last ordered to forward march in single file down to the wharf on the Potomac River, where the happy sight of the New York truce boat, with her outstretched gang plank to welcome and bid us enter, greeted our tired eyes and worn out frames. We went aboard cheerfully, with a sigh of great relief and without the glittering bayonets to "move us lively." After all were aboard the boat with its load of dirty and worn out paroled prisoners, we gave one old-fashion "rebel yell" and joined with one accord in "Dixie."

The thoughts of home in the Southland and the meeting again of the loved ones, cheered our hearts and gave us joy, and no man can describe in the English language the feelings of prisoners of war when paroled with anticipations of breathing the free air of their native home, though it be ever so poor. Taking a retrospective view, it would seem an impossibility to understand just what prisoners had to do, and setting my eyes homeward and bidding old Point Lookout a final adieu, I agreed with the great General Sherman, that "war is h--l."

138

Early in the war, prisoners were fortunate enough to have hopes of exchange, but agreement between North and South floundered over the question of the return of former slaves who were serving in the Union Army. Additionally, both sides were loath to have captured men return to full military status on the enemy side. *(Valentine Museum, Richmond, Virginia.)*

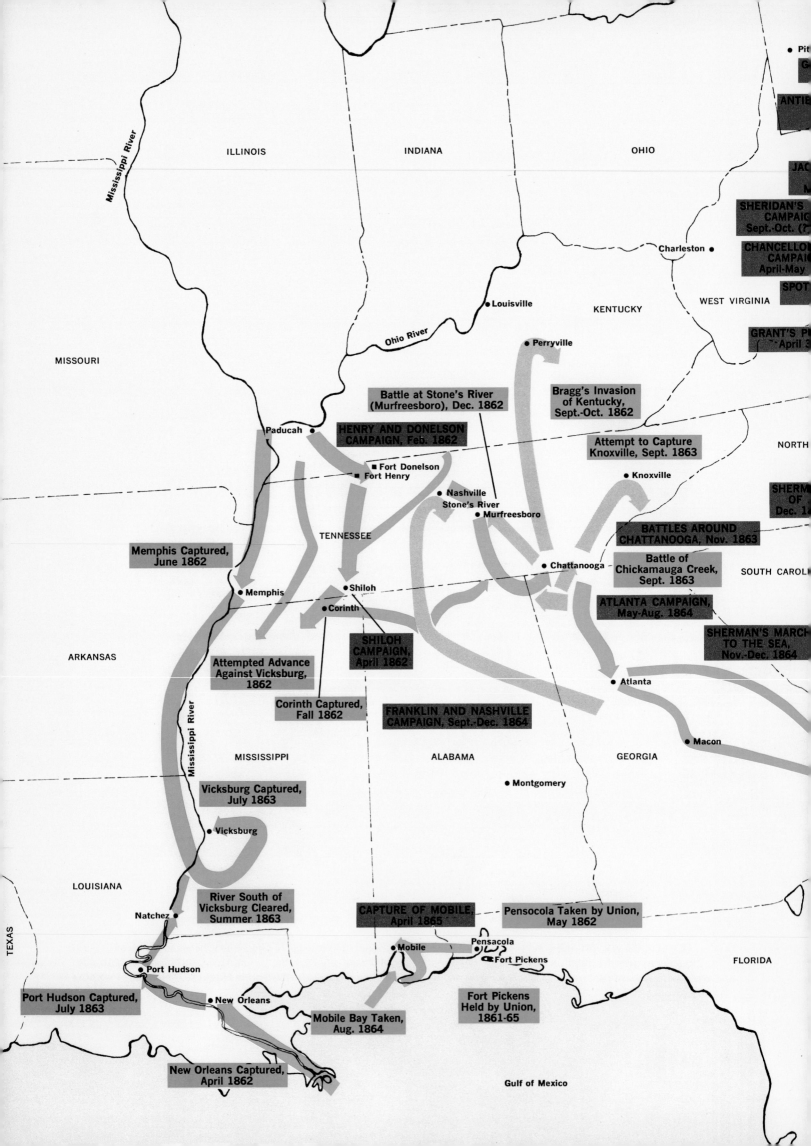

ILLINOIS

INDIANA

OHIO

Mississippi River

MISSOURI

Louisville •

Ohio River

Perryville •

Charleston •

WEST VIRGINIA

KENTUCKY

NORTH

Paducah •

Fort Donelson
Fort Henry

Nashville
Stone's River
Murfreesboro •

TENNESSEE

Knoxville •

SHER
OF
Dec. 1

Battle at Stone's River
(Murfreesboro), Dec. 1862

HENRY AND DONELSON
CAMPAIGN, Feb. 1862

Bragg's Invasion
of Kentucky,
Sept.-Oct. 1862

Attempt to Capture
Knoxville, Sept. 1863

ANTIE

JAC

SHERIDAN'S
CAMPAIG
Sept.-Oct. (?

CHANCELLO
CAMPAIG
April-May

SPOT

GRANT'S P
April 3

Memphis Captured,
June 1862

Memphis •

Shiloh •

Corinth •

Chattanooga •

BATTLES AROUND
CHATTANOOGA, Nov. 1863

Battle of
Chickamauga Creek,
Sept. 1863

SOUTH CAROL

ARKANSAS

Attempted Advance
Against Vicksburg,
1862

SHILOH
CAMPAIGN,
April 1862

ATLANTA CAMPAIGN,
May-Aug. 1864

SHERMAN'S MARCH
TO THE SEA,
Nov.-Dec. 1864

Corinth Captured,
Fall 1862

Atlanta •

Mississippi River

MISSISSIPPI

FRANKLIN AND NASHVILLE
CAMPAIGN, Sept.-Dec. 1864

ALABAMA

GEORGIA

Macon •

Vicksburg Captured,
July 1863

Montgomery •

Vicksburg •

LOUISIANA

River South of
Vicksburg Cleared,
Summer 1863

Natchez •

CAPTURE OF MOBILE,
April 1865

Pensocola Taken by Union,
May 1862

TEXAS

Port Hudson •

Mobile •

Pensacola
Fort Pickens

FLORIDA

Port Hudson Captured,
July 1863

New Orleans •

Fort Pickens
Held by Union,
1861-65

Mobile Bay Taken,
Aug. 1864

New Orleans Captured,
April 1862

Gulf of Mexico

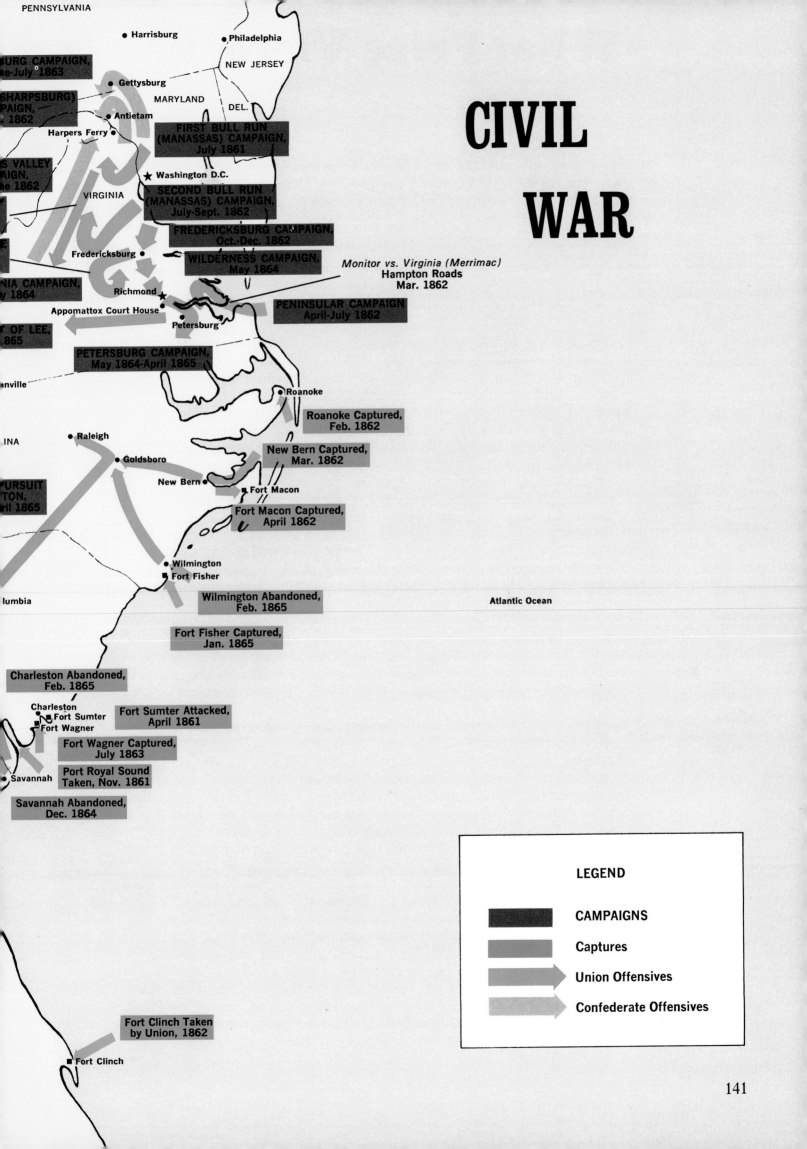

CIVIL WAR

PENNSYLVANIA

● Harrisburg
● Philadelphia

NEW JERSEY

BURG CAMPAIGN,
e-July 1863

● Gettysburg
MARYLAND
DEL.

SHARPSBURG)
PAIGN,
1862

● Antietam

Harpers Ferry ●

**FIRST BULL RUN
(MANASSAS) CAMPAIGN,
July 1861**

VALLEY
AIGN,
e 1862

★ Washington D.C.

VIRGINIA

**SECOND BULL RUN
(MANASSAS) CAMPAIGN,
July-Sept. 1862**

**FREDERICKSBURG CAMPAIGN,
Oct.-Dec. 1862**

Fredericksburg ●

**WILDERNESS CAMPAIGN,
May 1864**

Monitor vs. Virginia (Merrimac)
Hampton Roads
Mar. 1862

NIA CAMPAIGN,
1864

Richmond ★

Appomattox Court House

Petersburg ●

**PENINSULAR CAMPAIGN
April-July 1862**

OF LEE,
865

**PETERSBURG CAMPAIGN,
May 1864-April 1865**

nville

● Roanoke

**Roanoke Captured,
Feb. 1862**

INA

● Raleigh

● Goldsboro

**New Bern Captured,
Mar. 1862**

New Bern ●

Fort Macon

PURSUIT
TON,
il 1865

**Fort Macon Captured,
April 1862**

● Wilmington

■ Fort Fisher

lumbia

**Wilmington Abandoned,
Feb. 1865**

Atlantic Ocean

**Fort Fisher Captured,
Jan. 1865**

**Charleston Abandoned,
Feb. 1865**

Charleston
■ Fort Sumter
■ Fort Wagner

**Fort Sumter Attacked,
April 1861**

**Fort Wagner Captured,
July 1863**

**Port Royal Sound
Taken, Nov. 1861**

● Savannah

**Savannah Abandoned,
Dec. 1864**

**Fort Clinch Taken
by Union, 1862**

■ Fort Clinch

LEGEND

CAMPAIGNS

Captures

Union Offensives

Confederate Offensives

141

What Price Victory

> **. . . Grant is the only man that can whip the Rebs every time, and he can do it every time that he tries it. We would not give our General Grant for all the generals that are in the Northern army. When his men go in a fight they know he is going to have us whip them.**

From a letter to Mary Englesby,
John F. Brobst, Twenty-fifth Wisconsin Regiment,
Vicksburg, Mississippi, July 5, 1863

President Lincoln agreed with enlisted man, Johnny Brobst. He had stood by Grant through all the pressures to relieve him after the surprise at Pittsburgh Landing, and sustained his faith in the general amidst rumor and report of Grant's heavy drinking and personal dissipation. Before the battle of Vicksburg the President wrote: "He doesn't worry and bother me. He isn't shrieking for reinforcements all the time. He takes what troops we can safely give him and does the best with what he has got."

Successive commanders in the East did not seem to have Grant's tenacity nor his concept of the technique necessary to the winning of a war. As the general expressed it: "Find out where your enemy is, get at him as soon as you can, and strike him as hard as you can, and keep moving." His victories in the West proved winning might be incredibly summed up in that simple statement. A weary commander in chief was willing to try it. In March 1864, Lincoln summoned the forty-three-year-old Grant to Washington and placed him in command as general in chief of all Union armies. He was given the rank of lieutenant general, a status held by only two previous Americans—George Washington and old Winfield Scott, general in chief of the army during the Mexican War, who had resigned in 1861.

It was spring again and the work of war was to begin immediately. Grant would go after Lee's army in Virginia, and William Tecumseh Sherman, now in command of the western armies would strike Joe Johnston's forces in Georgia.

Across the Rapidan and into Virginia, Grant and his 115,000 Federals found themselves in that dense thicket known as the Wilderness. Lee plunged his inferior numbers into the forest, and in the two-day battle which followed, minié balls and musket fire which seemingly came from nowhere and had no visible object, set the forest afire, and many soldiers died from smoke and entrapment in the blazing brush. The usual Union retreat did not follow. At dusk on the following day Grant marched his men around Lee's line south toward Spotsylvania Court House, with the intention of placing himself between Richmond and Lee's army. The wily Lee arrived first. Union losses amounted to nearly twenty thousand for the battles at the Wilderness and Spotsylvania. Grant accepted the fact of attrition: "I . . . purpose to fight it out on this line, if it takes all summer." Many would die, but they would be replaced. Carnage was cruel, but ultimate victory a necessity.

Through the horrible battles at Bloody Angle, probably the fiercest hand-to-hand combat of the war, south to Cold Harbor, where Grant

Lieutenant General Ulysses S. Grant, by Leon Job Vernet, 1870. *(Courtesy Chicago Historical Society.)*

ordered a suicidal charge like that of Pickett at Gettysburg, "the most awful thirty minutes known to the Union Army," the Federals moved toward Petersburg, an essential rail center for supplies to the Army of Northern Virginia. Lee again arrived with the remnants of his troops to rendezvous with Beauregard. It would be a siege: Grant would destroy the rail links; he was well dug in and prepared to starve the rebel army.

With a crumbling economy and an army in the South incapable of attack, the Confederacy held only one hope—that the North would tire of the war and call for a negotiated end—perhaps by voting Lincoln out of office in the upcoming election of 1864. Partially to this end, Lee dispatched forces under General Jubal Early to attack Washington. Grant poured in thousands of Federals to defend the capital and after minor fighting Early retreated to the Shenandoah Valley, a primary source of Confederate supply. In September, "Little Phil" Sheridan and his cavalry ran him to ground and destroyed the fertile valley of Jackson's earlier successes.

Lincoln was in the midst of campaigning for re-election against the veteran General George McClellan. Sheridan's rout in the Shenandoah helped his chances, but impatient Northerners demanded more decisive victories. When Rear Admiral David Farragut took Mobile Bay with his famous cry: "Damn the torpedoes! Full speed ahead!" hopes brightened. When Sherman marched into Atlanta in September, "Little Mac" knew there would be no contest. The President's victory at the polls was assured.

During the winter, fighting had slowed for the Army of the Potomac, but Sherman had captured and evacuated Atlanta and had begun his infamous March to the Sea. On Christmas day 1864, the nation received a telegram from the general: "I beg to present you as a Christmas gift, the city of Savannah."

Christmas and the winter of 1864 had their pitiable contrasts at Petersburg. Lee's army was literally starving, while the Army of the Potomac was comfortable and well fed. Lincoln visited the troops encamped at City Point, and Grant's wife and children joined him there for occasional visits. Lee expected calamity, and while his troops deserted in increasing numbers, many remained to suffer the deprivations their commander shared. A peace mission failed. The President wanted one nation, and the price was not negotiable.

Sherman was marching North and the Confederate commander was forced to recommend the evacuation of Richmond, which its citizens partially burned and pillaged, while drunken mobs roamed the streets. Within a day President Lincoln was dining at the White House of the Confederacy, while the gallant Lee's men straggled westward to safety.

On April 9, at the tiny village of Appomattox Court House in the parlor of Wilmer McLean's home, the two military antagonists met in a spirit of mutual respect, Grant not so much to claim victory, Lee not coming in shame to surrender, but both to gain the peace so long pursued and at such a cost to the nation.

On April 26, Joe Johnston surrendered to Sherman in Durham, North Carolina, and when a Michigan regiment took Jefferson Davis into custody, the Confederate government died. The final meeting between Northern and Southern combatants occurred near Browns-

Major, 1861-1862
1st Virginia Volunteer Cavalry
(K/S Historical Publications.)

Private, 1859-1868
United States Marine Corps
(K/S Historical Publications.)

The Confederate cruiser *Alabama* had taken more than sixty Federal ships in eleven months. She finally went down off the coast of France, a victim of the U.S.S. *Kearsarge* on June 19, 1864. Edwin Hayes rendered the Alabama's final dramatic moments as the yacht *Deerhound* moved in to aid in the rescue of survivors. *(Courtesy Chicago Historical Society.)*

ville, Texas, on May 26, and then the fires of war, those of musket and those of campside were extinguished forever on American soil.

President Lincoln rejoiced in victory and in peace, his mission accomplished, but the conspiracy that detective Allan Pinkerton had once feared in Baltimore would come to successful fruition by other hands. As the President enjoyed an innocuous play at Ford's Theater in Washington on the night of April 14, the madman, the frustrated actor and brother of the great Edwin Booth, John Wilkes Booth, shot the President in the head. At 7:22 the following morning, the doctor attending spoke three solemn words; "He is gone."

John Brobst remembered: "He was given to us to do the great work which was before us to do. He has done it well, with a good, pure and forgiving heart, and when the day began to dawn in the far East, noble man he was called to go . . . . They have slain mercy, and now they must abide by the sterner master, Justice."

The war ended only a few days after this young rebel lost his life in the trenches at Petersburg. *(Library of Congress.)*

It is difficult to believe that at the beginning of the war, Ulysses S. Grant had trouble receiving a commission to serve, for after his victory at Fort Donelson in 1862, the initials U.S. stood, in the popular mind, for "Unconditional Surrender." He possessed skill and a grim tenacity. Like Lee he had a faculty for choosing subordinates: Sherman, Sheridan and Thomas displayed their own daring and special genius. The President agreed with Grant that the winning of the war depended not upon the capture and securing of land targets, but upon the destruction of the opposing army, and to that task he set the hero of the western campaigns.

From *Personal Memoirs of U.S. Grant:*

[The commission of lieutenant general of the army] was delivered to me at the Executive Mansion by President Lincoln in the presence of his Cabinet, my eldest son, those of my staff who were with me and a few other visitors.

The President in presenting my commission read from a paper . . . .

General Grant, the nation's appreciation of what you have done, and its reliance upon you for what remains to be done in the existing great struggle, are now presented, with this commission constituting you lieutenant-general in the Army of the United States. With this high honor, devolves upon you, also, a corresponding responsibility. As the country herein trusts you, so, under God, it will sustain you. I scarcely need to add, that, with what I here speak for the nation, goes my own hearty personal concurrence.

To this I replied:

Mr. President, I accept the commission, with gratitude for the high honor conferred.

With the aid of the noble armies that have fought in so many fields for our common country, it will be my earnest endeavor not to disappoint your expectations. I feel the full weight of the responsibilities now devolving on me; and I know that if they are met, it will be due to those armies, and above all, to the favor of that Providence which leads both nations and men.

The Confederates were assured that Grant would not show the reluctance of his predecessors, and rumors in the camps became prophecy as the spring campaigns took their grim tolls. The North was inching forward at a slower pace than anticipated. "More desperate fighting has not been witnessed on this continent than that of the 5th and 6th of May," wrote Grant after the jungle warfare of the Wilderness, but *he would go on until Lee was trapped at Petersburg, desperate and nearly beaten.*

From Frank Moore's *The Rebellion Record: A Diary of American Events:*

And through a thicket, [in the Wilderness] blind and interminable; over abattis of fallen trees; through swamps, and ditches and brush-heaps; and once—a glorious breathing-space—across a half acre of open field, the obedient troops move on . . . . Sometimes the eyes of the men sink to note a by-path in the forest, like that which many a one has travelled in old days to some old spring of home-like memory. And here is the "birr" of a bullet, like that which startled one who heard it one summer afternoon, when a brother hunter was careless, and fired at a partridge as he stood in range. The bee-like sounds are thicker on this ridge; in the forest, a little way

As the determined Grant continued his drive into Virginia, he again faced General Lee's army at Spotsylvania Court House, but failed to break through Confederate lines as Southern resistance stiffened. *(Valentine Museum, Richmond, Virginia.)*

ahead, there is a crackling, roaring tumult, seasoned with wild cheers . . . .

The air is stifling, the sun sends its rays down through the jagged limbs of the chapparal around like red hot spears. This march is long, these bullets from an unseen foe are staining some sleeves and jackets too soon . . . .

They are there at last; the bushwhackers, thick as the sprigs and leaves that partly hide their treacherous faces . . . .

The fighting—who shall describe it? Not a thousand men can be seen at once, yet for miles in the front thousands are engaged. The volleyed thunders of the combat roll among the glens and ravines hoarser and higher than the voices of an Eastern jungle. The woods are alive with cries and explosions, and the shrill anvil-clatter of musketry. One cannon, pitched afar, times the wild tumult like a tolling bell. The smoke is a shroud about our heroes; there is not wind enough to lift it into a canopy . . . .

From *Personal Memoirs of U.S. Grant:*

More desperate fighting has not been witnessed on this continent than that of the 5th and 6th of May. Our victory consisted in having successfully crossed a formidable stream, almost in the face of an enemy, and in getting the army together as a unit. We gained an advantage on the morning of the 6th, which, if it had been followed up, must have proven very decisive. In the evening the enemy gained an advantage; but was speedily repulsed. As we stood at the close, the two armies were relatively in about the same condition to meet each other as when the river divided them. But the fact of having safely crossed was a victory.

Our losses in the Wilderness were very severe. Those of the Confederates must have been even more so; but I have no means of speaking with accuracy upon this point . . . .

The fighting at Spotsylvania became particularly savage on May 12 at a point called "the Salient" or "Bloody Angle." Closely packed yankees battled in fierce hand-to-hand combat with the rebels only a few feet away. *(Library of Congress.)*

Federals rally round the flag in William E. Winner's *Union Assault of Confederate Works*. Many young men died in an effort to keep their colors aloft during battle. *(The West Point Museum Collections, United States Military Academy.)*

From George Agassiz's *Meade's Headquarters 1863-1865, Letters of Colonel Theodore Lyman from the Wilderness to Appomattox:*

As General Grant sat under a pine tree, stoically smoking his briarwood pipe, I heard him say: "Tonight Lee will be retreating south." Ah! General, Robert Lee is not Pemberton; he will retreat south, but only far enough to get across your path, and then he will retreat no more, if he can help it. In fact, orders were out for the whole army to move at dark on Spotsylvania Court House. But Lee knew it all: he could see the wagons moving, and had scouts besides. As night fell, his troops left their works and were crowding down the Parker's Store road, towards Spotsylvania—each moment worth untold gold to them! Grant had no longer a Pemberton!

"His best friend," as he calls him. And we marched also . . . .

From a letter of Lieutenant General Ulysses S. Grant to Major General Henry Halleck, May 11, 1864:

We have now ended the 6th day of very hard fighting. The result up to this time is much in our favor. But our losses have been heavy as well as those of the enemy. We have lost to this time eleven general officers killed, wounded and missing, and probably twenty thousand men. I think the loss of the enemy must be greater—we having taken over four thousand prisoners in battle, whilst he has taken from us but few except a few stragglers. I am now sending back to Belle Plain all my wagons for a fresh supply of provisions and ammunition, and purpose to fight it out on this line if it takes all summer . . . .

The Museum of the Confederacy, in war years the Confederate White House in Richmond, holds the effects of Jeb Stuart, including his plumed hat, leather gloves and LeMat revolver, here resting on the Stars and Bars, which flew over the headquarters of the South's most flamboyant cavalry officer. *(The Museum of the Confederacy.)*

Grant had placed Philip Sheridan in command of the cavalry of the Army of the Potomac. On the day following the dispatch to Halleck in Washington, Sheridan and Confederate General J.E.B. "Jeb" Stuart fought it out near Richmond at Yellow Tavern. Stuart—the spectacular cavalry officer regarded by Lee as the "eyes of the army," received a mortal wound. As he was being carried off the field, he witnessed the retreat of his men and shouted "Go back! Go back! and do your duty as I have done mine, and our country will be safe. Go back! Go back! I had rather die than be whipped!"

Stuart was carried to a private home in Richmond where Jefferson Davis visited him, and the gallant cavalryman assured the President that he was "willing to die if God and my country think I have fulfilled my destiny and done my duty." In the evening, he requested that the hymn "Rock of Ages" be sung for him and death swiftly followed.

From James B. Sheeran's *Confederate Chaplain, A War Diary:*

May God grant that I may never again experience such sensations or witness such scenes as I this night felt and beheld. We passed over the ground enclosed in the angle where Grant broke through our lines on the morning of the 12th. The thousands of Yankees slaughtered on that memorable morning are lying there decomposed and unburied. The ground is low and swampy. The atmosphere is densely impregnated with the offensive effluvia of the dead bodies of men and horses. The sights are shocking. The smell is still more offensive. We are moving through a dense sea of corrupted atmosphere. I became faintish. Doctor Martin, my immediate companion, complained of being similarly affected. Fortunately he brought with him a flask of brandy, a small portion of which enabled us to bear up under the offensive pressure.

The flashing drama of Southern cavalry in action is portrayed in Charles Hoffbauer's stirring mural of
James E. B. "Jeb" Stuart and his men. Until his death at Yellow Tavern, near Richmond, in 1864, Stuart's cunning and
bold maneuvers outwitted the Army of the Potomac on countless occasions. He became a legend of Southern
courage. (*Virginia Historical Society, Richmond*.)

William Sheppard's intense rendering of a *Confederate Battery in Action*, by the portrayal of a single instant in battle, captured the ferocity, excitement, pain and horror of the war. *(The Museum of the Confederacy.)*

Lee now blocked Grant's line of march southward at Cold Harbor, and in an ill advised and deadly maneuver, the Federal commander ordered the charge of three of his corps against the entrenched rebels. Terrified, but dauntless, the yankees pinned slips of paper containing their names and addresses to their coats. In a battle which was over in an instant, seven thousand Union troops lost their lives. Grant admitted his mistake. Now he would begin the siege of Petersburg, and at its end Richmond, the elusive target of so many Federal generals, would fall.

From William Swinton's *Army of the Potomac:*

Next morning, with the first gray light of dawn struggling through the clouds, the preparations [for

Union Soldiers at Cold Harbor or *The Skirmish Line,* by Gilbert Gaul. Grant's plan to capture the impregnable rebel defenses at Cold Harbor on June 3, 1864, was a costly failure. Union infantrymen came against such heavy fire that seven thousand were lost within a half an hour during the deadly charge. *(The West Point Museum Collections, United States Military Academy.)*

the battle at Cold Harbor] began: from behind the rude parapets there was an upstarting, a springing to arms, the muffled commands of officers forming the line. The attack was ordered at half-past four, and it may have been five minutes after that, or it may have been ten minutes, but it certainly was not later than forty-five minutes past four, when the whole line was in motion, and the dark hollows between the armies were lit up with the fires of death.

It took hardly more than ten minutes of the figment men call time to decide the battle. There was along the whole line a rush—the spectacle of impregnable works—a bloody loss—then a sullen falling back, and the action was *decided* . . . .

From *Personal Memoirs of U.S. Grant:*

I have always regretted that the last assault at Cold Harbor was ever made. I might say the same thing of the assault of the 22nd of May, 1863, at Vicksburg. At Cold Harbor no advantage whatever was gained to compensate for the heavy loss we sustained. Indeed, the advantages other than those of relative losses, were on the Confederate side. Before that, the Army of Northern Virginia seemed to have acquired a wholesome regard for the courage, endurance, and soldierly qualities generally of the Army of the Potomac. They no longer wanted to fight them "one Confederate to five Yanks." Indeed, they seemed to have given up any idea of gaining any advantage of their antagonist in the open field. They had come to much prefer breastworks in their front to the Army of the Potomac. This charge seemed to revive their hopes temporarily; but it was of short duration. The effect upon the Army of the Potomac was the reverse. When we reached the James River, however, all effects of the battle of Cold Harbor seemed to have disappeared.

Foraging, from Winslow Homer's *Campaign Sketches. (Courtesy, Museum of Fine Arts, Boston, gift of Charles G. Loring.)*

After Congress had passed the legislation necessary for the enlistment of blacks in 1862, recruitment posters directed toward them were in wide circulation. "Come Join Us Brothers" was the appealing slogan. *(Courtesy Chicago Historical Society.)*

Grant was supremely confident, even after Cold Harbor, but Lee, although not prepared to give in, was facing the old problems of recruitment.

Indeed, on both homefronts, there were increasing numbers of those who wanted a negotiated end to the war, and decreasing numbers willing to enlist.

From George Agassiz's *Meade's Headquarters 1863-1865, Letters of Colonel Theodore Lyman from the Wilderness to Appomattox:*

. . . There is, and can be, no doubt of the straits to which these people are now reduced; particularly, of course, in this distracted region; there is nothing in modern history to compare with the conscription they have. They have swept this part of the country of all persons under 50, who could not steal away. I have just seen a man of 48, very much crippled with rheumatism, who said he was enrolled two days ago. He told them he had thirteen persons dependent on him, including three grandchildren . . . but they said that made no difference; he was on his way to the rendezvous, when our cavalry crossed the river, and he hid in the bushes till they came up. I offered him money for some of his small vegetables; but he said: "If you have any bread, I would rather have it. Your cavalry have taken all the corn I had left, and, as for meat, I have not tasted a mouthful for six weeks."

Drunkenness was one of the Civil War soldiers' most common offenses. An ingenious method of punishment for the man so drunk he was unable to stand is shown above. Bayonets, tied in the mouth, served in place of a cloth gag. *(Library of Congress.)*

If you had seen his eyes glisten when I gave him a piece of salt pork, you would have believed his story. He looked like a man who had come into a fortune. "Why," said he, "that must weigh four pounds—that would cost me forty dollars in Richmond! They told us they would feed the families of those that were taken; and so they did for two months, and then they said they had no more meal."

From a letter of General Robert E. Lee to Secretary of War James A. Seddon, August 23, 1864:

The subject of recruiting the ranks of our army is growing in importance and has occupied much of my attention. Unless some measures can be devised to replace our losses, the consequences may be disas-

trous. I think that there must be more men in the country liable to military duty than the small number of recruits received would seem to indicate . . . .

I recommend that the facts of the case be investigated and that if the officers and men engaged in enrolling have finished their work, with the exceptions indicated, they be returned to the army, where their presence is much needed . . . . Our numbers are daily decreasing, and the time has arrived in my opinion when no man should be excused from service, except for the purpose of doing work absolutely necessary for the support of the army. If we had there a few thousand men more to hold the stronger parts of our lines where an attack is least likely to be made, it would enable us to employ with good effect our veteran troops. Without some increases in our strength, I cannot see how we are to escape

Although whimsical in execution, William Sheppard's *A Rabbit in Camp* illustrates the more serious fact that scarcity of food was becoming a serious and demoralizing problem for the Southern armies. *(The Museum of the Confederacy.)*

the natural military consequences of the enemy's numerical superiority.

From George Cary Eggleston's *A Rebel's Recollections:*

Union Soldier. Aren't times rather hard over there, Johnny?

Confederate Soldier. Not at all. We've all the necessaries of life.

U. S. Yes; but how about luxuries? You never see any coffee nowadays, do you?

C. S. Plenty of it.

U. S. Isn't it pretty high?

C. S. Forty dollars a pound, that's all.

U. S. Whew! Don't you call that high?

C. S. Well, perhaps it is a trifle uppish, but then you never saw money so plentiful as it is with us. We hardly know what to do with it, and don't mind paying high prices for things we want.

And that was the universal feeling. Money was so easily got, and its value was so utterly uncertain, that we were never able to determine what was a fair price for anything. We fell into the habit of paying whatever was asked, knowing that tomorrow we should have to pay more . . . .

A facetious friend used to say prices were so high that nobody could see them . . . . He held, however, that the difference between the old and the new order of things was a trifling one. "Before the war," he said, "I went to market with the money in my pocket, and brought back my purchases in a basket. Now I take the money in the basket, and bring the things home in my pocket."

When the Union commander of Fort Pillow, Tennessee, refused to surrender to Major General Nathan Forrest, rebel troops attacked with glee. Northern newspapers called it a "massacre," accusing Forrest of killing black and white soldiers after they had surrendered. *(The Granger Collection.)*

Following the Emancipation Proclamation, Southern blacks deserted plantations and shanties in growing numbers, straggling along to fight with whatever Federal unit happened to be passing by. In addition, more and more Negro regiments were commissioned.

The thought of black troops fighting on Southern soil against their former masters and protectors became an unbearable insult to the Confederate army, officers and enlisted men alike.

In 1864, Fort Pillow, on the Mississippi, was in Federal control, held by the Thirteenth Tennessee Cavalry. General Nathan Bedford Forrest, former slave dealer and supremely competent cavalry officer attacked them in April. The assault was called "inhuman, fiendish butchery" by Harper's Weekly. *It is still regarded by many as a massacre.*

Following the war, General Forrest became one of the organizers of the first branch of the Ku Klux Klan formed in Richmond, Virginia, to rid the city of its carpetbagger mayor. Later, however, he apparently disassociated himself from the group's activities.

From Charles C. Coffin's *Four Years of Fighting:*

The negroes came from all the surrounding plantations. Old men with venerable beards, horny hands, crippled with hard work and harder usage; aged women, toothless, almost blind, steadying their steps with sticks; little negro boys, driving a team of skeleton steers—mere bones and tendons covered with hide—or wall-eyed horses, spavined, foundered, and lame, attached to rickety carts and wagons, piled with beds, tables, chairs, pots and kettles, hens, turkeys, ducks, women with infants in their arms, and a sable cloud of children trotting by their side.

"Where are you going?" I said to a short, thickset, gray-bearded old man, shuffling along the road; his toes bulging from his old boots, and a tattered straw hat on his head—his gray wool protruding from the crown.

"I do'no, boss, where I's going, but I reckon I'll go where the army goes."

"And leave your old home, your old master, and the place where you have lived all your days?"

"Yes, boss; master, he's gone. He went to Richmond. Reckon he went mighty sudden, boss, when he heard you was coming. Thought I'd like to go along with you."

His face streamed with perspiration. He had been sorely afflicted with the rheumatism, and it was with difficulty that he kept up with the column; but it was not a hard matter to read the emotions of his heart. He was marching towards freedom. Suddenly a light had shined upon him. Hope had quickened in his soul. He had a vague idea of what was before him. He had broken loose from all which he had been accustomed to call his own—his cabin, a mud-chinked structure, with the ground for a floor, his garden patch—to go out, in his old age, wholly unprovided for, yet trusting in God that there would be food and raiment on the other side of Jordan . . . .

Lieutenant Mack J. Leaming quoted in *War of the Rebellion: . . . Official Records of the Union and Confederate Armies:*

The rebel charge was immediately sounded; when, as if rising from out the very earth on the center and north side, within 20 yards of our works, the rebels received our first fire, wavered, rallied again and finally succeeded in breaking our lines, and in thus gaining possession of the fort. At this juncture, one company of the Sixth U. S. Heavy Artillery, colored troops, rushed down the bluff, at the summit of which were our works, and many of them jumped into the river, throwing away their arms as they fled.

Seeing that . . . the enemy had now gained possession of our works, and in consequence that it would be useless to offer further resistance, our men threw down their arms and surrendered. For a moment the fire seemed to slacken. The scene which followed, however, beggars all description. The enemy carried our works at about 4 P.M., and from that time until dark, and at intervals throughout the night, our men were shot down without mercy and almost without regard to color. This horrid work of butchery did not cease even with the night of murder, but was renewed again the next morning, when numbers of our wounded were basely murdered after a long night of pain and suffering on the field where they had fought so bravely . . . .

The rebels were very bitter against these loyal Tennesseans, terming them "home-made Yankees," and declaring they would give them no better treatment than they dealt out to the negro troops with whom they were fighting . . . .

Of the number, white and black, actually murdered after the surrender I cannot say positively; however, from my own observation, as well as from prisoners who were captured at Fort Pillow and afterward made their escape, I cannot estimate that number at anything less than 300.

Nathan Bedford Forrest rose from the rank of private to major general in the Confederate service. The former slave dealer became active in the Ku Klux Klan following the war. *(The Museum of the Confederacy.)*

An engraving by Thomas Nast portrayed sentimental vignettes in the life of the ubiquitous drummer boy. *(Library of Congress.)*

General Nathan Bedford Forrest quoted in *War of the Rebellion: ... Official Records of the Union and Confederate Armies:*

Arrived there . . . on the morning of the 12th and attacked the place with a portion of McCulloch's and Bell's brigades, numbering about 1,500 men, and after a sharp contest captured the garrison and all of its stores. A demand was made for the surrender, which was refused. The victory was complete, and the loss of the enemy will never be known from the fact that large numbers ran into the river and were shot and drowned. The force was composed of about 500 negroes and 200 white soldiers (Tennessee Tories). The river was dyed with the blood of the slaughtered for 200 yards . . . .

It is hoped that these facts will demonstrate to the northern people that negro soldiers cannot cope with Southerners.

> *Farther south, Sherman and Joe Johnston waited it out for the most part. Johnston, outrationed and outnumbered, knew he was better off holding a defensive position. There were heavy skirmishes at Resaca, at Kennesaw Mountain, the two armies always inching toward Atlanta.*
>
> *Jefferson Davis wanted Sherman's forces destroyed, and it seemed Johnston was not the man who would do it. He replaced him with the bolder John Bell Hood, who responded with several fruitless but costly attacks.*

From a letter of Private John Brobst to Mary Englesby, 1864:

They [the Rebels] must soon fight or leave . . . entirely. If they stop and fight they will have to leave, and if they don't fight they will have to leave, so I think the best thing for them is to go without fighting. It would suit me the best anyway, for they shoot careless as can be. They had just as leave hit and kill us as not. It is all wrong, decidedly wrong, but they say that a continual dropping of water will wear away a rock, and if this is true, we will soon have them all worn out, for they are wearing away all the time. Every man and woman down here is loyal as soon as a soldier comes around the house. They will say, "I am Union and always have been. You will not take my chickens and turkeys, will you?" But we have no respect of persons down here. They must all suffer alike.

The people up north do not know what war is. If they were to come down here once, they would soon find out the horror of war. Wherever the army

General John Bell Hood was chosen by President Davis to replace General Joseph Johnston and fight it out with Sherman's army poised before Atlanta. On September 2 he surrendered the city to the seemingly invincible Northern forces. *(The Museum of the Confederacy.)*

goes, they leave nothing behind them, take all the horses, all the cattle, hogs, sheep, chickens, corn and in fact, everything, and the longer the rebs hold out the worse it is for them.

From *Memoirs of General W. T. Sherman:*

About 10 A.M. of that day (July 18th), when the armies were all in motion, one of General Thomas's staff-officers brought me a citizen, one of our spies, who had just come out of Atlanta, and had brought a newspaper of the same day, or of the day before, containing Johnston's order relinquishing the command of the Confederate forces in Atlanta, and Hood's order assuming the command. I immediately inquired of General Schofield, who was his classmate at West Point, about Hood, as to his general character, etc., and learned that he was bold even to rashness, and courageous in the extreme; I inferred that the change of commanders meant "fight." Notice of this important change was at once sent to all parts of the army, and every division commander was cautioned to be always prepared for battle in any shape. This was just what we wanted, viz., to fight in open ground, on any thing like equal terms, instead of being forced to run up against prepared intrenchments; but, at the same time, the enemy having Atlanta behind him, could choose the time and place of attack, and could at pleasure mass a superior force on our weakest points. Therefore, we had to be constantly ready for sallies.

From Chauncy Cook's *A Soldier Boy's Letters 1862-1865:*

Dear Folks at Home: I enclose a lot of leaves torn from my water soaked diary written morning, noon and night, just as I happened to have time . . . .

After the Rebel army retreated last night, and we got into their trenches, we found that they had suffered a bigger loss than our side. Blood stains along the breastworks, the barked trees and plowed earth works showed the work of the grape and cannister of our batteries, and the knapsacks and guns that were picked up told the story of their loss. They did not have time to carry away all their dead. I stood guard last night for two hours under the shadow of a big tree within 20 feet of a fine looking fellow. He lay stretched out on his back. Both arms extending straight out from his body. He was killed by a bayonet or minnie ball thrust thru his heart. His comrades had torn his vest and shirt front open to hunt for the fatal wound. The bars on his sleeve showed that he was sergeant. His face with the moon on it had a ghastly look. A Missouri boy, who stood next to me, took the flap of his coat, after pulling it out from under him, and covered his face . . . .

Just as the bugle blew for the noon halt, I went to a near plantation for water or milk. There were a lot of women and children, but no men save one very old man . . . . When some of the fellows came to the door as if to go in, a youngish black eyed girl took a stand square in the door way. Her black eyes looked so hard that Ed Coleman said he dodged every time she looked at him. One of the boys asked about the road to Marietta. She said it was nine miles. She had "hearn tell twas a good road but she had never been there." Tho she was born in that neighborhood. Just to be saying something the boys asked a lot of questions about the rebel army. She said we would find out all about it 'fore we got across the Chatahoochee river.

sting the wounded on the field of Battle

Alfred R. Waud was no stranger to the agonies of those injured in the fighting. In this graphic pencil and wash drawing, field surgeons perform an amputation as citizen volunteers assist in aiding the wounded on the field of battle. *(Library of Congress.)*

Mathew Brady photographed General Sherman in 1865. The general's concept of "total war" was meant to destroy the spirit and the means of Southern resistance. Grant agreed, and gave him permission to "make Georgia howl." *(Courtesy Chicago Historical Society.)*

Now began the siege and bombardment of Atlanta, the cutting and burning of rail ties which were then twisted into what the Federals began to call "Sherman's neckties." After a last attack by Hood to defend his only remaining supply line, the city was evacuated. What was left of it belonged to the Union.

But staying in Atlanta was not to Sherman's liking. In October he telegraphed to General Grant requesting permission to pursue and "to make Georgia howl." Sherman meant that he wanted total warfare, that economic resources were legitimate targets for confiscation and destruction. Stealing, euphemistically known as foraging, was not a new concept, but now Grant officially acquiesced.

The Special Field Orders No. 120 Sherman issued sound reasonable today in terms of modern warfare, but the orders of a commander are subject to the special needs and often liberal interpretations of subordinate officers.

In November the army moved South, slashing a wide swathe of total destruction through the most fertile farmlands of the Confederacy. After the capture of Savannah, they struck northward into South Carolina, dealing the same blows to the state that had led the secession movement. Southerners would never forget the hated name of William Tecumseh Sherman.

From a letter of Private John Brobst to Mary Englesby, September 26, 1864:

. . . Sherman is our guide, like Moses of old was guide for the children of Israel, but he did not smite the waters of the Chattahoochee River as Moses did the Red Sea, but we had to wade, swim or roll through it, any way to get through, and when we got out of meat he called for chickens, turkeys, geese, pigs, sheep, and anything that we could take, from the rebs in place of the Egyptians, better than quails. In place of smiting the rock for water, he smites the cellar doors, and the wine, brandy, gin, and whiskey flows in the place of water. Sherman is rather ahead of Moses if he gets us through the wilderness all right, I think.

From a letter of Private John Brobst to Mary Englesby, July 11, 1864:

. . . And I think Atlanta will soon be ours. For when part of an army gets a foothold the remainder will soon get the same, and when our army gets all on this side of the river, we can push forward and the rebels will not have any more mountains to help them to defend the city of Atlanta, but the country will be comparatively level, which will give us a much better chance than what we have been having. It is thought that they will not try to hold the city, as we would destroy it if they did so, and if not we would save the place for our own use.

We have very good news from General Grant's army. I hope he will get Richmond soon, for I am satisfied that we will soon have Atlanta, and then I think the rebs will begin to talk peace, but they must come to our terms or have no peace. Some of them say they will fight as long as there is one of them left. We tell them that is what we want. We want to kill them all off and cleanse the country, but they are very few that talk so. Once in a long time we find one hot-headed one. The most of them say that they are tired of war and want peace, even at our terms.

From *Memoirs of W. T. Sherman:*

. . . General Hardee was gone, and we all pushed forward along the railroad south, in close pursuit, till we ran up against his lines at a point just above Lovejoy's Station. While bringing forward troops and feeling the new position of our adversary, rumors came from the rear that the enemy had evacuated Atlanta, and that General Slocum was in the city. Later in the day I received a note in Slocum's own handwriting, stating that he had heard during the night the very sounds that I have referred to; that he had moved rapidly up from the bridge about daylight, and had entered Atlanta unopposed. His letter was dated inside the city, so there was no doubt of the fact. General Thomas's bivouac was but a short distance from mine, and, before giving notice to the army in general orders, I sent one of my staff-officers to show him the note. In a few minutes the officer returned, soon followed by Thomas himself, who again examined the note, so as to be perfectly certain that it was genuine. The news seemed to him too good to be true. He snapped his fingers, whistled, and almost danced, and, as the news spread to the army, the shouts that arose from our men, the wild hallooing and glorious laughter, were to us a full recompense for the labor and toils and hardships through which we had passed in the previous three months.

From General William T. Sherman's Special Field Orders, No. 120, November 1865:

The army will forage liberally on the country during the march. To this end, each brigade commander

(continued on page 169)

Left: The last train north from Atlanta was overflowing with refugees and bundles of goods to be saved from the yankees. *(Missouri Historical Society, St. Louis.)*
Below: Confederate fortifications before Atlanta. Wood houses such as the two in the picture were shorn of their siding to provide materials needed for the defenses. *(Missouri Historical Society, St. Louis.)*

(continued from page 167)

will organize a good and sufficient foraging party, under the command of one or more discreet officers, who will gather, near the route traveled, corn or forage of any kind, meat of any kind, vegetables, corn-meal, or whatever is needed by the command, aiming at all times to keep in the wagons at least ten days' provisions for his command, and three days' forage. Soldiers must not enter the dwellings of the inhabitants, or commit any trespass; but, during a halt or camp, they may be permitted to gather turnips, potatoes, and other vegetables, and to drive in stock in sight of their camp. To regular foraging parties must be intrusted the gathering of provisions and forage, at any distance from the road traveled.

To corps commanders alone is intrusted the power to destroy mills, houses, cotton-gins, etc; and for them this general principle is laid down: In districts and neighborhoods where the army is unmolested, no destruction of such property should be permitted; but should guerrillas or bushwhackers molest our march, or should the inhabitants burn bridges, obstruct roads, or otherwise manifest local hostility, then army commanders should order and enforce a devastation more or less relentless, according to the measure of such hostility.

As for horses, mules, wagons, etc., belonging to the inhabitants, the cavalry and artillery may appropriate freely and without limit; discriminating, how-

General Sherman (at rear of cannon) and his staff meet after the capture of Atlanta in September 1864. The general's elation over the taking of this Southern prize would soon wane, and his armies would begin the devastating March to the Sea. *(Missouri Historical Society, St. Louis.)*

ever, between the rich, who are usually hostile, and the poor and industrious, usually neutral or friendly. Foraging parties may also take mules or horses, to replace the jaded animals of their trains, or to serve as pack-mules for the regiments or brigades ....

Negroes who are able-bodied and can be of service to the several columns may be taken along; but each army commander will bear in mind that the question of supplies is a very important one, and that his first duty is to see to those who bear arms ....

From John Trowbridge's *A Picture of the Desolated States and the Work of Restoration:*

... A gentleman of Jones County said: "I had a noble field of corn, not yet harvested. Old Sherman came along and turned his droves of cattle right into it, and in the morning there was no more corn there than there is on the back of my hand. His devils robbed me of all my flour and bacon and corn meal. They took all the pillow-slips, ... dresses, ... sheets and bed quilts they could find in the house to tie their plunder in. You couldn't hide anything but they'd find it."

A lady living near Milledgeville was the president of a soldiers' aid society. At the time of Sherman's visit she had in her house a box full of stockings knit by patriotic ladies for the feet of the brave defenders of their country. This box she buried in a field which was afterwards ploughed, in order to obliterate all marks of concealment. A squadron of cavalry arriving at this field formed in line, charged over it, and discovered the box by a hollow sound it gave forth under the hoofs. The box was straightway brought to light, to the joy of many a stockingless invader, who had the fair ladies of Milledgeville to thank for his warm feet that winter.

From John Trowbridge's *A Picture of the Desolated States and the Work of Restoration:*

According to a tradition which I found current in middle Georgia, General Sherman remarked, while on his grand march through the state, that he had his gloves on as yet, but that he would take them off in South Carolina .... At mention of this, however, many good Georgians ... blazed with indignation: "If he had his gloves on here, I should like to know what he did with his gloves off!"

A Confederate brigadier general said to me: "One could track the line of Sherman's march all through Georgia and South Carolina by the fires on the horizon. He burned the ginhouses, cotton presses, railroad depots, bridges, freighthouses and unoccupied dwellings, with some that were occupied. He stripped our people of everything. He deserves to be called the great robber of the nineteenth century ...."

From *Memoirs of W. T. Sherman:*

Before I had reached Savannah, and during our stay there, the Rebel officers and newspapers represented the conduct of the men of our army as simply infamous; that we respected neither age nor sex; that we burned everything we came across—barns, stables, cotton-gins, and even dwelling houses; that we ravished the women and killed the men, and perpetrated all manner of outrages on the inhabitants. Therefore it struck me as strange that Generals Hardee and Smith should commit their families to our custody, and even bespeak our personal care and attention. These officers knew well that these reports were exaggerated in the extreme, and yet tacitly assented to these publications, to arouse the drooping energies of the people of the South.

170

As Sherman and his men marched to the sea, they tore railroad lines and twisted them into "Sherman's neckties." The army laid bare all that fell before it as it slowly moved toward Savannah in December. *(Library of Congress.)*

From a letter of President Abraham Lincoln to General William T. Sherman, December 26, 1864:

Many, many thanks for your Christmas gift—the capture of Savannah.

When you were about to leave Atlanta for the Atlantic coast, I was anxious, if not fearful; but feeling that you were the better judge, and remembering that 'nothing risked, nothing gained,' I did not interfere, Now, the undertaking being a success, the honor is all yours . . . .

Please make my grateful acknowledgements to your whole army, officers and men.

From John Trowbridge's *A Picture of the Desolated States and the Work of Restoration:*

Warned by the flying cavalry, and the smoke and flames of plantations on the horizon, the panic-stricken inhabitants thought only of saving their property and their lives from the invaders. Many fled from their homes carrying the most valuable of their possessions, or those which could be most conveniently removed. Mules, horses, cattle, sheep, hogs were driven wildly across the country, avoiding one foraging party perhaps only to fall into the hands of another. The mother caught up her infant; the father, mounting, took his terrified boy upon the back of his horse behind him; the old man clutched his moneybag and ran; not even the poultry, not even the dogs were forgotten; men and women shouldered their household stuffs, and abandoned their houses to the mercies of the soldiers, whose waving banners and bright steel were already appearing on the distant hilltops.

From Sidney Andrews' *The South Since the War: As Shown by 14 Weeks of Travel and Observation in Georgia and the Carolinas:*

A city of ruins, of desolation, of vacant houses, of widowed women, of rotting wharves, of deserted warehouses, of weed-wild gardens, of miles of grass-grown streets, of acres of pitiful barrenness—that is Charleston wherein rebellion loftily reared its head five years ago . . . .

We can never again have the Charleston of the decade previous to the war . . . . Five millions of dollars could not restore the ruin of these past four years; and that sum is . . . far beyond the command of the city . . . . Yet, after all, Charleston was Charleston because of the hearts of its people. Now one marks how few young men there are, how generally the young women are dressed in black. The flower of their proud aristocracy is buried on scores of battle-fields. If it were possible to restore the broad acres of crumbling ruins to their foretime style and uses, there would even then be but the dead body of Charleston.

In late summer of 1864, Major General Philip Sheridan had received his orders to destroy the fertile Shenandoah Valley. When he met the rebel forces of Jubal Early at Cedar Creek on September 19, the Federals were nearly routed, but Sheridan, shown above, galloped fourteen miles from Winchester, reversing the retreat and rallying the troops. His action was immortalized in Thomas Buchanan Read's poem "Sheridan's Ride." *(Library of Congress.)*

Despite problems on the domestic front, Lincoln, boosted by the key military victories of Sheridan, Sherman and Farragut, won his reelection in November 1864. With characteristic sensitivity for the feelings of his constituents and equally characteristic eloquence, he addressed the nation deploring the continuing war and intimating that the South would receive not retribution, but mercy, at the time peace should come. Lincoln's thoughts regarding Reconstruction were temperate. He favored liberal terms for surrender and the readmission of the Confederate states to the Union. He would not live to see that some politicians in Congress were waiting in the wings to subvert his call for "malice toward none" and "charity for all."

From President Abraham Lincoln's Second Inaugural Address, March 4, 1865:

On the occasion corresponding to this four years ago, all thoughts were anxiously directed to an impending civil war. All dreaded it—all sought to avert it. While the inaugural address was being delivered from this place, devoted altogether to saving the Union without war, insurgent agents were in the city seeking to destroy it without war—seeking to dissolve the Union, and divide effects, by negotiation. Both parties deprecated war; but one of them would make war rather than let the nation survive; and the other would accept war rather than let it perish. And the war came.

One-eighth of the whole population were colored slaves, not distributed generally over the Union, but localized in the Southern part of it. These slaves constituted a peculiar and powerful interest. All knew that this interest was, somehow, the cause of the war. To strengthen, perpetuate, and extend this interest was the object for which the insurgents would rend the Union, even by war; while the Government claimed no right to do more than to restrict the territorial enlargement of it. Neither party expected for the war the magnitude or the duration which it has already attained. Neither anticipated that the cause of the conflict might cease with, or even before, the conflict itself should cease. Each looked for an easier triumph, and a result less fundamental and astounding . . . .

With malice toward none, with charity for all; with firmness in the right, as God gives us to see the right, let us strive on to finish the work we are in; to bind up the nation's wounds; to care for him who shall have borne the battle, and for his widow, and his orphan—to do all which may achieve and cherish a just and lasting peace among ourselves, and with all nations.

The victories of Sherman and Sheridan assured
Lincoln's reelection in 1864. *(Courtesy Chicago Historical Society.)*

From a letter of Lieutenant General Ulysses S. Grant to his father, Jesse, March 19, 1865:

. . . We are now having fine weather and I think will be able to wind up matters about Richmond soon. I am anxious to have Lee hold on where he is a short time longer so that I can get him in a position where he must lose a great portion of his army. The rebellion has lost its vitality and if I am not much mistaken there will be no rebel army of any great dimensions in a few weeks hence. Any great catastrophe to any one of our armies would of course revive the enemy for a short time. But I expect no such thing to happen.

From David Bates' *Lincoln Stories:*

In March, 1865, Sheridan, with his chief of staff, Captain Forsyth, rode over from White House to City Point. Robert Lincoln informed his father, who was on the River Queen, that "Little Phil" had arrived. The President hastened ashore and went to Colonel Bower's tent to express his personal congratulations to Sheridan, which he did in the most sincere and graceful manner, winding up with this remark, "General Sheridan, when this peculiar war began I thought a cavalryman should be at least six feet four high; but," still holding Sheridan's hand in his earnest grasp and looking down upon the little general, "I have changed my mind—five feet four will do on a pinch." Sheridan measured five feet four and a half, and at this time weighed only one hundred and forty-one pounds; but in the saddle "he weighed a ton," as his soldiers were wont to say. At the meeting with Lincoln he appeared without sword, sash, belt, or epaulets, and with his old brown slouch-hat in his hand.

Not long afterward, Sheridan won an important victory at Five Forks, breaking the lines of Lee, who was forced to retreat. The Confederate general recommended the immediate evacuation of Richmond. Jefferson Davis described the hurried preparations to leave Richmond for Danville, Virginia. His friend and neighbor, Mr. Grant recalled in later years his own impressions of that day so fateful to the Confederacy.

The First of May 1865 or *General Moving Day in Richmond, Virginia.* (Library of Congress.)

From a letter of President Jefferson Davis to his wife, Varina, April 5, 1865:

I have in vain sought to get into communication with General Lee . . . . On last Sunday I was called out of church to receive a telegram announcing that General Lee could not hold his position longer than till night and warning me that we must leave Richmond, as the army would commence retiring that evening. I made the necessary arrangements at my office and went to our house to have the proper dispositions made there . . . but little could be done in the few hours which remained before the train was to leave.

I packed up the bust and gave it to John Davis who offered to take it and put it where it should never be found by a Yankee—I also gave him charge of the painting "Heroes of the Valley"—both were removed after dark. The furniture of the house was left and very little of the things I directed to be put up, bedding and groceries, were saved.

Mr. Grant was afraid to take the carriage to his house & etc. & etc. I sent it to the depot to be put on a flat . . . .

I do not wish to leave Virginia, but cannot decide on my movements until those of the army are better developed . . . .

From a letter of W.E. Grant to Edward Valentine, circa 1903: [The Davis, Grant and Valentine families all lived on Richmond's Clay Street.]

It is impossible for me to give you anything like a connected account of the occurrences of the latter days of the war which came under my observation. You will readily appreciate this when you know I am only mentioning *events* which would appeal to a boy between the ages of five and nine years. Of course I saw many of the officers, first of the Con-

After the halocaust of April 3, the once proud and elegant city of Richmond lay in ruin. Crumbling brickwork and ashes gave a mute protest to the ignorance of those who had ravished its charm and beauty. *(Valentine Museum, Richmond, Virginia.)*

Citizens of Richmond fled the city in disorganized panic on the night of April 2, 1865. Civil and military authorities had ordered the burning of rebel supplies, but the fires got quickly out of hand, while milling incendiaries robbed and pillaged. Union soldiers restored order and brought the blaze under control. *(Valentine Museum, Richmond, Virginia.)*

federate army & after the evacuation of Richmond, those of the yankee army.

My first recollection was of a public gathering on the Capital Square, when Mr. Davis made a speech from the Washington Monument to a large audience. This is stamped on my memory from the fact that Mr. Davis used my father's carriage drawn by his two white horses Frank and John. Frank was a pure white, without a black spot and driven on the left; John was heavier and flea bitten, also had a better disposition . . . . I played with Jeff and Maggy Davis and now remember the piles of rocks we gathered to throw at the yankees if they should ever come to Richmond . . . . During the battles around Richmond I with the older members of the family often stood on the top of our house from which we could see the smoke of battle and at night we have seen the flashes of the guns.

I was in St. Paul's Church when Mr. Davis was called out on that memorable Sunday. I saw him

leave church. Later, when on the corner of 12th and Clay, some ladies asked me to go in and ask Mr. Davis "if Richmond was to be evacuated?" This I declined to do. Of course there was great excitement everywhere. After dinner, when the older heads were engaged, I drifted down the gully, and when I returned to the house, was told that Mr. Davis had been to say goodbye and left something for me to remember him by. This was the rose wood desk ornament with brass finish, inkstand, pen holder and match box, representing a cannon on wheels . . . .

I heard the magazines blow up and saw the first yankees who came up to the White House.

There are many other childish recollections as the foregoing. One that I forgot to mention was when the fire bells would ring during the war, to announce the approach of the enemy and the teachers would let out school, what excitement there was, and how delighted we were. The scholars were always wishing for the yankees to come . . . .

Within a few days of Richmond's fall, President Lincoln left by boat for the city. Many of the finest and most historic buildings survived, including the spectacular capitol designed by Thomas Jefferson. A captain of a Massachusetts regiment had his men surround the famous hilltop site and gave them orders to shoot anyone with intentions of destroying the seat of rebel government.

The President wished especially to see the Davis mansion on Clay Street and he wandered slowly through the elegance of its Victorian rooms, pausing to sit at the Confederate President's desk, and staying to dine and to reflect upon the life of a man who had to make decisions similar and equal to his own.

Everywhere he went the streets were filled with cheering throngs, black and white alike. Negroes fell to their knees, causing the President to caution them to "kneel only before God." Only days earlier, the city had been the official and symbolic center of the great rebellion. Now it welcomed with abandon the leader of the Union who brought with him the hope of an imminent peace.

Richmond in ruin.
(Valentine Museum, Richmond, Virginia.)

Thomas Thatcher Graves quoted in Robert Underwood Johnson's and Clarence Buell's *Battles and Leaders of the Civil War:*

On passing out from Clay Street, from Jefferson Davis's house, I saw a crowd coming, headed by President Lincoln, who was walking with his usual long, careless stride, and looking about with an interested air and taking in everything. Upon my saluting he said, "Is it far to President Davis's House?" I accompanied him to the house, which was occupied by General Weitzel as headquarters . . . .

At the Davis house, he was shown into the reception room, with the remark that the housekeeper had said that that room was President Davis's office. As he seated himself he remarked, "This must have been President Davis's chair," and, crossing his legs, he looked far off with a serious, dreamy expression. At length he asked me if the housekeeper was in the house. Upon learning that she had left he jumped up and said, with a boyish manner, "Come let's look at the house!" We pretty much went over it . . . and he seemed interested in everything. As we came down the staircase General Weitzel came in, in breathless haste, and at once President Lincoln's face lost its boyish expression as he realized that *duty* must be resumed . . . .

From Stephen Vincent Benét's *John Brown's Body:*

Richmond is fallen—Lincoln walks in its streets,
Alone, unguarded, stops at George Pickett's house,
Knocks at George Pickett's door. George Pickett has gone
But the strange, gaunt figure talks to George Pickett's wife
A moment—she thinks she is dreaming, seeing him there—
"Just one of George Pickett's old friends, m'am."
                                        He turns away.
She watches him down the street with wondering eyes.
The red light falls upon him from the red sky.
Houses are burning, strange shadows flee through the streets.
A gang of loafers is broaching a liquor-barrel
In a red-lit square. The liquor spills on the cobbles.
They try to scoop it up in their dirty hands.
A long, blue column tramps by, shouting "John Brown's Body."
The loafers scatter like wasps from a half-sucked pear,
Come back when the column is gone.
                                        A half-crazy slave
Mounts on a stoop and starts to preach to the sky.
A white-haired woman shoos him away with a broom.
He mumbles and reels to the shadows.
                                        A general passes,
His escort armed with drawn sabres. The sabres shine
In the red, low light.
                        Two doors away, down the street,
A woman is sobbing the same long sob all night
Beside a corpse with crossed hands.
                                        Lincoln passes on.

J. Balldwin, wearing the uniform of the Union army, in a formal portrait. *(Courtesy Chicago Historical Society.)*

As spring came to the Virginia country-side and Jefferson Davis remained in Danville, hoping somehow to reestablish the crumbling government, Lee's broken, badly clothed and hungry army followed. An earlier attempt to join the forces of Johnston had failed and the Confederate general had no illusions about the futility of further fighting. In February he had written Confederate Secretary of War Seddon: "The physical strength of the men, if their courage survives, must fail. . . . You must not be surprised if calamity befalls us."

Grant also had no illusions. His troops were ecstatic at the prospect of victory.

On April 7, 1865, in the pastoral setting near Appomattox Court House, the Federal commander requested the surrender of the Army of Northern Virginia. The two leaders exchanged several dispatches in the careful language of the soldier as diplomat. On April 9 Lee accepted Grant's terms. They were magnanimous, as President Lincoln had directed.

On Palm Sunday, the two met in the living room of Wilmer McClean's sturdy, but unpretentious home. Except for a few remaining complexities the war was ended. The time was at hand to bind up the nation's wounds, and to implement the peace.

From *Personal Memoirs of U.S. Grant:*

The much talked of surrendering of Lee's sword and my handing it back, this and much more that has been said about it is the purest romance. The word sword or side arms was not mentioned by either of us until I wrote it in the terms. . . .

General Lee, . . . before taking his leave, remarked that his army was in a very bad condition for want of food . . . that his men had been living for some days on parched corn exclusively, and that he would have to ask me for rations. . . . I told him "certainly," and asked for how many men he wanted rations. His answer was "about twenty-five thousand." I authorized him to send . . . to Appomattox Station, two or three miles away, where he could have, out of the trains we had stopped, all the provisions wanted. . . .

When news of the surrender first reached our lines our men commenced firing a salute of a hundred guns in honor of the victory. I at once sent word . . . to have it stopped. The Confederates were now our prisoners, and we did not want to exult over their downfall.

After Appomattox, Lee's battle-wearied veterans wept openly for their defeated leader. In Richard Norris Brooke's *Furling the Flag*, Confederates gently retired their colors for the final time. Lee then urged his men toward "the restoration of the country and the reestablishment of peace." *(The West Point Museum Collections, United States Military Academy.)*

General Robert E. Lee's farewell to his troops, April 10, 1865:

After four years' of arduous service, marked by unsurpassed courage and fortitude, the Army of Northern Virginia has been compelled to yield to overwhelming numbers and resources. I need not tell the survivors of so many hard-fought battles, who have remained steadfast to the last, that I have consented to this result from no distrust of them; but, feeling that valour and devotion could accomplish nothing that could compensate for the loss that would have attended the continuation of the contest, I have determined to avoid the useless sacrifice of those whose past services have endeared them to their countrymen. By the terms of the agreement, officers and men can return to their homes and remain there until exchanged. You will take with you the satisfaction that proceeds from the consciousness of duty faithfully performed; and I earnestly pray that a merciful God will extend to you His blessing and protection. With an increasing admiration of your constancy and devotion to your country, and a grateful remembrance of your kind and generous consideration of myself, I bid you an affectionate farewell.

General Long quoted in Captain Robert E. Lee's *Recollections and Letters of General Robert E. Lee:*

It is impossible to describe the anguish of the troops when it was known that the surrender of the army was inevitable. Of all their trials, this was the greatest and hardest to endure. There was no consciousness of shame; each heart could boast with honest pride that its duty had been done to the end, and that still unsullied remained its honor. When, after his interview with General Grant, General Lee again appeared, a shout of welcome instinctively went up from the army. But instantly recollecting the sad occasion that brought him before them, their shouts sank into silence, every hat was raised, and the bronzed faces of thousands of grim warriors were bathed in tears. As he rode slowly along the lines, hundreds of his devoted veterans pressed around the noble chief, trying to take his hand, touch his person, or even lay their hands upon his horse, thus exhibiting for him their great affection. The general then with head bare, and tears flowing freely down his manly cheeks, bade adieu to the army. . . .

Subsequent to the surrender of the Army of Northern Virginia, Union soldiers gathered captured muskets and prepared to ship them to the North. *(Valentine Museum, Richmond, Virginia.)*

Above: The sleepy town of Appomattox Court House, Virginia, provided the pastoral setting in which General Lee surrendered to his tenacious antagonist, Lieutenant General Ulysses S. Grant. In Wilmer McClean's modest home (right center) four years of carnage at long last came to an end. *(National Park Service.)* Below: Lee and Traveller share the final moments of the bitter day in a photograph known as *Sunset after Appomattox. (The Museum of the Confederacy.)*

While Booth remained unfound for the eleven days after Lincoln's assassination, posters were circulated offering large rewards for capture of the murderer and his accomplices. *(Cyr Color Photo Agency, photo by L.L.T. Rhodes.)*

The glorious days of rejoicing over the victory and the peace were short-lived. On the evening of April 14, President Lincoln attended a performance of Our American Cousin *at Ford's Theater. The play is remembered only for its associations with that fateful evening.*

John Wilkes Booth had previously tried to assassinate the President. He had planned to poison him, but the plan had failed. He had schemed to abduct him, but the attempt was abortive. On this evening he succeeded in entering the Lincoln box and, with a single pistol shot, inflicting the mortal wound.

Booth's fellow conspirators were to kill Vice President Andrew Johnson and Secretary of State William H. Seward, but they bungled their objectives.

Booth himself was cornered in a barn near Bowling Green, Virginia, on April 26.

He either committed suicide or was shot to death as soldiers burned the building.

When the Radical Republicans in Congress clamored for the blood of Southerners in retribution for the war, they did not get it. Jefferson Davis would not hang, but Booth's associates, some convicted on the flimsiest of evidence, were publicly hung, giving some satisfaction to the North's desire for vengeance.

From Walt Whitman's *Specimen Days:*

There is a scene in the play representing a modern parlor, in which two unprecedented English ladies are informed by the impossible Yankee that he is not a man of fortune, and therefore undesirable for marriage-catching purposes; after which, the comments being finished, the dramatic trio make exit, leaving the stage clear for a moment. . . . Through

Abraham Lincoln (1809-1865), sixteenth President of the United States. Secretary Stanton, present at Lincoln's deathbed in the early morning hours of April 15, pronounced the great man's most fitting epitaph: "Now he belongs to the ages." *(Philadelphia War Museum and Library. Cyr Color Agency, photo by L.L.T. Rhodes.)*

the general hum following the stage pause, with the change of positions, came the muffled sound of a pistol-shot, which not one-hundredth part of the audience heard at the time—and yet a moment's hush—somehow, surely, a vague startled thrill—and then, through the ornamented, draperied, starred and striped space-way of the President's box, a sudden figure, a man, raises himself with hands and feet, stands a moment on the railing, leaps below to the stage (a distance of perhaps fourteen or fifteen feet), falls out of position, catching his boot-heel in the copious drapery (the American flag), falls on one knee, quickly recovers himself, rises as if nothing had happened (he really sprains his ankle, but unfelt then)—and so the figure, Booth, the murderer, dressed in plain black broadcloth, bareheaded, with full, glossy, raven hair, and his eyes like some mad animal's flashing with light and resolution, yet with a certain strange calmness, holds aloft in one hand a large knife—walks along not much back from the footlights—turns fully toward the audience his face of statuesque beauty, lit by those basilisk eyes, flashing with desperation perhaps insanity—launches out in a firm and steady voice the words *Sic semper tyrannis*—and then walks with neither slow nor very rapid pace diagonally across to the back of the stage, and disappears. . . .

A moment's hush—a scream—the cry of *murder*—Mrs. Lincoln leaning out of the box, with ashy cheeks and lips, with involuntary cry, pointing to the retreating figure, *He has killed the President.*

Walt Whitman, *O Captain! My Captain!*

O Captain! my Captain! our fearful trip is done,
The ship has weathered every rack, the prize we sought is won,
The port is near, the bells I hear, the people all exulting,
While follow eyes the steady keel, the vessel grim and daring;
    But O heart! heart! heart!
      O the bleeding drops of red,
        Where on the deck my Captain lies,
          Fallen cold and dead.

O Captain! my Captain! rise up and hear the bells;
Rise up—for you the flag is flung—for you the bugle trills,
For you bouquets and ribboned wreaths—for you the shores
      a-crowding
For you they call, the swaying mass, their eager faces turning;
    Here Captain! dear father!
      This arm beneath your head!
        It is some dream that on the deck
          You've fallen cold and dead.

My Captain does not answer, his lips are pale and still,
My father does not feel my arm, he has no pulse nor will,
The ship is anchored safe and sound, its voyage closed and done,
From fearful trip the victor ship comes in with object won;
    Exult O shores, and ring O bells!
      But I, with mournful tread,
        Walk the deck my Captain lies,
          Fallen cold and dead.

An engraving of the funeral car which bore the body of President Lincoln appeared in *Frank Leslie's Illustrated Newspaper.* The President's train was met by thousands as it passed along nearly the same route which had borne him to Washington in 1861. On May 4, 1865, the man who had led the country through the most wounding years in its brief history was laid to rest in Springfield, Illinois. *(Courtesy Chicago Historical Society.)*

The stage of Ford's Theater in Washington was not used for theatrical performances for over a century after the tragedy of President Lincoln's assassination. Alfred R. Waud sketched the figures of the President and his wife in their box and John Wilkes Booth on stage at the point where he fell on that most fateful of April evenings in 1865. *(Library of Congress.)*

The soldiers waited to go home and soon they would. When John Brobst returned to Wisconsin, he married the girl he had fallen in love with by letter, Mary Englesby. When Leander Stillwell found his way back to Otterville, Illinois, he saw that things had not changed much at all. And so it was with most: They quickly resumed the chores of life in a country once again at peace. It was now the war which seemed unreal. One year before, the familiar sites of home and wives and children were the cherished and shadowy vision. Peace was the illusion. Now it was reality. The war was indeed over and home was the fixed point in their small and suddenly precious universe.

From John Greenleaf Whittier's *Laus Deo:*

It is done!
Clang of bell and roar of gun
Send the tidings up and down.
How the belfries rock and reel!
How the great guns, peal on peal,
Fling the joy from town to town!

It is done!
In the circuit of the sun
Shall the sound thereof go forth.
It shall bid the sad rejoice,
It shall give the dumb a voice,
It shall belt with joy the earth!

Ring and swing,
Bells of joy! On morning's wing
Send the song of praise abroad!
With a sound of broken chains
Tell the nations that He reigns,
Who alone is Lord and God!

The war was over. Those men who had survived the long years of conflict returned to the bosom of their families and to the more mundane concerns of building a new life in times of peace. *(Library of Congress.)*

From a letter of Private John Brobst to Mary Englesby, April 22, 1865:

The worst news that we have is the loss of our President. We would all rather heard of a large defeat of some of our armies than to heard of this sad disaster, even of Sherman's army that never has known what defeat was and never will know what it is. Yet we would be willing to suffer one defeat than to have lost our good, honest, and patriotic President, Abraham Lincoln.

Our army, that is, the army of Sherman, has been successful in every move that it has made since the commencement of this war, and we believe it always will be, with Sherman to command it.

The weather is very pleasant and warm. Everything looks pleasant, too pleasant to be wearing life away in this lonely place. We have a very pleasant place for a camp, and have everything comfortable as can be in camp life, and after all it is a disagreeable life to live, no society, no good times, only what we can get up in the way of stories, and they have become old long ago. We all hope there is a better time coming now, and soon. [The] human mind is never easy, always longing for something new. Home and its pleasures and endearments are all our thoughts now, all our talk, and all our desire. . . .

General Sherman comes around to see us occasionally. He tells us he hopes to soon march one of the best armies in the world home in a few days.

From Leander Stillwell's *The Story of a Common Soldier, or Army Life in the Civil War:*

I arrived at the little village of Otterville [Illinois] about sundown. It was a very small place in 1865. There was just one store, (which also contained the post office,) a blacksmith shop, the old stone schoolhouse, a church, and perhaps a dozen or so private dwellings. There were no sidewalks, and I stalked up the middle of the one street the town afforded, with my sword poised on my shoulder, musket fashion, and feeling happy and proud. . . .

I now had only two miles to go, and was soon at the dear old boyhood home. My folks were expecting me, so they were not taken by surprise. There was no "scene" when we met, nor any effusive display, but we all had a feeling of profound contentment and satisfaction which was too deep to be expressed by mere words.

When I returned home I found that the farm work my father was then engaged in was cutting and shocking corn. So, the morning after my arrival, September 29th, I doffed my uniform of first lieutenant, put on some of my father's old clothes, armed myself with a corn knife, and proceeded to wage war on the standing corn. The feeling I had while engaged in this work was sort of queer. It almost seemed, sometimes, as if I had been away only a day or two, and had just taken up the farm work where I had left off.

The guiding force of the Union was gone. His counterpart in the Confederacy, Jefferson Davis, remained a fugitive until his capture on May 10 in Florida. He was then imprisoned for two years at Fort Monroe, but never tried because no one expected conviction from a Virginia jury. A vengeful Northern press commented, "At about three o'clock yesterday, all that is mortal of Jeff'n Davis, late so-called 'President of the alleged Confederate States' was duly, but quietly and effectively committed to that living tomb prepared within the impregnable walls of Fortress Monroe . . . . He is buried alive."

Davis was very embittered because he would never be able to defend his views in a public trial. His defense would be in print as he retired to Mississippi to write The Rise and Fall of the Confederate Government. Citizenship was never granted to the former President, and he died in 1889, essentially a man without a country.

Robert E. Lee, probably the greatest figure of the war, whose reputation for gallantry and nobility extended the boundaries created by the savage conflict of the previous years, became the president of a small Virginia college, now known as Washington and Lee University. He worked diligently to restore the broken South, but his own health was failing rapidly, and indeed had been since 1863, when he had contracted what the doctors termed "a rheumatic inflamation of the sac around the heart." Lee died on October 12, 1870, and the deathbed scene as described by Colonel William Preston Johnston is also a stirring eulogy to the character and dignity of the hero of the South.

Colonel William Preston Johnson quoted in Reverend J.W. Jones' *Personal Reminiscences of General Robert E. Lee:*

. . . General Lee's closing hours were consonant with his noble and disciplined life. Never was more beautifully displayed how long and severe education of mind and character enables the soul to pass with equal step through this supreme ordeal; never did the habits and qualities of a lifetime, solemnly gathered into a few last sad hours, more grandly maintain themselves amid the gloom and shadow of approaching death . . . .

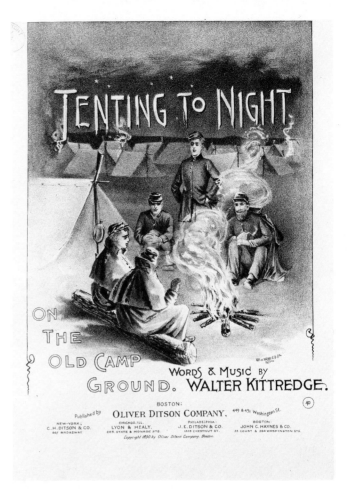

Tenting Tonight, with its subdued melody and lyrics that evoked the soldier's weariness of war, was one of the fighting man's most cherished songs. *(Library of Congress.)*

As the old hero lay in the darkened room, or with his lamp and hearth-fire casting shadows upon his calm, noble front, all the massive grandeur of his form, and face, and brow remained; and death seemed to lose its terrors, and to borrow a grace and dignity in sublime keeping with the life that was ebbing away. The great mind sank to its last repose, almost with the equal poise of health . . . but as long as consciousness lasted there was evidence that all the high, controlling influences of his whole life still ruled . . . . A Southern poet has celebrated in song those last significant words, "Strike the tent": and a thousand voices were raised to give meaning to the uncertain sound, when the dying man said, with emphasis, "Tell Hill he must come up!" These sentences serve to show most touchingly through what fields the imagination was passing . . . .

Deeds which required no justification must speak for him. [At the end] his voiceless lips, like the shut gates of some majestic temple, were closed, not for concealment, but because that within was holy. Could the eye of the mourning watcher have pierced the gloom that gathered about the recesses of that great soul it would have perceived a presence there of an ineffable glory. Leaning trustfully upon the all-sustaining Arm, the man whose stature, measured by mortal standards, seemed so great, passed from this world of shadows to the realities of the hereafter.

189

Waves of blue ranks paraded down Pennsylvania Avenue as veterans of the Army of the Potomac passed in Grand Review on May 23, 1865. All of Washington came to honor the men who had defended them through four arduous years. *(Library of Congress.)*

Lee's old adversary, Ulysses S. Grant, was rewarded by a grateful people with the Presidency of the United States. Not so magnanimous in power as he was in victory, his administration resulted in military rule in the South, and Federal troops remained on Southern soil until 1877. Grant admitted that he was not fit for the political life, and his two terms, rampant with civil corruption in all levels of government, proved him correct.

At the end of his tenure in 1876, after an "extended" tour of Europe and a short stay in his old home of Galena, Illinois, Grant retired to Mount McGregor near Saratoga, New York. Bad investment found the ex-President bankrupt in 1884. He was aware at this time that he had cancer of the throat, and desperately sought for a way to save his family from destitution after his death.

Mark Twain, a family friend, urged the failing general to write his memoirs and offered him a $25,000 advance royalty for each volume. He began by dictating, but by the fall of 1884 could no longer speak. Beyond this time, his condition steadily weakening, he wrote constantly and could be seen on the front porch of his cottage, bundled in blanket and stocking cap, pencil and paper in hand. Personal Memoirs of U.S. Grant was completed one week before his death on July 23, 1885. He had written nearly 295,000 words, and assured not only the security of his family, but a dual immortality, for his actions on the field of battle and his eminently readable book will never be forgotten.

The problem of what to do with the defeated South was going to remain with the nation for over a decade, but initially it was up to Andrew Johnson to deal with it. Radical Republicans wanted revenge and the way Johnson talked it seemed they would get it. They also wanted to do something about adjusting the newly freed blacks into society, but Johnson had no particular feelings on the black issue, except perhaps negative ones.

The new President did not wait for Congress to convene in December before initiating Reconstruction policies. Not an astute politician, Johnson never understood the art of the possible, nor did he have the skill for compromise. The most saliant point of his policies hinged on

his plebian hatred of the planter aristocracy. His childhood had been one of extreme poverty. Amnesty would be offered to Southerners with certain exceptions, among them Confederate civil and military officers, but more importantly those whose taxable property was valued at $20,000 or more.

President Grant was photographed only four days before his death from cancer as he sat on the porch of his Mount McGregor, New York, home. He had just completed his two-volume *Personal Memoirs of U.S. Grant*, written at the urging of family friend, Mark Twain. The work would save his family from bankruptcy. *(Courtesy Chicago Historical Society.)*

However, those in this class could apply for special *pardons. The end result was that the President signed pardons by the thousands, possibly because it made the rich and the powerful beg to a man who remembered his humble origins only too well. Consequently, as elections were held in the South in 1865, the old leadership* again rose to the top. There simply had not been time, the time the Radicals knew would be needed, for new leadership to develop. Early in 1866, the Southern legislatures began to pass the "Black Codes," designed to keep the Negro in his place, a position so near to slavery there was little distinction.

Freedmen in New Orleans, under the supervision of white officials, cast their votes in 1867. *(The Granger Collection.)*

From the Louisiana Labor Contract Act, 1865:

Section Nine: Be it further enacted, &c., That, when in health, the laborer shall work ten hours during the day in summer, and nine hours during the day in winter, unless otherwise stipulated in the labor contract; he shall obey all proper orders of his employer or his agent; take proper care of his work-mules, horses, oxen, stock; also of all agricultural implements; and employers shall have the right to make a reasonable deduction from the laborer's wages for injuries done to animals or agricultural implements committed to his care, or for bad or negligent work. Bad work shall not be allowed. Failing to obey reasonable order, neglect of duty, and leaving home without permission will be deemed disobedience; impudence, swearing, or indecent language to or in the presence of the employer, his family, or agent or quarreling and fighting with one another, shall be deemed disobedience. For any disobedience a fine of one dollar shall be imposed on and paid by the offender. For all lost time from work-hours, unless in case of sickness, the laborer shall be fined twenty-five cents per hour. For all absence from home without leave he will be fined at the rate of two dollars per day. Laborers will not be required to labor on the Sabbath unless by special contract.

Five generations of this black family were born on the South Carolina plantation of J. J. Smith. For many Negroes the transition from bondage to freedom would be difficult and painful, compounded by long-held racial prejudices. *(Library of Congress.)*

From the Mississippi Vagrant Law, 1865:

Section Two: All freedmen, free negroes and mulattoes in this State, over the age of eighteen years, found on the second Monday in January, 1866, or thereafter, with no lawful employment or business, or found unlawfully assembling themselves together, either in the day or night time, and all white persons so assembling themselves with freedmen, free negroes or mulattoes, or usually associating with freedmen, free negroes or mulattoes, on terms of equality, or living in adultery or fornication with a freed woman, free negro or mulatto, shall be deemed vagrants, and on conviction thereof shall be fined in a sum not exceeding, in the case of a freed-man, free negro or mulatto, fifty dollars, and a white man two hundred dollars, and imprisoned at the discretion of the court, the free negro not exceeding ten days, and the white man not exceeding six months . . . .

From the Penal Laws of Mississippi, 1865:

Section One: Be it enacted . . . . That no freedman, free negro or mulatto, not in the military service of the United States government, and not licensed so to do by the board of police of his or her county, shall keep or carry fire-arms of any kind, or any ammunition, dirk or bowie knife, and on conviction thereof in the county court shall be punished by fine . . . .

Radical Republicans, although their motives were sometimes allied with various economic interests, did want gradual Reconstruction and their rhetoric regarding the rights which should be extended to the black man sounds genuinely convincing and almost contempory to that of our own times. Said House leader Thaddeus Stevens: "This is not a white man's government. To say so is political blasphemy, for it violates the fundamental principles of our gospel of liberty. This is man's government; the government of all men alike."

With the elections in the fall of 1866, the Republicans captured two-thirds of each house, giving Radicals effective control of Reconstruction. In the South, "radical" Reconstruction meant carpetbaggers (those who carried all their earthly belongings in one bag, but probably needed more copious baggage to bring home the spoils); it meant blacks serving in legislatures; it meant the Ku Klux Klan and lynchings, but it was an attempt at reunion, at educating black children and at providing for the indigent Negro through the Freedmen's Bureau. The period of Reconstruction was a bitter one, and the South held firm. President Rutherford B. Hayes removed the last Federal troops from Southern soil in 1877. White rule was reestablished.

It would remain for another President Johnson to put teeth into the amendments passed to guarantee the black man his rights under law by proposing the Civil Rights Act of 1964, nearly one hundred years after the close of the American Civil War.

From Sidney Andrews' *The South Since the War: As Shown by 14 Weeks of Travel and Observation in Georgia and the Carolinas:*

There are many Northern men here already, though one cannot say that there is much Northern society, for the men are either without families or have left them at home. Walking out yesterday with a . . . Charlestonian . . . he pointed out to me the various "Northern houses"; and I shall not exaggerate if I say that this classification appeared to include at least half the stores on each of the principal streets. "The presence of these men," said he, "was at first very distasteful to our people, and they are not liked any too well now; but we know they are doing a good work for the city."

I fell into some talk with him concerning the political situation . . . . When I asked him what should be done, he answered: "You Northern people are making a great mistake in your treatment of the South. We are thoroughly whipped; we give up slavery forever; and now we want you to quit reproaching us. Let us back into the Union, and then come down here and help us build up the country."

From the report of a Federal Grand Jury to Congress, South Carolina, 1871:

In closing the labors of the present term, the grand jury beg leave to submit the following : . . . During the whole session we have been engaged in investigations of the most grave and extraordinary character—investigations of the crimes committed by the organization known as the Ku Klux Klan. The evidence . . . has been voluminous, gathered from the victims themselves and their families, as well as those who belong to the Klan and participated in its crimes. The jury has been shocked . . . at the number and character of the atrocities committed, producing a state of terror and a sense of utter insecurity among a large portion of the people, especially the colored population . . . .

The jury has been appalled as much at the number of outrages as at their character, it appearing that eleven murders and over six hundred whippings have been committed in York County alone. Our investigation in regard to the other counties named has been less full; but it is believed, from the testimony, that an equal or greater number has been committed in Union . . . .

We are of the opinion that the most vigorous prosecution of the parties implicated in these crimes is imperatively demanded; that without this there is great danger that these outrages will be continued, and that there will be no security to our fellow-citizens of African descent.

We would say further, that unless the strong arm of the Government is interposed to punish these crimes . . . , there is every reason to believe that an organized and determined attempt at retaliation will be made, which can only result in a state of anarchy and bloodshed too horrible to contemplate.

From W.E.B. Du Bois' *The Souls of Black Folk:*

. . . Guerrilla raiding, the ever-present flickering after-flame of war, was spending its forces against the Negroes, and all the Southern land was awakening as from some wild dream to poverty and social revolution. In a time of perfect calm, amid willing neighbors and streaming wealth, the social uplift-

The Ku Klux Klan, specializing in the terrorization of blacks, began its harrassment in December of 1866. Although the organization declined in power at times, its lynchings, acts of arson and cross burnings surfaced periodically, the most recent resurgence being in response to civil rights demands of blacks in the early 1960's. *(The Granger Collection.)*

ing of four million slaves to an assured and self-sustaining place in the body politic and economic would have been a herculean task; but when to the inherent difficulties of so delicate and nice a social operation were added the spite and hate of conflict, the hell of war; when suspicion and cruelty were rife, and gaunt Hunger wept beside Bereavement—in such a case, the work of any instrument of social regeneration was in large part foredoomed to failure. The very name of the [Freedmen's] Bureau stood for a thing in the South which for two centuries better

men had refused even to argue—that life amid free Negroes was simply unthinkable, the maddest of experiments. . . . Curiously incongruous elements were left arrayed against each other—the North, the government, the carpet-bagger, and the slave, here; and there, all the South that was white, whether gentleman or vagabond, honest man or rascal, lawless murderer or martyr to duty.

Thus it is doubly difficult to write of this period calmly, so intense was the feeling, so mighty the human passions that swayed and blinded men.

Aged and ill blacks received rations from the Freedmen's Bureau, established by the government in 1865. The agency, while it did valuable relief work, was also entrusted with assuring Negroes protection of their civil rights. *(Valentine Museum, Richmond, Virginia.)*

From Kenneth M. Stampp's *The Era of Reconstruction, 1865-1877:*

. . . We come to the idealistic aim of the radicals to make Southern society more democratic, especially to make the emancipation of the Negroes something more than an empty gesture. In the rural South the basic socioeconomic pattern was not destroyed, for share-cropping replaced the antebellum slave-plantation system. Most of the upper-class large landowners survived the ordeal of war and reconstruction, and the mass of Negroes remained a dependent, propertyless peasantry. After Reconstruction, in spite of the Fourteenth and Fifteenth Amendments, the Negroes were denied equal civil and political rights. In 1883 the Supreme Court invalidated the Civil Rights Act of 1875; in 1894 Congress repealed the Force Acts [enacted to deal with Southern opposition to Reconstruction laws, pri-

marily the Fourteenth and Fifteenth Amendments]; and in 1896 the Supreme Court sanctioned social segregation if Negroes were provided "Equal accommodations." Thus Negroes were denied Federal protection, and by the end of the nineteenth century the Republican party had nearly forgotten them. In place of slavery a caste system reduced Negroes to an inferior type of citizenship; social segregation gave them inferior educational and recreational facilities; and a pattern of so-called "race etiquette" forced them to pay deference to all white men. Negroes, in short, were only half-emancipated.

. . . Thus Negroes were no longer denied equality by the plain language of the law, as they had been before radical reconstruction, but only by coersion, by subterfuge, by deceit, and by spurious legalisms. For a time, of course, the denial of equality was as effective one way as the other . . . .

But Not in Vain

You, reader, who shouldered your musket and fought like the hero you are, for the Union and the old flag, if you had been bred at the South, and had understood your duty as the Southerners did theirs, would have fought quite as bravely for secession as you did against it; and you would have been quite as truly a hero in the one case as in the other, because in either you would have risked your life for the sake of that which you held to be the right.

George Cary Eggleston, from
A Rebel's Recollections, *1878*

Stacked Arms, by Conrad Wise Chapman. *(Valentine Museum, Richmond, Virginia.)*

All who had fought in the great war, North or South, had gambled with their lives for a cause they had felt to be just. Many had forfeited the game, and many returned home maimed by wounds or disabled by disease. Those whose luck had run well came back to family and job and the business of everyday living.

199

Now came the time for the veterans to tell their tales of battle and bivouac, not around the campfires and picket posts, but by the hearthside, to awed wives and children, and to old cronies from the field. It was the time for embellishment of brave deeds and for the flight of the more painful realities to the subconscious.

It was a time to build memorials to the honored dead. In nearly every city and town were erected fitting monuments with pious inscriptions written with the noblest intentions, but such cenotaphs not only praised the dead who lay elsewhere; they perpetuated the glory of war and as such, war itself.

Nevertheless the costly horror of the previous years was finished. General Sherman marched his troops in glorious array down Pennsylvania Avenue in Washington, and in his farewell to the armies of Tennessee admonished: "To such as go home, I will only say that our favored country is so grand, so extensive, so diversified in climate, soil and productions, that every man can find a home and occupation suited to his tastes, and none should yield to the natural impotence sure to result from our past life of excitement and adventure."

Grant told his armies to "hope for perpetual peace and harmony with the enemy, whose manhood, however mistaken the cause, drew forth such Herculean deeds of valor."

General Lee, who pleaded for amnesty from the United States Government, but never received it, still had the grace to say, "I believe it to be the duty of everyone to unite in the restoration of the country and the reestablishment of peace and harmony."

To these men and their entreaties toward conciliation and the earliest possible return to the status quo must go the credit for an expeditious peace. When they spoke, the men who served and loved them listened, and the specter of interminable guerilla fighting, common to the ending of civil wars, did not haunt the United States.

In the North the Industrial Age rumbled forward, and the South, in time, would find a more balanced economic base, but there, a mythological web began to spin itself around the bygone days of the antebellum years and to envelop the great Southern struggle itself. Perpetuated by tradition, by novelists and playwrights, the Old South took on ethereal and sentimentalized hues, still appealing to the contemporary reader and visitor.

This vision had one exclusion, the black man, around whose freedom and rights the conflict had raged. Over a century later, his struggle is with us, North and South, for each found its own ways of denying the gains won by the fearful bloodshed. As historian Robert Cruden has suggested, the war has thus far never ended.

No observer of those awful, swift years was more sensitive than American poet Walt Whitman, and perhaps he has written their best epitaph:

> Such was the war. It was not a quadrille in a ballroom. Its interior history will not only never be written—its practicality, minutiae of deeds and passions, will never even be suggested. The actual soldier of 1862-'65, North and South, with all his ways, his incredible dauntlessness, habits, practices, tastes, language, his fierce friendship, his appetite, rankness, his superb strength and animality, lawless gait, and a hundred unnamed lights and shades of camp, I say, will never be written—perhaps must not and should not be.

William Ludwell Sheppard depicted citizens decorating the graves of Confederate soldiers at Richmond's Hollywood Cemetery in 1867. The grave of Jeb Stuart is shown in the upper left detail. *(Valentine Museum, Richmond, Virginia.)*

From Bell Irvin Wiley's *The Life of Johnny Reb:*

. . . The average Rebel private belonged to no special category. He was in most respects an ordinary person. He came from a middleclass rural society, made up largely of non-slaveholders, and he exemplified both the defects and the virtues of that background. He was lacking in polish, in perspective and in tolerance, but he was respectable, sturdy and independent.

He was comparatively young, and more than likely unmarried. He went to war with a lightheartedness born of detachment and of faith in a swift victory. His moral wavered with the realization that the conflict was to be long and hard. He was nostalgic and war-weary. He felt the blighting hand of sickness, and it was then that his spirit sank to its lowest ebb. His craving for diversion caused him to turn to gambling and he indulged himself now and then in a bit of swearing. But his tendency to give way to such irregularities was likely to be curbed by his deep-seated conventionality or by religious revivals.

He complained of the shortcomings of officers, the scantiness of clothing, the inadequacy of rations, the multiplicity of pests and numerous other trails that beset him, but there was little depth to his complaints, and his cheerfulness outweighed his dejection. Adaptability and good-nature, in fact, were among his most characteristic qualities. He was a gregarious creature, and his attachment to close associates was genuine.

He had a streak of individuality and of irresponsibility that made him a trial to officers during periods of inactivity. But on the battlefield he rose to supreme heights of soldierhood. He was not immune to panic, nor even to cowardice, but few if any soldiers have had more than he of *élan,* of determination, of perseverance, and of the sheer courage which it takes to stand in the face of withering fire.

He was far from perfect, but his achievement against great odds in scores of desperate battles through four years of war is an irrefutable evidence of his prowess and an eternal monument to his greatness as a fighting man.

From Bell Irvin Wiley's *The Life of Billy Yank:*

. . . Johnny Reb made a better showing on the battlefield during the first half of the war, but his superiority was attributable in the main to better leadership. There is no reason to believe, however, that he ever possessed more of determination, courage, pride, loyalty to fellows and other basic characteristics that go to make a good soldier. Such differences as existed in combat effectiveness had disappeared by the autumn of 1863, if not sooner, and on the basis of the whole war record it cannot be said that the common soldier of one side was any better or any worse fighter than the one who opposed him . . . .

In sum, it may be stated that the similarities of Billy Yank and Johnny Reb far outweighed their differences. They were both Americans, by birth or by adoption, and they both had the weaknesses and the virtues of the people of their nation and time. For the most part they were of humble origin, but their conduct in crisis compared favorably with that of more privileged groups and revealed undeveloped resources of strength and character that spelled hope for the country's future.

While it is indeed regrettable that people so similar and basically so well-meaning found it necessary to resort to arms in settling their differences, now that their doing so is a matter of history their descendants can point with justifiable pride to the part played in the struggle by both the Blue and the Gray.

From a report of Lieutenant General Ulysses S. Grant to Secretary of War Edwin M. Stanton:

It has been my fortune to see the armies of both the West and the East fight battles, and from what I have seen I know there is no difference in their fighting qualities. All that it was possible for men to do in battle they have done. The Western armies commenced their battles in the Mississippi Valley, and received the final surrender of the remnant of the principal army opposed to them in North Carolina. The armies of the East commenced their battles on the river from which the Army of the Potomac derived its name, and received the final surrender of their old antagonists at Appomattox Court House, Virginia. The splendid achievements of each have nationalized our victories, removed all sectional jealousies (of which we have unfortunately experienced too much), and the cause of crimination and recrimination that might have followed had either section failed in its duty. All have a proud record, and all sections can well congratualte themselves and each other for having done their full share in restoring the supremacy of law over every foot of territory belonging to the United States. Let them hope for perpetual peace and harmony with the enemy, whose manhood, however mistaken the cause, drew forth such herculean deeds of valor.

From a letter of General Robert E. Lee to Josiah Tattnall, September 7, 1865:

. . . . The war being at an end, the Southern states having laid down their arms and the questions at issue between them and the Northern states having been decided, I believe it to be the duty of everyone

to unite in the restoration of the country and the reestablishment of peace and harmony. These considerations governed me in the counsels I gave to others and induced me on the 13th of June to make application to be included in the terms of the amnesty proclamation. I have not received an answer and cannot inform you what has been the decision of the President. But whatever that may be, I do not see how the course I have recommended and practised can prove detrimental to the former president of the Confederate States.

It appears to me that the allayment of passion, the dissipation of prejudice, and the restoration of reason will alone enable the people of the country to acquire a true knowledge and form a correct judgment of the events of the past four years. It will, I think, be admitted that Mr. Davis has done nothing more than all the citizens of the Southern states and should not be held accountable for acts performed by them in the exercise of what had been considered by them unquestionably right. I have too exalted an opinion of the American people to believe that they will consent to injustice; and it is only necessary, in my opinion, that truth should be known for the rights of everyone to be secured. I know of no surer way of eliciting the truth than by burying contention with the war.

As soon as news of Lee's surrender at Appomattox reached General Sherman, he arranged a meeting with his Georgia antagonist, Joseph Johnston near Durham, North Carolina. The purpose was to sign an armistice, which the two men did, but President Johnson, considering the terms too generous, rejected the proposal, to the avowed bitterness of the commander of the March to the Sea.

William Tecumseh Sherman died in 1891, and his former foe, Joe Johnston, insisted on attending the funeral. The weather was of the kind that had plagued both armies throughout the war years, but Johnston, out of respect for his former adversary, stood hatless at the ceremonies, and from the exposure contracted pneumonia, only to die within a month of the man he had come to honor.

From a letter of General William T. Sherman to James E. Yeatman, May 21, 1865:

You will have observed how fiercely I have been assailed for simply offering to the President "terms" for his approval or disapproval, according to his best judgment—terms which, if fairly interpreted, mean, and only mean, an actual submission by the rebel armies to the civil authority of the United States. No one can deny I have done the State some service in the field, but I have always desired that strife should cease at the earliest possible moment. I confess, without shame, I am sick and tired of fighting—its glory is all moonshine; even success the most brilliant is over dead and mangled bodies, with the anguish and lamentations of distant families, appealing to me for sons, husbands, and fathers. You, too, have seen these things, and I know you also are tired of the war, and are willing to let the civil tribunals resume their place. And, so far as I know, all the fighting men of our army want peace; and it is only those who have never heard a shot, never heard the shrieks and groans of the wounded and lacerated (friend or foe), that cry aloud for more blood, more vengeance, more desolation. I *know* the rebels are whipped to death, and I declare before God, as a man and a soldier, I will not strike a foe who stands unarmed and submissive before me, but would rather say—*"Go, and sin no more."*

From Bruce Catton's *Never Call Retreat:*

. . . Something had been won; but it was nothing more, and at the same time nothing less, than a chance to make a new approach toward a goal that had to be reached if the war and the nation that had endured it had final meaning. The ship was moving through Lincoln's dream, toward a dark indefinite shore, it had a long way to go, and the sky contained no stars the oridnary mortal could see. All that was certain was that the voyage was under way.

Walt Whitman, *To the Leaven'd Soil They Trod:*

To the leaven'd soil they trod calling I sing for the last,
(Forth from my tent emerging for good, loosing, untying the
        tent-ropes,)
In the freshness the forenoon air, in the far-stretching circuits
        and vistas again to peace restored,
To the fiery fields emanative and the endless vistas beyond, to
        the South and the North,
To the leaven'd soil of the general Western world to attest my
        songs,
To the Alleghanian hills and the tireless Mississippi,
To the rocks I calling sing, and all the trees in the woods,
To the plains of the poems of heroes, to the prairies spreading
        wide,
To the far-off sea and the unseen winds, and the sane impal-
        pable air;
And responding they answer all, (but not in words,)
The average earth, the witness of war and peace, acknowl-
        edges mutely,
The prairie draws me close, as the father to bosom broad the
        son,
The Northern ice and rain that began me nourish me to the
        end,
But the hot sun of the South is to fully ripen my songs.

Walter Williams, who saw service in the Confederate army, was the last veteran survivor of the Civil War. He died in Houston, Texas, December 19, 1959. *(Wide World Photos.)*

From *Barne's Centenary History: One Hundred Years of American Independence:*

. . . On July 4, 1868, the ninety-second anniversary of the national birthday, a pardon was proclaimed to all engaged in the late war, except those already indicted for treason or other felony. On Christmas of the same year—a day most fitting for acts of goodwill and mercy to erring brethren—a UNIVERSAL AMNESTY was declared.

Though the nation was still agitated by political strife—the ground-swell, as it were, of the recent terrible storm—the country was rapidly taking on the appearance and ways of peace. The South was slowly adjusting herself to the novel conditions of free labor. The soldiers retained somewhat their martial air; but "blue-coats" and "gray-coats" were everywhere to be seen engaged in quiet avocations. The ravages of war were fast disappearing. Nature had already sown grass and quick-growing plants upon the battlefields where contending armies had struggled.

"There were domes of white blossoms where swelled the white tent;
There were plows in the track where the war-wagons went;
There were songs where they lifted up Rachel's lament."

Strangely symbolical of the new era of growth which had dawned on the nation, a wanderer over the cannon-plowed slope of Cemetery Ridge found a broken drum, in which a swarm of bees were building their comb and storing honey gathered from the flowers growing on that soil so rich with Union and Confederate blood.

From Francis Trevelyan Miller's *The Photographic History of the Civil War:*

Of untold benefit have been the meeting of the Philadelphia Brigade and Pickett's men at Gettysburg, the visits of Massachusetts soldiers to Richmond, and of Virginia Confederates to Boston, and many similar occasions. These, . . . and a thousand similar incidents, have resulted in those acts that passed in Congress by unanimous votes, one providing for a Confederate section of Arlington Cemetery, the other looking to the care of the Confederate dead at Arlington and around the Federal Prisons to the North . . . .

And all over the land there are monuments to the dead of the Civil War, bearing inscriptions that will outlast the marble and bronze upon which they are written. Such is the legend on the monument built by the State of Pennsylvania to its dead at Vicksburg, "Here brothers fought for their principles, here heroes died to save their country, and a united people will forever cherish the precious legacy of their noble manhood."

Another such is on a monument erected by the State of New Jersey, and the survivors of the Twenty-third New Jersey Volunteers at Salem Church, Virginia. On one side is an appropriate inscription to their own dead; on the other, a bronze tablet bearing this magnanimous tribute, "To the brave Alabama boys who were our opponents on this field and whose memory we honor, this tablet is dedicated." That is a tribute, not by a Government, but directly by the men who fought to the men who fought them. It is truly noble.

From W.E.B. Du Bois' *The Souls of Black Folk:*

I have seen a land right merry with the sun, where children sing, and rolling hills lie like passioned women wanton with harvest. And there in the King's Highway sat and sits a figure veiled and bowed, by which the traveller's footsteps hasten as they go. On the tainted air broods fear. Three centuries' thought has been the raising and unveiling of that bowed human heart, and now behold a century new for the duty and the deed. The problem of the twentieth century is the problem of the color-line.

From Robert Cruden's *The War That Never Ended:*

. . . The unresolved issue of the Civil War casts its shadow a century later. White America's failure to honor the commitment to equality in the past (except during Reconstruction) bequeaths to the present generation of whites the psychic conflict involved in adherence to the nation's principles and the practise of racism. For blacks this has meant a dilemma of their own. For long now they have sought equality—but always with the consciousness that their struggle was circumscribed by the limits set by white society. Struggle as they might, blacks realized bitterly that they were not masters of their own fate. The consequence of past decisions has been an abrasive coexistence of the races, in which the black minority ever feels at a disadvantage.

But if it is true that the past conditions the present, it is equally true that the past does not determine the present. Man makes his own history, each generation shaping the heritage it will pass along to future generations. Who knows, the present generation of young Americans, both white and black, may so contribute as to bring to an end the war that thus far has never ended.

From Stephen Vincent Benét's *John Brown's Body:*

John Brown's body lies a-mouldering in the grave.
Spread over it the bloodstained flag of his song,
For the sun to bleach, the wind and the birds to tear,
The snow to cover over with a pure fleece
And the New England cloud to work upon
With the grey absolution of its slow,
                                    most lilac-smelling rain,
Until there is nothing there
That ever knew a master or a slave
Or, brooding on the symbol of a wrong,
Threw down the irons in the field of peace.
John Brown is dead, he will not come again,
A stray ghost-walker with a ghostly gun.
Let the strong metal rust
In the enclosing dust
And the consuming coal
That was the furious soul
And still like iron groans,
Anointed with the earth,
Grow colder than the stones
While the white roots of grass and little weeds
Suck the last hollow wildfire from the singing bones.

Bury the South together with this man,
Bury the bygone South.
Bury the minstrel with the honey-mouth,
Bury the broadsword virtues of the clan,
Bury the unmachines, the planters' pride,
The courtesy and the bitter arrogance,
The pistol-hearted horsemen who could ride
Like jolly centaurs under the hot stars.

Bury the whip, bury the branding-bars,
Bury the unjust thing
That some tamed into mercy, being wise,
But could not starve the tiger from its eyes
Or make it feed where beasts of mercy feed.
Bury the fiddle-music and the dance,
The sick magnolias of the false romance
And all the chivalry that went to seed
Before its ripening.

And with these things, bury the purple dream
Of the America we have not been,
The tropic empire, seeking the warm sea,
The last foray of aristocracy
Based not on dollars or initiative
Or any blood for what that blood was worth
But on a certain code, a manner of birth,
A certain manner of knowing how to live,
The pastoral rebellion of the earth
Against machines, against the Age of Steam,
The Hamiltonian extremes against the Franklin mean,
The genius of the land
Against the metal hand,
The great, slave-driven bark,
Full-oared upon the dark,
With gilded figurehead,
With fetters for the crew
And spices for the few,
The passion that is dead,
The pomp we never knew,
Bury this, too.

In the National Cemetery at Gettysburg, decorated for Memorial Day, lie both Union and Confederate men who perished there in July of 1863. *(Eastern National Park and Monument Association.)*

CHRONOLOGY OF THE WAR YEARS

December 24, 1860: South Carolina secedes from the Federal Union.

February 8, 1861: Confederate States of America formed; Jefferson Davis chosen as President, Alexander Stephens as Vice-President.

February 18, 1861: Inauguration of Jefferson Davis.

March 4, 1861: Inauguration of Abraham Lincoln to the Presidency of the United States.

April 12, 1861: Confederate batteries under the command of General Pierre Beauregard open fire on Union-held **Fort Sumter,** South Carolina.

April 14, 1861: Evacuation of Fort Sumter by Major Robert Anderson and his men.

April 15, 1861: President Lincoln calls for 75,000 volunteer militia to suppress the rebellion.

May 4, 1861: Congress of the Confederate States issues a declaration of war against the Federal Union.

July 21, 1861: At the battle of **Bull Run** or **Manassas,** Confederates under Generals Beauregard, Thomas J. (Stonewall) Jackson and Joseph Johnston rout the Union forces of General Irvin McDowell.

July 27, 1861: Major General George B. McClellan assumes command of the Army of the Potomac.

November 1, 1861: General Winfield Scott resigns as general in chief of the Union armies and Major General McClellan assumes full command.

February 6-16, 1862: Federals take command of **Fort Henry** on the Tennessee River, General Ulysses S. Grant, gets unconditional surrender of **Fort Donelson** from General Simon Buckner.

March 7-8, 1862: The battle of **Pea Ridge** in northwestern Arkansas preserves Missouri for the Union.

March 9, 1862: The first naval engagement in history between ironclad ships, the Union **Monitor** and the Confederate **Merrimac** (renamed the *Virginia*), is fought at Hampton Roads, Virginia, and makes wooden navies obsolete.

April 6-7, 1862: At the battle of **Shiloh,** or **Pittsburgh Landing,** Generals Grant and Buell turn a surprise attack by Generals Albert Sidney Johnston and Pierre Beauregard into a costly Union victory. General Johnston is killed and the Confederates retreat to Corinth, Mississippi.

March 17—July 3, 1862: General McClellan advances toward Richmond and repulses Confederate General Joseph E. Johnson's attack at the battle of **Seven Pines,** or **Fair Oaks.** Johnston is wounded and General Robert E. Lee assumes command of the Army of Northern Virginia.

June 25—July 1, 1862: **The Seven Days' Battles** end McClellan's Peninsular Campaign to capture Richmond. After ten battles, his army retreats. McClellan is replaced by General John Pope.

August 29-30, 1862: Generals Jackson and Lee deal a sound blow to the Army of the Potomac at the second battle of **Bull Run,** or **Second Manassas.** General Pope is relieved and the command returned to McClellan.

September 17, 1862: Lee's first invasion of the North is intercepted by McClellan at **Sharpsburg,** Maryland, on **Antietam** Creek. In the bloodiest day of the war, the armies fight to a stalemate; General Lee retreats to Virginia.

September 22, 1862: President Lincoln issues his preliminary Emancipation Proclamation.

December 13, 1862: Major General Ambrose Burnside, new commander of the Army of the Potomac, is defeated at **Fredericksburg.**

January 1, 1863: The **Emancipation Proclamation** becomes official.

December 31, 1863—January 2, 1863: The battle of **Stone's River,** or **Murfreesboro,** results in heavy losses on both sides and no gains. General Braxton Bragg's Tennessee army retires from the area after heavy engagements with General William Rosecrans' Federals.

May 1-4, 1863: General Lee wins his greatest victory as he and General Jackson meet General Joseph Hooker's army in the Wilderness of north-central Virginia at **Chancellorsville.** After the battle, Jackson is mistakenly shot by his own men.

July 1-3, 1863: Lee moves into the North to resupply his ravaged troops and makes contact with the Army of the Potomac, under General George G. Meade, at **Gettysburg,** Pennsylvania. For three days Lee attacks Federal lines. The last charge, by General George E. Pickett, fails and ends the battle. Lee's damaged army retreats.

July 4, 1863: Lieutenant General John Pemberton surrenders the city of **Vicksburg,** Mississippi, to General Grant after forty-seven days of continuous bombardment and seige.

November 19, 1863: President Lincoln delivers his Gettysburg Address at the dedication of the National Cemetery.

September 19-20, 1863: General Rosecrans' army pursues General Bragg's forces to **Chickamauga.** A determined effort by General George Thomas, which earns him the nickname "Rock of Chickamauga," saves the Federals from complete disaster and allows them to retreat to Chattanooga.

November 23-27, 1863: Braxton Bragg besieges the Union forces occupying Chattanooga. General Grant and reinforcements arrive and the Federals take the offensive, winning battles at **Lookout Mountain** and **Missionary Ridge.**

March 1864: President Lincoln promotes Grant to general in chief with the rank of lieutenant general. He joins the Army of the Potomac and begins a war of attrition against the Army of Northern Virginia.

May 5-6, 1864: Fires blaze in the dense woods of the **Wilderness** as Lee and Grant fight for two days. Hundreds of soldiers burn to death in the battle before Grant moves southeastward toward Spotsylvania.

May 8-12, 1864: Lee and Grant fight a costly and indecisive battle at **Spotsylvania Court House.**

June 3, 1864: At **Cold Harbor,** Grant suffers his worst defeat of the war. Seven thousand Union men fall in one half-hour of the assault. It is the Army of Northern Virginia's last great victory.

June 14, 1864—April 2, 1865: Thwarted from striking Richmond, General Grant moves his forces to the James River and attacks **Petersburg.** Lee holds firm and Grant lays siege to the vital rail center for nine months at a cost of 42,000 men—the longest and the last siege of the war.

May 7—September 2, 1864: General William Tecumseh Sherman and his armies fight their way to **Atlanta,** which falls to the Federals on September 2. After ten weeks, Sherman begins his March to the Sea in a successful effort to sever the Deep South and crush the Confederates.

May 11, 1864: Cavalry officer J.E.B. (Jeb) Stuart is mortally wounded in a clash with General Philip Sheridan at **Yellow Tavern.**

August 5, 1864: Rear Admiral David Farragut takes **Mobile Bay,** the most important remaining Confederate port on the Gulf of Mexico.

September 1864: General Sheridan's cavalry defeats General Jubal Early's forces in the Shenandoah Valley and devastates the entire area, which is Lee's main source of food for the Army of Northern Virginia.

November 1864: President Lincoln defeats Major General George B. McClellan in the Presidential election.

December 15-16, 1864: Confederate General John Hood, outnumbered two to one by the forces of General George Thomas, sustains heavy losses south of **Nashville.** It is nearly the end of Southern resistance in the west.

February 3, 1865: The Confederacy proposes unacceptable peace terms to President Lincoln on board ship off Hampton Roads, Virginia.

March 4, 1865: President Lincoln is inaugurated into his second term of office.

March 25, 1865: General Lee makes an abortive last attempt to break from Petersburg and join with the forces of General Joseph Johnston.

April 3-4, 1865: Richmond is abandoned by its citizens and the leaders of the Confederacy. President Lincoln visits the rebel capital.

April 9, 1865: General Lee surrenders the forces of the Army of Northern Virginia to General Grant at **Appomattox Court House,** Virginia.

April 14, 1865: President Abraham Lincoln is assassinated at Washington's Ford Theater by actor and Southern sympathizer, John Wilkes Booth.

Bloody Lane at Antietam battlefield, forever at peace, belies the history of a September day in 1863 when the site was littered with the corpses of its Confederate defenders. *(Black Star, Photo by Charles L. Moore.)*

A SELECTIVE BIBLIOGRAPHY

Agassiz, George, ed. *Meade's Headquarters, 1863-1865, Letters of Colonel Theodore Lyman from the Wilderness to Appomattox.* Boston: Books for Libraries Press, Inc., 1922.

Alcott, Louisa M. *Hospital Sketches and Camp and Fireside Stories.* Boston: Roberts Brothers, 1869.

Beitzell, Edwin. *Point Lookout Prison Camp for Confederates.* Abell, Maryland: 1972.

Benét, Stephen Vincent. *John Brown's Body.* Garden City, New York: Doubleday, Doran and Company, Inc., 1927.

Botkin, B.A., ed. *A Civil War Treasury of Tales, Legends and Folklore.* New York: Random House, Inc., 1960.

Bowman, Colonel S.M. and Irwin, Lieutenant Colonel R. B. *Sherman and His Campaigns: A Military Biography.* New York: Charles B. Richardson, 1865.

Catton, Bruce. *The Coming Fury.* Garden City, New York: Doubleday and Company, Inc., 1961.

————. *Never Call Retreat.* Garden City, New York: Doubleday and Company, Inc., 1965.

————. *Terrible Swift Sword.* Garden City, New York: Doubleday and Company, Inc., 1965.

Cavada, F.F. *Libby Life: Experiences of a Prisoner of War.* Philadelphia: 1864.

Charnwood, Lord Godfrey Rathbone Benson. *Abraham Lincoln.* Garden City, New York: Garden City Publishing Company, 1917.

Cruden, Robert. *The War That Never Ended: The American Civil War.* Englewood Cliffs, New Jersey: Prentice-Hall, Inc., 1973.

Dannett, Sylvia, ed. *Noble Women of the North.* New York: Thomas Yoseloff, 1959.

Darby, George. *Incidents and Adventures in Rebeldom.* Pittsburgh: Rawsthorne Engraving and Printing Company, 1899.

Dodd, William E. and Macy, Jesse. *The Days of the Cotton Kingdom: The Anti-Slavery Crusade,* Vol. 28, The Yale Chronicles of America Series. New Rochelle, New York: United States Publishers Association, 1919.

Donald, David. Introduction to *A Rebel's Recollections,* by George Cary Eggleston. Bloomington, Indiana: University of Indiana Press, 1959.

Durkin, Reverend Joseph T., ed. *Confederate Chaplain: A War Journal of Rev. James B. Sheeran.* Milwaukee: The Bruce Publishing Company, 1960.

Fuller, John F. C. *Grant and Lee: A Study in Personality and Generalship.* Bloomington, Indiana: Indiana University Press, 1957.

Grant, Ulysses S. *Personal Memoirs of U.S. Grant,* 2 vols. New York: 1885-1886.

Harris, William C. *Prison Life in the Tobacco Warehouse at Richmond.* Philadelphia: Childs, 1862.

Hyde, Thomas W. *Following the Greek Cross; or, Memories of the Sixth Army Corps.* Boston: 1894.

Johnson, Robert Underwood and Buell, Clarence Clough, eds. *Battles and Leaders of the Civil War,* 4 vols. New York: 1884-1888.

McClellan, George B. *McClellan's Own Story: The War for the Union.* New York: 1887.

McClure, Alexander K. *Abraham Lincoln and Men of War Times.* Philadelphia: 1892.

Miller, Francis Trevelyan, ed. *Photographic History of the Civil War,* 10 vols. New York: 1911.

Minnigerode, Meade. *The Fabulous Forties 1840-1850: A Presentation of Private Life.* New York: G. P. Putnam's Sons, 1924.

Moore, Frank, ed. *The Rebellion Record: a Diary of American Events,* 12 vols. New York: 1868.

Morgan. W. H. *Personal Reminiscences of the War of 1861-5.* Lynchburg, Virginia: J. P. Bell Company, 1911.

Poe, J. C., ed. *The Raving Foe: The Civil War Diary of Major James T. Poe, C.S.A. and the 11th Arkansas Volunteers.* Eastland, Texas: Lonhorn Press, 1967.

Pryor, Sara Rice. *Reminiscences of Peace and War.* Select Bibliographies Reprint Series. Freeport, New York: Books for Libraries Press, Inc., 1908.

Roth, Margaret Brobst, ed. *Well, Mary: Civil War Letters of a Wisconsin Volunteer.* Madison, Wisconsin: University of Wisconsin Press, 1960.

Rowland, Dunbar, ed. *Jefferson Davis Constitutionalist: His Letters, Papers and Speeches.* Jackson, Mississippi: State of Mississippi Department of Archives and History, 1923.

Sandburg, Carl. *Abraham Lincoln: the War Years,* 4 vols. New York: Harcourt Brace Jovanovitch, Inc., 1939.

Stampp, Kenneth M. *The Era of Reconstruction, 1865-1877.* New York: Random House, Inc., 1965.

Stillwell, Leander. *The Story of a Common Soldier, or Army Life in the Civil War.* Erie, Kansas: 1917.

Swinton, William. *Campaigns of the Army of the Potomac.* New York: 1882.

United States War Department. *War of the Rebellion: A Compilation of the Official Records of the Union and Confederate Armies.* Series I. Washington, D.C.: 1902.

Wiley, Bell Irvin. *The Life of Billy Yank.* Indianapolis: The Bobbs-Merrill Company, Inc., 1952.

————. *The Life of Johnny Reb.* Indianapolis: The Bobbs-Merrill Company, Inc., 1943.